ACCLAIM FOR LEE FANG'S
THE MACHINE

"Lee Fang documents in lively detail the cogs, axles, sockets, levers, and output of the most insidious political machine in our history—the resurgent right. The reach of this machine is hair-raising, but in order to overcome it, one must know it. With his years of reporting and insight, Fang presents a compelling field guide for smart progressives. A must-read for the left and anyone concerned about the takeover of democracy by the wealthy few."

*—Jennifer Granholm, former governor
of Michigan*

"Fang is one of America's best and most prolific investigative journalists, and in this brilliant and insightful work he tells a vital story of the takeover of American politics by a small band of billionaires. An absolute must-read."

—Thom Hartmann, radio host and author of
The Last Hours of Ancient Sunlight

"With our lawmakers more beholden than ever to dark money, Lee's book couldn't have come at a better time. . . . Reformers need to arm themselves with the best information available, and this expertly researched book is a great place to start."

—*Bob Edgar, president of Common Cause*

"Few people have done more in-depth research, reporting, and writing on the post-Obama conservative movement than Lee Fang. *The Machine* goes beyond the headlines and explores exactly how this ideological movement operates."

—*Amanda Terkel, senior political reporter,*
The Huffington Post

"Fang's riveting account offers readers not only a guide for understanding how the mechanisms of right-wing power operate, but also a roadmap for developing countermeasures to effectively challenge them."

—*Christine Trost, program director of the Berkeley Center for Right-Wing Studies and co-editor of* Steep:
The Precipitous Rise of the Tea Party

"Lee Fang is a fearless American muckraker who exposes secret political machinations often overlooked by the mainstream press. Anyone interested in understanding why Washington doesn't work should read *The Machine*."

—*Jane Mayer, staff writer,* The New Yorker

Photo credit: VIKRUM AIYER

Lee Fang is a reporting fellow with the Investigative Fund at The Nation Institute and a contributing writer at *The Nation*. A former investigative blogger for ThinkProgress, Fang has written for national publications including the *Boston Globe* and is a regular commentator on MSNBC and NPR. His work has led to calls for investigations in Congress and the FEC. This is his first book. Fang lives in San Francisco and Washington, D.C.

THE
MACHINE

A FIELD GUIDE
TO THE
RESURGENT RIGHT

LEE FANG

THE NEW PRESS

NEW YORK
LONDON

Requests for permission to reproduce selections from this book should be mailed to:
Permissions Department, The New Press, 38 Greene Street, New York, NY 10013.

Published in the United States by The New Press, New York, 2013
Distributed by Perseus Distribution

ISBN 978-1-59558-639-1 (pbk)
ISBN 978-1-59558-692-6 (e-book)
CIP data is available

The New Press publishes books that promote and enrich public discussion and understanding of the issues vital to our democracy and to a more equitable world. These
books are made possible by the enthusiasm of our readers; the support of a committed
group of donors, large and small; the collaboration of our many partners in the independent media and the not-for-profit sector; booksellers, who often hand-sell New
Press books; librarians; and above all by our authors.

www.thenewpress.com

Composition by Bookbright Media
This book was set in Janson Text

Printed in the United States of America

10 9 8 7 6 5 4 3 2 1

Dedicated to the most important women in my life,
my mother and Maytak

CONTENTS

ACKNOWLEDGMENTS

Many people were very kind to me during the long research and writing process that went into this book. I want to first and foremost thank my editors as well as my friends and family for their support during the months I spent working on this project. The New Press decided to invest in this endeavor, and I deeply appreciate their patience, assistance, and advice along the way.

I began the effort while still reporting for ThinkProgress, and much of my research was shaped in part through the mentorship of Faiz Shakir, who at the time served as editor in chief of the blog. Through ThinkProgress, I traveled the country, attending countless Tea Parties, gun rallies, Conservative conferences, and lobbying presentations. My reporting work for the blog became the basis for this book.

I want to also thank the many writers who have closely covered the right-wing movement, both before and during the Obama era. While much of this book is based on my

own reporting, I also depend on the articles and research by
dozens of reporters—from both traditional newspaper outlets and independent media—who have covered the conservative movement for several decades.

INTRODUCTION

The morning of November 5, 2008, America woke to news of a seismic shift. It wasn't just the election of the first African American president. The conservative era, which had begun with Richard Nixon's culture war and seemed ascendant with Ronald Reagan's supply-side radicalism and permanent after George W. Bush's masterful 2004 reelection, appeared to be over. The combination of Barack Obama's commanding victory and the second consecutive cycle of Democratic gains in both houses of Congress redrew the political map.

The GOP had lost up and down the ballot, from local assembly races to the U.S. Senate, making the Republicans almost inconsequential overnight. Within hours of the election results, *Bloomberg* reported that an all-out "bloodbath" erupted within the party as competing factions vied for power. "Among Republicans, there is no energy, no fresh thinking, no ability to capture the concerns and feelings of millions of people," noted the *New Yorker*'s George Packer earlier that year in a widely read article about the slow death of American conservatism.

The election was read as a sign of future Democratic dominance. Obama had not only captured "new South" states like Virginia and North Carolina, he gained a majority of newly registered young voters and Latinos, as well as white-collar professionals. Some called it a realignment. "This majority," former Clinton strategist James Carville declared, "will guarantee that the Democrats remain in power for the next forty years."

And the evidence of GOP decline was everywhere. The states of New England no longer sent a single Republican to the House of Representatives; in New Mexico, Democrats gained control of the entire congressional delegation.

There were calls for Obama to enact a second New Deal, to seize this moment of partisan dominance and public support to pass broad reforms. Anything was suddenly possible.

But the euphoria soon came to an end. Exactly one year later, on the morning of November 5, 2009, attention was not at the White House, but focused on the steps of the Capitol. Thousands of Tea Party activists, many of them bused in by a group called Americans for Prosperity, had assembled on the West Lawn to listen to Republican lawmakers denounce health reform.

Republican leader John Boehner boomed that the bill was the "greatest threat to freedom" he had ever seen in his career. Representative Michele Bachmann held court over the center of the stage, as partisans took turns exciting the crowd. "You are our fighting force," screamed Texas Congressman John Carter, pointing to the legislative office buildings for his colleagues in the House. "Go get 'em!"

The crowds marched dutifully toward the white concrete buildings across the street to lobby lawmakers. Many Democrats had endured months of pressure from lobbyists, ad campaigns, and well-organized protests. Despite campaigning on a promise to enact health reform, lawmakers like Georgia's John Barrow and Pennsylvania's Jason Altmire buckled and refused to support the legislation. Two days after the "House Call" rally on Capitol Hill, Speaker Nancy Pelosi called for a vote and passed the bill with a razor-slim margin of five votes. Thirty-nine Democrats joined Republicans in voting against the bill.

At this point, the big Obama agenda seemed to be holding on by a thread. The Democrats had lost public opinion, lost control of the narrative, and the entire legislative program was suddenly in jeopardy. The jubilation in November 2008 turned to deep despair and disappointment by November 2009. Health reform was eventually signed into law, but after being significantly delayed, watered down, and disparaged. Other legislative priorities were stripped down or forgotten altogether.

And one year later, on November 5, 2010, the window of opportunity for Obama's first administration had closed. President Obama's party received the greatest rebuke since the Great Depression. Democrats had suffered poor midterm elections in the past, but 2010 resulted in a greater loss than 1948, 1966, or 1994, the Gingrich Revolution. The Republicans were not only back, but in many states, like North Carolina, were in stronger numbers than before. In Wisconsin, nearly every position of power switched to the GOP's column, up and down the ballot.

In no time at all, the politics of hope were reduced to a historical footnote. Obama's bold plans became a relic of the past as Republicans, given back the reins of power from the American people, busted unions, demanded austerity, and passed corporate tax cuts. Prospects of reforming labor, addressing global warming, or breaking up the big banks were wiped off the table—in fact, these problems became worse.

One could argue that Obama simply faced too many barriers, too much corruption, and an economy that was poisoned by his predecessor. Yes, big-business groups were happy to oblige an opposition party promising to obstruct any Obama idea. Yes, the Supreme Court decided to unlock the floodgates of unlimited corporate money in the election system only one year into the young president's term. Yes, the entrenched special interests in Washington were never terribly pleased to welcome the junior senator and former community organizer from Illinois into the White House.

But the story of the right's revival and the almost overnight rebirth of the Republican Party stems from a series of key decisions. Effective strategies from the left would be duplicated. Corporate lobbying would have to better cohere with right-wing ideology and Republican partisanship. Young activists and populists would need to be harnessed. The religious right coalition, central to GOP gains for three decades but in obvious decline since the last years of the Bush administration, would need to be replaced. The political infrastructure that had catapulted the right to dominance, starting in the late 1970s, would have to be redesigned and rebuilt.

This book covers the plutocrats, strategists, front groups, and decision makers who were pivotal in making sure that America's choice in 2008—to set a bold, progressive course for the country—was more an aberration than a new beginning.

1

THE TRUE HISTORY OF THE TEA PARTY

Who would have guessed that a legion of Americans, some dressed in tricorner colonial-style hats, would usher in one of the greatest midterm upsets in American history, while smashing the domestic policy agenda of Barack Obama? The true history of the Tea Party, how it revived the conservative movement and reestablished Republican rule, is rooted in circumstance and hidden planning.

The Bush presidency ended in a political implosion. For over thirty years, the religious right had formed the backbone of the modern conservative movement. But scandal after scandal—from Congressman Mark Foley's (R-FL) sexual advances on male pages to Ted Haggard's meth-fueled relationship with a gay prostitute to Senator Larry Craig's (R-ID) attempted tryst in a men's bathroom—eroded the evangelical movement's enthusiasm for the Republican Party. To make matters worse, John McCain, the party's 2008 standard-bearer, maintained a tense relationship with Christian right leaders. In 2000, McCain denounced Christian Broadcasting Network president Pat Robertson and Moral Majority founder Rev. Jerry Falwell as "agents of intolerance." McCain spent much of the campaign trying to mend fences with the religious right, kowtowing to various Christian right organizations and extremist preachers like John Hagee. Even so, he never fully earned their trust, despite his selection of Sarah Palin, a favorite among the Christian right. While evangelicals did not shift their allegiance to the Democratic Party, many either stayed home or did not enthusiastically mobilize their friends and family for the Republican ticket, as they had for Bush and for Republican candidates since the early eighties.

Moreover, the Republican Party brand was in tatters. According to Gallup, 2008 showed the highest level of support for the generic Democratic Party over the Republicans since the firm began regularly tracking measures of party support in 1991. By the time of the election, 52 percent of Americans identified as Democrats or said they leaned to the Democratic Party, compared to only 40 percent who identified with or leaned toward the Republicans.[1] Toward the end of the 2008 campaign, by a two-to-one ratio, Americans blamed Republicans and Republican policies for the financial crisis.

The weakening of its grassroots religious right base, coupled with an unprecedented level of unpopularity, caused great consternation among Republican Party elders. But for others, it was a golden opportunity. A small group of libertarian-minded Republicans and corporate lobbyists had always detested the dominance of the religious right over the Republican Party. Former Republican Majority Leader Dick Armey had long sought a grassroots base centered on libertarian principles of small government and less regulation, not right-wing Christian values such as opposition to gay marriage or abortion.

Although he considered himself a very pro-life legislator, Armey particularly resented having to rely on religious right power brokers. In a post denouncing the influence of the Christian right posted on the FreedomWorks website in October of 2006, Armey called Focus on the Family leader James Dobson a "bully." Armey detailed a specific incident with Dobson, which Armey believed exemplified the arrogance of the religious right: "As Majority Leader, I remember vividly a meeting with the House leadership where Dobson scolded us for having failed to 'deliver' for Christian conservatives, that we owed our majority to him, and that he had the power to take our jobs back. This offended me, and I told him so."

Armey's feuding with Dobson, a key figure who could make or break Republican politicians, seemed like a quixotic campaign in 2006. But shortly after the 2008 election results were in, Dobson's Focus on the Family organization announced steep cuts and a layoff of more than two hundred employees. Obama had scored a series of high-profile evangelical endorsements, including one from Rev. Kirbyjon Caldwell, the pastor for a Texas megachurch, who had officiated at Jenna Bush's wedding. Although Obama failed to capture much of the white evangelical vote, 2008 marked a tectonic shift for the role of the religious right in the GOP.

In his broadside against the religious right, Armey also mocked the Republican-led intervention into the case of Terri Schiavo. In 2005, GOP leaders called a special session of Congress to pass a law forcing doctors to reinsert a feeding tube for the brain-dead Schiavo against the wishes of Schiavo's husband. The press obtained a memo from a staffer to Republican Senator Mel Martinez that detailed how the entire charade was a gimmick to excite the pro-life Christian

base. Armey, however, wanted his own movement independent of preachers and pastors as proxies. That was part of
the reason that, after he retired from Congress, he quickly
signed up as chairman of Citizens for a Sound Economy, an
antigovernment grassroots group funded by a variety of corporate interests and billionaire David Koch.

The schism between the libertarian, antigovernment right
and the religious right had existed since the beginning of the
modern conservative movement. Ayn Rand, the objectivist
founder of American libertarianism, dismissed Christianity
as "superstition" and religious faith in general as "extremely
detrimental to human life." While Ronald Reagan's leadership is credited with helping to bridge the divide between
the religious and economic right, the rift grew as libertarians
found themselves increasingly sidelined during the second
Bush administration. Although signature Bush agenda items,
like the Iraq and Afghanistan wars, Medicare Part D, and the
Patriot Act, seemed anathema to core small-government beliefs, most libertarians stuck by Bush because of his dogmatic
efforts to privatize Social Security, strip businesses of regulations, oppose labor unions, and cut corporate and individual
tax rates.

For Republicans and their corporate patrons, the Christian
right presented a worldview that Republicans could campaign
on: outlawing abortions, preserving heterosexual marriage,
and introducing Christianity into areas of public life, such
as public schools or public displays of the Ten Command-
ments. In exchange for support for religious social issues, big
business–minded Republicans would count on evangelicals
and conservative Catholics first and foremost to deliver millions of votes, but also to support corporate tax cuts, deregulation, and other pillars of supply-side economics. But in the

dawn of the Obama presidency, with this tidy relationship falling apart, Republicans needed a new vanguard. The story of creation is one of the most central and defining narratives for a culture. By basing its values in the story of creation offered by the Christian right, the Republican Party could claim the moral high ground for any of its candidates or positions. However, with the Christian right drifting away, Republicans searched for a new story, a new narrative, a new moral clarity. And libertarian operatives were ready with their own version of creation—this one rooted in national, rather than religious, identity.

Libertarian mythology explained that the Founding Fathers were all laissez-faire capitalists, and that the colonial rebellion against the British centered entirely on high taxes and government regulation. The Ludwig von Mises Institute, one of the bedrock institutions of libertarian ideas, churns out essays and opinion pieces almost every year—beginning well before Obama's rise to the presidency—about how the American Revolutionary War was rooted in libertarian ideals. "You could justifiably say that the American Revolution occurred, not because we objected to taxes without representation, but because we objected to taxes, period," a typical von Mises essay by writer Charles Adams exclaimed in 2006.[2] By redefining the founding story of America, libertarians sidestepped both political parties and aimed directly for the American psyche.

THE TEA PARTY OF 1773 VS.
THE TEA PARTY OF TODAY

Fierce competition from the Dutch and a variety of other factors pushed the British East India Company to near bankruptcy in the mid- to late eighteenth century. Members of Parliament, as well as the King and his family, were large shareholders of the East India Company. So with little hesitation, in 1767 the British government began passing a series of laws called the Townshend Acts to help the East India Company solidify its monopoly over the market in the American colonies as well as in England. American shipping companies competed directly with the East India Company by opening new trading lines, and small American retailers purchased products in bulk from the Dutch. To mitigate the East India Company's competition, the Townshend laws included harsh measures to give the corporation new powers to search American homes and businesses for smuggled goods. Other Townshend Acts imposed new fees and taxes for various goods, including glass items and paint. Of course, none of these laws were passed with the colonists' democratic input or consent.

To the colonists, perhaps the most insulting measure was the Tea Act passed in May of 1773. The Tea Act was a tax cut for the East India Company that allowed the corporation to bypass any duties and taxes on tea so it could sell directly to the colonists. The tax loophole applied only to the East India Company and allowed the company to severely undercut the price on tea imported by private American businesses.

Popular disgust at the East India Company rippled through the colonies. As news broke of the Tea Act, the May 27, 1773, edition of the *Alarm*, an insurgent paper bent on agitation, circulated around the colonies. The newsletter charged that the East India Company, through "Barbarities, Extortions and Monopolies," had stolen land in Asia and forced famine in colonized countries for the sake of profit. The newsletter, signed by the anonymous "Rusticus," asked the question:

"Are we in like manner to be given to the disposal of the East India Company, who have now the Assurance, to step forth in Aid of the Minister, to execute his Plan, of enslaving America?"[3] The colonial press buzzed with similar furor at the Tea Act, spurring a broad coalition of opposition.

The first shipments of the untaxed East India Company tea met well-organized resistance in November and December of 1773. In Charleston, South Carolina, protesters forced customs officials to keep the tea on the dock, and eventually the East India ship sailed back to England. In Philadelphia, a confrontation with the captain of the East India Company ship arriving there stalled the tea from making delivery. And in Boston, more than one hundred protesters, led by Samuel Adams, boarded the East India Company ship and dumped containers of the company's tea, worth nearly two million in present-day dollars, into the harbor. The so-called Boston Tea Party faced down employees of the East India Company, many of whom acted as spies for their employer, as well as the military force of the British Empire, which at that time served the interests of the company. As the East India Company demanded repayments for their lost property, a series of escalating confrontations between British soldiers, acting on orders from the East India Company, and American colonists resulted in America's war for independence.

Popular American myths about the Boston Tea Party define it as simply a protest against "taxation without representation." However, as author Thom Hartmann has noted, much of the "real Boston Tea Party was a protest against huge corporate tax cuts for the British East India Company, the largest trans-national corporation then in existence." While the colonists demanded their own representative government to levy taxes, they also demanded a competitive marketplace where small businesses and entrepreneurs could thrive against profit-seeking behemoths. But what about the twenty-first-century Tea Party, a movement seemingly consumed with the iconography and rhetoric of the original protest in Boston?

On a crisp November morning, the day after the 2010 midterm elections, I was one of a small handful of reporters in the National Press Club for the first celebratory press conference hosted by Tea Party leaders. Newly elected Republicans "are not in a mood for compromise," boomed Mark Meckler, a spokesman for the Tea Party Patriots, at the time one of the largest Tea Party groups in the country. Meckler, a California lawyer and highly successful distributor of Herbalife, a direct-selling business widely viewed as a pyramid scheme, added that the Tea Parties would be a permanent political force well after the Obama presidency.[4] Americans were taxed too much, tired of "big government," and were yearning for a "constitutional conservative" awakening, the Tea Party Patriot leaders said.

Fair enough. But after hearing over and over that the anti-Obama Tea Party movement was "fed up" with "taxes and regulations," I decided to raise my hand and ask a question. "Last year in 2009, ExxonMobil paid nothing in corporate income taxes," I said. "Google paid, I believe, 2 percent. Does the Tea Party believe those corporations, many of which pay essentially nothing in corporate income taxes, were really taxed too much?" Meckler nodded and replied, "We've been suggesting a corporate tax holiday to allow these companies to come in and create jobs." According to these self-styled patriots, ExxonMobil, which made over $19 billion in profits and paid nothing in federal corporate income taxes in 2009, deserved a tax holiday. It wasn't an anomaly. I asked another

Tea Party Patriots volunteer in the lobby if he thought it was fair that hedge-fund managers are taxed at 15 percent, using the carried-interest loophole, while nurses and engineers who make a fraction of a hedge fund manager's earnings are taxed at nearly double the rates. He said that was fine. Hedge-fund managers, he was sure, created much-needed jobs.

Stepping outside of the press conference, I interviewed Jenny Beth Martin, a former low-level Republican staffer from Georgia who rose to prominence as one of the most visible leaders of the Tea Party movement. I asked her about the Republican pledge to defund the Consumer Protection Agency, one of the hallmarks of Obama's financial regulatory reform law. My question was open-ended: "What do you think about that?" She buried her face in her hands and yelped, "I have no idea." Later, she said she would have someone from a conservative think tank, such as the American Enterprise Institute, "come in and talk about Wall Street reform" so that she could make a decision. I pointed out that Wall Street billionaire Bruce Kovner and other titans of the financial services industry chair the American Enterprise Institute, so their advice might be biased. She shrugged.

For a fiery populist movement, these Tea Party leaders seemed awfully obedient to the interests of big business. Corporate conglomerates, which like the East India Company of 1773 dodged taxes at any opportunity, were still taxed too much, according to these Tea Partiers. The modern anti-Obama Tea Party was full of passion and anti-elite sentiment, but upon examination, there was little substance and absolutely no interest in taking on corporate monopolies.

Other than the hollow responses to my questions about policy, the most revealing aspect of the press conference came about two-thirds of the way in. After rather boilerplate remarks about repealing Obama's reforms and promises to "take the country back," the Tea Party Patriot leaders at the press conference stepped aside and let the only man in the front of the room wearing a crisp suit speak.

Colin Hanna, the silver-haired chairman of the Republican front group Let Freedom Ring, approached the podium and announced that his group had covertly provided training and resources to the Tea Party Patriots throughout the election. Young men working for Hanna handed out pamphlets to the reporters in the room detailing their efforts, which included providing the Tea Party Patriots with a small army of election lawyers, training for over 1,748 Tea Party Patriot "poll watchers," and state-of-the-art technology from the Republican consulting firm Edge Targeting. Hanna's group paid for the Tea Party Patriots' automated phone calls, which reached over 1.6 million households focusing on twenty-three swing congressional districts. Hanna said his Let Freedom Ring group, which had aired a series of million-dollar ads supporting establishment Republican John McCain in 2008, was itself part of the Tea Party revolution.

Let Freedom Ring was not the only group propping up the Tea Party Patriots. Staffers from FreedomWorks, the front group led by Dick Armey, had managed the Tea Party Patriots' listserv. Corporate front groups like Americans for Prosperity and the Heartland Institute provided many of the talking points and speakers used by the Tea Party Patriots and its affiliates.[5] Free training seminars and online tutorials for grassroots organizing were provided to the Tea Party Patriots by the Leadership Institute, which is funded by the billionaire Koch family as well as by other corporate interests, including Amway. Even the Tea Party Patriots' website was sponsored by a who's who of Republican front groups, including Regular Folks United, FreedomWorks, and Americans for Tax Reform. A mysterious donor granted Tea Party Patriots an additional $1 million for increased election-season outreach.

Shortly before the election, a memo from the Tea Party Patriots leaked. The Tea Party Patriots had attended a meeting of the Council for National Policy, a secretive group of conservative donors, and presented a wish list with dollar amounts attached. The Tea Party Patriots asked the donors to underwrite their campaign efforts. To fund the Tea Party Patriots' "traditional" get-out-the-vote walk and phone lists, they asked for $150,000, as well as $250,000 for "GPS-enabled smart-phone walk lists and technology," $125,000 for help setting up house parties, and finally $250,000 for "collateral material." It didn't end there. For efforts after the election, the memo demanded $110,000 for help protesting possible legislation during the lame-duck session of Congress, $175,000 for a summit to entertain newly elected Tea Party politicians, $300,000 for "Younger Generation Outreach," at least $500,000 for a renewed advertising budget, $200,000 for help organizing tax-day Tea Parties in 2011, and a litany of other high-priced requests.

Aside from their somewhat casual attire, Mark Meckler, Jenny Beth Martin, and the Tea Party Patriots leadership were indistinguishable from any ordinary Republican consultants with high-priced demands and orthodox supply-sider beliefs. With donors from the Reagan-era Council for National Policy and allies like Koch Industries and Let Freedom Ring, the Tea Party Patriots were like any other Republican group. However, to the media and to millions of Americans, they were still rag tag protesters fighting against the grain of the establishment.

Even after the victory of scores of Tea Party Republicans, the *New York Times* still referred to the Tea Party as "insurgents," the *Washington Post* called them "outsiders," and CNBC referred to Tea Partiers as heroic "rebels." Unlike the Republican Party brand, which hadn't improved significantly since the defeat of John McCain, the Tea Party appealed to many segments of American society. Throughout 2009 and 2010, polls showed that the Tea Party was more popular than the Republican Party, and independents gravitated quickly toward the idea of Tea Party–aligned candidates. An exhausted electorate disillusioned with political institutions and the two parties found a fresh alternative with the Tea Parties, the only widespread and seemingly new political movement in the twenty-first century.

On national television, Tea Party leaders declared that they sought an outright elimination of Social Security, a repeal of the Seventeenth Amendment, and even mass deportation of undocumented immigrants. At Tea Party rallies, explicit racism and racist signs became not only commonplace, but were accepted. Photoshopped images of Obama dressed as a witch doctor, complete with a bone through his nose, were often seen at Tea Party rallies. During an anti–health reform protest on Capitol Hill, Tea Party members accosted African American lawmakers with curse words, racial epitaphs, and even spit. Congressman Barney Frank, an openly gay Democrat, was called a "faggot" by Tea Party members and was taunted by grown men who lisped their heckles in an effort to mock Frank's sexual orientation. Despite their deeply unpopular policy positions and the vile behavior demonstrated regularly at Tea Party rallies, poll after poll showed the American people held a positive view of the Tea Parties. At one point, 51 percent of Americans viewed the Tea Party in a favorable light. In a sense, the Boston Tea Party, as a symbol, is as American as the bald eagle or the Stars and Stripes. How could anyone oppose it?

The Tea Party's fervent nationalism and antigovernment radicalism encapsulated the kind of movement-based free-market economics that libertarians had dreamed of for years. As a political identity, the Tea Party provided a proxy for voters disgusted with the Republican Party's track record to still vote for the GOP, as long as the candidate pledged allegiance to the Tea Party rather than the ill-defined "establishment." The Tea Party's stunningly successful bid winning primary elections for its candidates also cemented its role as the new kingmaker of the Republican Party. The estimated hundreds of thousands of Tea Party volunteers who showed up at rallies, placed phone calls to Congress, and worked tirelessly for Republican candidates easily supplanted the loss of evangelical enthusiasm. While Republican planners had fretted that core religious right issues—like traditional marriage—didn't appeal to young voters, the Tea Party's antigovernment sentiment struck a chord with almost every demographic group. In every practical sense, the Tea Party had replaced the thirty-year reign of the religious right within the conservative movement.

LAYING THE GROUNDWORK
Efforts to co-opt the memory of the Boston Tea Party for political gain are a tried-and-true American tradition. Throughout history, the Tea Party has been invoked to justify radical action, violence, protest, and extralegal activity. As historian Benjamin Carp noted, partisans of every stripe and ideology, from lynch mobs to Abraham Lincoln, used the Tea Party to justify their ends:

Colorado farmers mentioned the Boston Tea Party in their protests against British enterprises in 1887. Abraham Lincoln cited the Tea Party as precedent when defending women who had destroyed a saloon in 1854, while William Randolph Hearst gave the Tea Party as an example of just disobedience to the Volstead Act in 1929. In the 1941 comedy *The Devil and Miss Jones*, a labor union organizer invokes the Tea Party in front of a magistrate. The list goes on: the anti-slavery *Liberator* in 1831, vigilante agrarian reformers in Kentucky in 1907, the Knights of Mary Phagan in 1915.[6]

In fact, one of the first attempts to launch a broad political movement based around Tea Party symbolism was hatched by progressives. In his second inaugural address, President Nixon promised to revitalize American self-confidence. "At every turn, we have been beset by those who find everything wrong with America and little that is right," he lamented. In a bid to win back American patriotism, Nixon set out to celebrate America's bicentennial with a dramatic reenactment of the Boston Tea Party in Boston Harbor. As Nixon courted corporate donors to help sponsor the event, antiwar activists led by Jeremy Rifkin established a "People's Bicentennial Commission." The leftist plan was to use Nixon's bicentennial as a springboard for their own Tea Party movement, called Tax Equity for Americans, the T.E.A. Party. Rifkin urged his cohorts to embrace symbols of the American Revolution, particularly the yellow Gladsden "Don't Tread on Me" flag, to denounce the Vietnam War as well as what was perceived as a creeping corporate takeover of America.

The leftist coup was a short-term success. According to Harvard historian Jill Lepore, who detailed this history of the liberal incarnation of the Tea Party in her book *The Whites of Their Eyes*, as forty thousand people gathered to watch a group of reenactors dump casks of tea into the harbor, the left-wing activists sprang into action:

> The National Organization for Women was picketing: "Taxation Without Equal Rights Is Tyranny." Another banner read "Gay American Revolution." . . . Minutes later, six protesters boarded the ship and unfurled a flag that read "Impeach Nixon." The Associated Press reported, "A member of the group, wearing a huge mask resembling President Nixon's face, circled the brig in a rowboat and waved his hands high in Nixon's familiar 'V' style." On board, they tarred and feathered an effigy of the President.

Protesters also dumped boxes labeled "Exxon" and "Gulf Oil" into the harbor to protest corporate power. Although the liberal agitators gained nationwide headlines by hijacking Nixon's event, the planned progressive T.E.A. Party movement never gained momentum.

In the eighties, the Boston Tea Party was still not perceived as an exclusively right-wing concept. In some cases, it was a cause for both sides of the ideological spectrum. According to Howard Kurtz, in his *Hot Air: All Talk, All the Time*, consumer rights advocate Ralph Nader teamed up with antitax lobbyist Grover Norquist to call for a Tea Party protest against a proposed congressional salary increase. As the story goes, talk radio host Roy Fox of Detroit's WXYT received a call from a listener suggesting that voters send tea bags to Washington and "attach a little message at the end of the string that says, 'No pay increase.'" The idea caught on. Coordinated by Nader and Norquist, radio hosts from Boston, Seattle, Los Angeles, San Antonio, Des Moines, and West Palm Beach rallied listeners to send 160,000 tea bags to Washington. The effort, culminating with a press event on the anniversary of the Boston Tea Party, caused enough bad publicity for Congress to scuttle their pay hike.

But the roots of the modern antigovernment, antitax Tea Party can be traced to carefully formulated plans concocted by the tobacco industry. In the late eighties and throughout the nineties, the tobacco industry faced an assault from all sides. Legislators, litigators, and ballot initiatives alike sought to prohibit tobacco advertising to children, ban indoor smoking, tax tobacco products, place warning labels on tobacco products, and fine the industry for intentionally misleading consumers about the health effects of its products. The tobacco industry's efforts to win the battle of public opinion by funding fake citizens' groups sympathetic to the tobacco industry, such as "smokers' rights" leagues, are well documented. It has also been reported that the industry made huge investments in conservative think tanks and bought off academics to produce junk studies casting doubt on the health effects of smoking. A less well-known tactic, however, was the attempt to create a "Tea Party" movement against government as a shield to protect the tobacco industry. Tobacco lobbyists, needing to win over public opinion—and perhaps inspired by antitax political operatives like Norquist, who was on the tobacco industry payroll—thought they could instigate a backlash against government regulation and taxes, and in doing so, stop government and consumer intrusion into the tobacco industry's business.

Memos from the American Tobacco Company, Philip Morris, and R.J. Reynolds detail a broad array of strategies to engineer an antigovernment backlash, using a "Boston Tea Party" theme. A campaign advertisement from tobacco giant Philip Morris sought to use former Republican Senator Howard Baker to compare curbs on tobacco products to infringements on freedom tantamount to the British repression that led to the Tea Parties. A document, dated 1989 and archived at the Legacy Tobacco Documents Library at the University of California, San Francisco, outlined an advertisement with the following script: "British policies of minority rule, increased government intervention, unfair taxation. . . . Ironically, those same issues face us again today. Excise taxes, advertising restrictions, franchise legislation, price supports, and smoking bans make it necessary to act to protect our rights as citizens of the United States." After a movie clip of colonists casting tea into the harbor, the advertisement proposal indicated that Senator Baker was supposed to say, "The Boston Tea Party was one of the sparks that ignited the Revolution." A call to resist government regulation of tobacco closed the video.

One attempt to create a national Tea Party phenomenon was defused when *O'Dwyer's Washington Report*, a trade publication for the public relations industry, exposed the plan. *O'Dwyer's* revealed a proposal from a tobacco industry group, Coalition Against Regressive Taxation (CART), to contract the public relations firm Burson-Marsteller to create a citizens' protest against a proposal to eliminate deductions on excise taxes on products such as tobacco. Burson-Marsteller said it would create a "Boston Tea Party theme" that included a "guerrilla campaign after Labor Day" aimed at the 1992 presidential candidates.[7] Burson-Marsteller's agents would hand out signs while wearing "attention-drawing accouter-ments" to create political buzz for the cause. One of the fake citizens' groups suggested in this campaign was Citizens for a Sound Economy, a corporate front group that would later play a dominant role in the anti-Obama Tea Parties (subsequent documents from the late nineties, naming the tobacco industry's "3rd party allies," showed that Philip Morris had budgeted up to $2 million a year for Citizens for a Sound Economy).[8]

The exposure of the CART document killed the Tea Party idea in 1992, but Tea Party themes from tobacco lobbyists continued to emerge in later years. When President Clinton proposed taxing cigarettes to fund his health reform plan, the tobacco industry needed citizen outrage. In June of 1994, the *New York Times* reported that "about 3,000 tobacco farmers mounted what was billed as a modern-day 'Boston Tea Party' today, cheering as bales of tobacco were tossed into the Kentucky River to protest proposals to increase taxes on tobacco products to help finance health care." The *Times* reporter, as well as dozens of other media outlets which carried the story, did not realize that the event was orchestrated by political operatives working for big tobacco. In an October 5, 1995, memo to Philip Morris, the PR firm Jack Guthrie and Associates of the Worldcom Group took credit for the event. The lobbyists at Jack Guthrie and Associates saw the Kentucky River protest as just a start. The memo outlined that a broad antigovernment Tea Party movement could be orchestrated as a political maneuver to kill proposed Food and Drug Administration regulations on tobacco products as well:

> It is conceivable that tens of thousands of people from the six states—representing hundreds of in-

RECOMMENDED PUBLIC RELATIONS PLAN
PHILIP MORRIS U.S.A.
Page 23

In addition, we recommend that the six MAN partners consider combining their third-party forces for a demonstration in Washington, D.C. It is conceivable that *tens of thousands* of people from the six states -- representing hundreds of industries and interests -- could carry a powerful message to the President, Congress and the FDA.

JGA will explore possible "themes" that could be associated with such rallies. (In June 1994, for example, JGA organized a re-enactment of the Boston Tea Party, where 6,000 farmers converged at the Kentucky state capital to hurl stalks of tobacco into the Kentucky River -- in protest to President Clinton's proposed tax increases on cigarettes to pay for health care reform. The event, organized on behalf of the Council for Burley Tobacco, was covered by nearly every national print and broadcast outlet.)

Phillip Morris' recommended PR plan

dustries and interests—could carry a powerful message to the President, Congress and the FDA. JGA (Jack Guthrie and Associates) will explore possible "themes" that could be associated with such rallies. (In June 1994, for example, JGA organized a reenactment of the Boston Tea Party, where 6,000 farmers converged at the Kentucky state capitol to hurl stalks of tobacco into the Kentucky River—in protest to President Clinton's proposed tax increases on cigarettes to pay for health care reform. The event, organized on behalf of the Council for Burley Tobacco, was covered by nearly every national print and broadcast outlet.)[9]

Ultimately, the anti-FDA Tea Party never took place. But the David vs. Goliath ethos of the Tea Party clearly took hold within the executive suites of the tobacco industry. "The government's plan to influence personal behavior through higher taxes is reminiscent of colonial times," wrote Philip Morris CEO Michael Miles in a letter to shareholders. He added, "back then" the people responded with the "Boston Tea Party."[10]

While the tobacco industry throughout the nineties featured Tea Party themes in leaflets and advertisements opposing government regulation, a radical set of Republican politicians began experimenting with a similar idea, on a broader scale. Leading the charge, Texas Representative Dick Armey believed he could eliminate the income tax and replace it with a national sales tax—an idea called the flat tax—by calling for a revolt based on the Boston Tea Party. Starting in 1993, Armey began staging stunts with other members of Congress to call attention to his antitax, antigovernment crusade. Working with Citizens Against Government Waste, Armey purchased advertisements in *Parade* magazine for a "second Boston Tea Party" and called for antitax activists to mail tea bags to legislators. On the steps of the Capitol, along with fellow Republican lawmakers Bob Walker, Chris Cox, and Mel Hancock, Armey stood beside volunteers dressed in colonial costumes to dump tea in front of the building. Armey's event, staged at the beginning of the 103rd Congress for maximum press coverage, was a dud. But he kept trying.

THE TRUE HISTORY OF THE TEA PARTY

In 1997, still working to drum up media support for his regressive tax proposals, Armey sent fellow Republican congressmen Billy Tauzin and Dan Schaefer to Boston for a slightly more elaborate stunt. The pair dumped the federal tax code into Boston Harbor and announced the beginning of a new antitax revolution. A few dedicated antitax protesters came to the event, but no nationwide movement sprung up. Conceding to a reporter from the *Los Angeles Times* that "we're not anywhere near" the votes in Congress needed to pass his tax proposal, Tauzin said he was hoping to build a grassroots movement.

The following year, on tax day, April 15, Armey, who was by then the Republican majority leader, traveled again to Boston with Tauzin. Organizers from the progressive organization United for a Fair Economy (UFE) showed up, with a dinghy marked "Working Family Life Raft" with a young man, a young woman, and a baby doll in it, while about fifteen other organizers in formal suits and dresses surrounded Armey and Tauzin. When the two lawmakers prepared to throw the tax code into the water, the man and woman in the dinghy yelled, "Don't throw it! You'll flatten us with your flat tax, and you'll sink us with your sales tax!" The UFE activists on the dock, who pretended to be wealthy elites, shouted, "Do it!" to the shocked congressmen. Armey and Tauzin eventually threw the tax code into the water.[11] The political jujitsu worked: the dinghy with the young couple sank, and the media cameras, including ones from CNN, captured the entire debacle, much to the delight of the progressive activists. A transcript from CNN indicates that the network provided only a few minutes of coverage, which revolved entirely around the UFE protest of Armey. Then, the reporters began talking about the so-called Y2K bug. In sum, the media spectacle Armey had hoped for was another flop.

The tobacco industry demonstrated that the Tea Party could be used to induce regular Americans to find common cause with corporate interests, and Armey's stunts showed willingness from the Republican Party to embrace the concept as their own. However, the nuts and bolts of how to create a self-perpetuating antigovernment Tea Party were designed primarily by three wealthy libertarians: real estate magnate Howie Rich and the billionaire owners of Koch Industries, Charles and David Koch.

The Koch brothers and Rich had worked together since the late seventies, when they were all active members of the Libertarian Party. By some estimates, David Koch provided half of the party budget in 1980, and he became the party's vice presidential candidate that year. The dismal election showing—Libertarian Party nominee Ed Clark received less than 1 percent of the vote—convinced the Koch brothers and Rich to pool their resources outside electoral politics and into think tanks, academic centers at major universities, and in an array of libertarian activist groups. According to Brian Doherty, a libertarian who interviewed the Koch brothers, the pair became sick of pure partisan politics and Charles Koch began to view electoral matches as "actors playing out a script."[12] Instead of finding the right actor, they concluded that better results could come from changing the script.

The Koch brothers and Rich paid a number of prominent libertarian activists from their days in the party to head up new groups. They hired Ed Crane, Koch's 1980 campaign manager, to lead the Cato Institute, and gave a former Libertarian Party activist named Eric O'Keefe grants to develop grassroots campaigns designed to limit the size and scope of government action. The first and most successful campaign was a multifaceted effort to create term limits for legislators on both the state and national level. Although the Supreme Court struck down federal limits, state-based term limits proliferated around the country.

For twenty years, front groups funded by the Kochs and Rich struggled with ways to engineer public support for their extremely unpopular ideas, such as slashing the size of state government, thus laying off teachers and firemen, and reducing services. Rich, in particular, favored a stealth lobbying approach. While working with other businessmen, Rich would funnel large donations through a series of foundations he controlled, then use the money to hire canvassers to place initiatives, like the so-called Taxpayer Bill of Rights (TABOR), a state constitutional amendment to limit the growth of government, on the ballot.[13] Then, a small group of Rich-funded organizers would show up with seemingly spontaneous protests and media stunts in support of the measure. A PBS investigation found that 99 percent of the advertising and campaign funds used for TABOR initiatives in Oklahoma, Missouri, and Arizona came from groups funded by Rich. The same giant paper-mâché pig paraded in public to denounce government spending was used for Rich-supported efforts in Michigan and Montana, despite the fact that local antitax groups claimed they had created it. Rich would latch on to local religious efforts to privatize schools, or lobbying campaigns to deregulate industry, or anything else that would help support his cause of limiting the size of government.

In many cases, Koch- and Rich-supported fronts provided a veneer of citizen support for far-right Republican objectives. While Armey gained little traction with his

Tea Party gimmick in Boston, Koch's Citizens for a Sound Economy (CSE) hosted a series of rallies to boost Armey's pet cause, the flat tax. CSE, of course, had flirted with the idea of creating a Tea Party protest, funded by the tobacco industry, in 1992.

In 2001, CSE began organizing antigovernment Tea Parties. The North Carolina affiliate of CSE organized a "Tar Heel Tea Party" against a proposed tax increase to plug a $167 million shortfall in the state budget. Busloads of CSE-organized protesters, with support from the North Carolina Republican Party and a local right-wing think tank called the John Locke Foundation, arrived in Raleigh.[14] Some wore colonial costumes; others carried "Don't Tread on Me" signs. Roughly six hundred protesters deluged the capital, yelling in the faces of lawmakers and throwing tea bags on the floor of the chamber. The tax hike was postponed, and as the *National Review* gloated in an article published several days later, "the taxpayers clearly had the upper hand."

CSE continued to organize Tar Heel Tea Parties the following year, and the experience served as a training ground for later Tea Parties organized by CSE operatives. During the 2002 round of CSE-sponsored Tea Parties, the organization founded the website USTeaParty.com to try to promote the idea nationally. But before CSE could organize more Tea Party rallies, the organization changed leadership and morphed because of an internal dispute in 2003.[15]

Dick Armey, the original proponent of right-wing Tea Party rallies, retired from Congress and became chairman of CSE. He soon clashed with David Koch and others financing CSE. Armey sought to use CSE as a vessel to promote the interests of his corporate clients at the lobbying firm he simultaneously worked for, DLA Piper. The leadership disagreements left CSE splintered—half the organization went off to become a new group chaired by David Koch, called Americans for Prosperity. The other half merged with a group called Empower America to form FreedomWorks, which Armey led.

Armey ruthlessly expanded FreedomWorks and leveraged its extensive resources to promote the clients paying him at DLA Piper. Before he became one of the leading voices of the anti-Obama Tea Party, Armey experimented with fake grassroots tricks by using FreedomWorks to set up phony student groups, town halls, and other public events to promote President Bush's effort to privatize Social Security. In December 2004, FreedomWorks operative Sandra Jacques introduced herself as merely a "single mom" from Iowa who supported Social Security privatization at a Bush town hall meeting. The *New York Times* pointed out that, "Ms. Jacques is not a random single mother. She is the Iowa state director" for FreedomWorks.[16] In 2006, FreedomWorks staffer John Hallman went to work organizing events to promote Social Security privatization all over Florida. In 2009, Hallman used the same network to organize anti-Obama Tea Parties as the Florida Tea Party field director. Other FreedomWorks staffers, including Max Pappas and Matt Kibbe, worked diligently to host a series of rallies for Senator Jim DeMint (R-SC) to promote Social Security "reform." In 2009, they repeated the strategy, this time promoting DeMint as the premier leader of the anti-Obama Tea Party.

After taking on a number of oil-related clients, including BP and Irving Oil, Armey used his FreedomWorks organization to promote offshore drilling. Once the American Council of Life Insurers began paying Armey, FreedomWorks mobilized its activist base to call for life insurance deregulation. While

FreedomWorks sometimes peppered its rhetoric with references to the Tea Party—like claiming in one publication its goal was to create "meaningful social change by reclaiming the lost art of grassroots activism, as Sam Adams understood it"—Armey largely abandoned the broad Tea Party activism during most of the Bush administration. However, as Armey integrated use of FreedomWorks to build public support for his DLA Piper clients into his business model, fronts controlled by the Kochs and Rich were thinking big picture.

In 2006, Americans for Limited Government held a conference for libertarian activists in Chicago. Funded by Rich, Americans for Limited Government used the conference to discuss and promote creative ways to undermine the government. According to reporter Laura Oppenheimer, attendees coalesced around a new theme: the Boston Tea Party. Mary Adams, an activist from rural Maine, accepted the activist-of-the-year award and dedicated it to Sam Adams, the colonial leader in charge of the eighteenth-century attack on the East India Company. Like many libertarians, she misinterpreted the Boston Tea Party as simply an antigovernment phenomenon. In any case, Sam Adams's heroic Tea Party was her inspiration, she said. The room, filled with anti–property tax activists, libertarian writers, and businessmen including Howard Rich, agreed. The Boston Tea Party could be a "blueprint" for an overarching antigovernment movement.

Shortly after the Americans for Limited Government conference, Rich, working with a cadre of former Republican operatives and longtime associates from his TABOR and term limits campaigns, founded a new group called the Sam Adams Alliance. The announcement read: "Those of you who were able to join us at the inaugural Action Conference in Chicago this August heard a lot of talk about Sam Adams" and his Tea

Party. One of the first videos from the group retold the story of the Boston Tea Party—from the libertarian perspective—juxtaposed with scenes of Sam Adams Alliance staffers working the phones and Sam Adams Alliance–supported antitax protesters marching with signs.

The Sam Adams Alliance, headed by longtime libertarian operative Eric O'Keefe, would motivate Tea Party activism by handing out cash grants to the most dynamic libertarian activists. The first set of awards, which continued annually, gave out more than $40,000 to various activists. For example, in 2007, Melyssa Donaghy won the "Tea Party award" for "staging numerous creative protests around the state in response to Indiana's increasing property tax burden."[17] In a posting later deleted from the Internet, the Sams Adams Alliance provided a grant to a local group called the Team Hammond Taxpayers' Group to "sponsor a Tea Party Tax Revolt at the Lake County Government Center in Crown Point, Indiana," in March of 2008.[18] Pictures posted online by Team Hammond showed antitax protesters in colonial garb mingling with people with Ron Paul 2008 signs. Other cash grants were given to innovative antigovernment activists in Tennessee, Oregon, Virginia, and elsewhere for blogging, creating documentaries, and confronting government officials (and promoting videos of the confrontations online).

Around the same time the Sam Adams Alliance began its search for Tea Party talent, David Koch's Americans for Prosperity (formerly Citizens for a Sound Economy) reactivated their Tea Party activism. In 2007, the Michigan branch of Americans for Prosperity formed a coalition with the Michigan Realtors Association and other business groups to host Tea Party rallies to support corporate tax cuts. "Our April 18th tax rally will have the tea bag as our theme to draw a parallel to the Boston tea party that sparked the American Revolution," blared the Americans for Prosperity announcement.

The renewed interest in the Tea Party as a vehicle to achieve antigovernment goals paralleled a true revolution in campaign tactics pioneered by Republican presidential candidate and strident libertarian Ron Paul. Paul for President supporters celebrated the 2007 anniversary of the Tea Party by rallying at the State House in Boston. Unlike previous attempts to co-opt the Tea Party—by tobacco lobbyists, anti–Vietnam War radicals, or even Dick Armey—Paul activists mobilized the event nationally using the Internet, with team leaders planning mini–Tea Party rallies simultaneously in cities across the country, such as Austin and Santa Monica. Rand Paul, speaking in Boston on behalf of his father, encouraged supporters by denouncing the Bush "imperial presidency," the Iraq war, and the loss of civil liberties in equally harsh terms as he attacked government programs. The bold message, coupled with a layered participatory strategy of live webcasts and online forums, helped Paul use the Tea Party anniversary to raise a record-breaking $6.6 million from 58,407 individual contributors in online donations that day.[19]

The Republican Party literally locked out Ron Paul supporters from their 2008 nominating convention in St. Paul, Minnesota. I attended the shadow Ron Paul campaign convention some ten miles away at the Target Center in Minneapolis, and watched, half baffled, as an amalgamation of libertarians in colonial costumes waving Revolutionary War flags bustled in and out of the lobby, screaming euphorically about limited government. Back in St. Paul, Republican delegates cheered over the selection of Sarah Palin, but the enthusiasm never met the wild screams over Austrian economics across town. In conversations during the convention, several Republican delegates told me how much they envied the Ron Paul campaign's energetic populism and grassroots fund-raising.

Republican Party operatives marveled at the Paul movement's use of the Internet, but the Paul campaign's strident libertarian views, particularly his stance opposing the war in Iraq and supporting gay marriage, made him an anathema to the party—at least in 2008. Forces outside the control of the traditional party structure, however, seized upon Paul's tactics as proof that a free-market-oriented populist movement had potential. The Ron Paul campaign techniques were discussed at length during the Sam Adams Alliance blogger convention in March of 2008. FreedomWorks snapped up Paul's online consultants, including a firm called Terra Eclipse, which had helped build Paul's digital tools and social networking platform.[20]

As the 2008 presidential campaign played out, Eric O'Keefe, the Koch brothers, and a group of bankers, oil tycoons, and corporate executives met in secret to plot the next stage of the libertarian movement. Using a service called DonorsTrust, many of the executives had anonymously invested vast amounts of money into organizations like the Sam Adams Alliance. With the end of the Bush presidency and the failure of John McCain, the Republican Party fell into turmoil. What better time for a libertarian resurgence than when other dominant factions of the right, like the Christian values voters, were in disarray? Moreover, the economic crisis left the country paralyzed and seething with anger at institutions they thought were there to protect them. The country was fertile ground for a new form of populism to take root.

BIRTH PANGS OF THE ANTI-OBAMA TEA PARTY

Relegated to deep minority status in Congress, Republican leaders knew they needed guerrilla tactics to stop Obama and his reforms. Republican congressman Pete Sessions, the incoming head of the National Republican Congressional Committee in charge of recruiting and electing new House Republicans, told editors at the *National Journal's* Hotline blog that the Taliban would serve as a model of opposition for the GOP. "Insurgency, we understand perhaps a little bit more because of the Taliban," Sessions explained. "And we need to understand that insurgency may be required when the other side, the House leadership, does not follow the same commands, which we entered the game with."

The right-wing grassroots insurgency Sessions sought started rather quietly, on message boards and Internet forums. As the Huffington Post's Alex Brant-Zawadzki reported, the Libertarian Party of Illinois, using a Yahoo listserv, began discussing the idea of a Chicago Tea Party on January 6, 2009, and one of its members, Chris Jenner, pondered "soliciting aid and support for the Tea Party concept from organizations like Sam Adams Alliance and the Illinois Policy Institute," a state-based conservative think tank. The party set up a MeetUp.com and Facebook group devoted to the Tea Party protest idea. Eric Odom, a veteran of several Republican campaigns before coming to the Sam Adams Alliance as director of new media, reportedly involved himself in these Tea Party discussions in early January.[21] Odom liked to brag that he specialized in "stealth-type marketing" that "some say" are "attack sites." On January 30, Odom, who had served for over a year at the Sam Adams Alliance working to establish relationships with hundreds of bloggers through its "Blogivists" and "Samsphere" networks, as well as with Americans for Prosperity's RightOnline new media initiative, announced his retirement from the group.[22] He noted, however, that he planned to continue "to work closely with SAA as a consultant on many of our endeavors."

On the same day as Odom's departure from Sam Adams Alliance, FreedomWorks held an activist training session in Tampa, Florida focused on "how leftist organizer Saul Alinsky's 'Rules for Radicals' can apply to the limited government movement." One of the attendees, Mary Rakovich, a fifty-three-year-old unemployed automotive engineer, caught the eye of FreedomWorks staffers Brendan Steinhauser and Tom Gaitens for her level of energy for the cause.[23] The next week, Steinhauser called Rakovich to organize a protest against President Obama, who had a town hall in Fort Meyers, Florida to tout his Recovery Act stimulus program. The February 10th protest lacked a coherent theme—FreedomWorks staffers suggested simply calling the stimulus "pork" and only one other person showed up to wave signs.

Despite the dull antipork theme and the fact only one other person joined her, Fox News's Neil Cavuto invited Rakovich on to his show to talk about opposition to Obama. Conservative blogger Michelle Malkin, who promoted Rakovich's protest, began publicizing similar protests against the stimulus, which she termed the "Porkulus," in Seattle and Denver. Right-wing media—first bloggers like Malkin and Instapundit, then radio hosts like Kirby Wilbur (a staffer for Americans for Prosperity) and David Boze—quickly converged to support the Seattle protest on February 16, and the Denver one the next day. Americans for Prosperity lent its other coordinators along with staffers from the Golden,

Colorado–based Independence Institute, to help organize the Denver event, which attracted almost three hundred people.

On February 19, 2009, in a televised rant still mired in controversy, CNBC contributor and commodities broker Rick Santelli set the fuse to the modern anti-Obama Tea Party movement. From the floor of the Chicago Mercantile Exchange, surrounded by a crowd of smirking traders, on live television Santelli suddenly launched into a vitriolic rant aimed at the administration's proposed Homeowner Affordability and Stability Plan, a program to offer refinancing assistance to millions of Americans suffering from falling home prices and foreclosure. "The government is promoting bad behavior," said Santelli, and compared the administration's approach to that of communist Cuba. Santelli, who hadn't thrown a fit of rage at the hundreds of billions offered to banks for its failures, sneered at the prospect of helping with the "losers' mortgages." The commodity traders at booths next to Santelli—who he lovingly referred to as "a pretty good statistical reflection of America, the silent majority" —cheered as Santelli yelled into the camera, "President Obama, are you listening?" He continued, "We're thinking of having a Chicago tea party in July. All you capitalists who want to show up to Lake Michigan, I'm going to start organizing." Santelli's emotional blast, despite coming from a wealthy trader, oozed populism, at least in terms of style.

Santelli's rant, which was placed on YouTube almost instantly, immediately gained wide coverage on the Drudge Report and other right-wing websites. A few hours later, Eric Odom registered the domain TaxDayTeaParty.com and Americans for Prosperity staff members registered TaxPayerTeaParty.com, both websites calling for Tea Party–themed protests against Obama. A Facebook page started by Americans for Prosperity's Phil Kerpen demanded Tea Party protests from coast to coast. The fast-moving nature of the campaign to promote Santelli's cry for a Tea Party revolt against Obama's progressive reforms sparked allegations that Santelli had conspired with the right beforehand. Journalists Mark Ames and Yasha Levine pointed out that another website went live only hours after Santelli's rant— ChicagoTeaParty.com. They argued that the timing shows that Santelli was in cahoots with conservative organizers in Chicago:

> The domain was registered in August 2008 by Zack Christenson, a dweeby Twitter Republican and producer for a popular Chicago right-wing radio host Milt Rosenberg—a familiar name to Obama campaign people. In August of 2008, Rosenberg, who looks like Martin Short's Irving Cohen character, caused an outcry when he interviewed Stanley Kurtz, the conservative writer who first "exposed" a personal link between Obama and former Weather Underground leader Bill Ayers. As a result of Rosenberg's radio interview, the Ayers story was given a major push through the Republican media echo chamber, culminating in Sarah Palin's accusation that Obama was "palling around with terrorists." That Rosenberg's producer owns the "chi cagoteaparty.com" site is already weird—but what's even stranger is that he first bought the domain last August, right around the time of Rosenburg's launch of the "Obama is a terrorist" campaign. It's as if they held this "Chicago tea party" campaign in reserve, like a sleeper-site. Which is exactly what it was.

The debate over whether Santelli's rant was planned has never been resolved conclusively. However, Santelli, Odom, members of the Libertarian Party of Illinois circulating the idea for a Chicago Tea Party, and the owners of the "sleeper-site" Tea Party website, Milt Rosenberg and Zack Christenson, all worked in the Chicago area in the months leading up to Santelli's "spontaneous" rant. Eric O'Keefe, of the Chicago-based Sam Adams Alliance, was even an acquaintance of Rosenberg's through Shimer College, where they both served as members of the board of trustees. David Brady of the Libertarian Party of Illinois later wrote a piece claiming "we gave Rick Santelli the idea for the Tax Day Tea Parties," and bemoaning that "this is all kind of frustrating because LP Illinois gets no credit for this [Tea Party] project. Eric Odom, member of LP Illinois, and our original group, created his own website and facebook group and aligned directly with Santelli." Odom admonished Brady in the comment section of his post, writing, "We need to knock it off with the 'who gets credit' nonsense and go take our government back."[24] Could Santelli have gotten the idea from Jonathan Hoenig, his colleague at CNBC who also worked in Chicago? Hoenig, author of *Greed is Good: The Capitalist Pig Guide to Investing*, was a devoted libertarian activist who attended Sam Adams Alliance events.

Santelli denied any affiliation with any of the political operatives responsible for the Tea Party rallies across the country, but basked in the right-wing media spotlight. In the days after his rant, he hit the conservative talk radio junket bragging, without a shred of evidence, that the White House must be out to get him and his children because of his bold dissent. Despite his announcement on September 2, 2008, two weeks before the market crash, that the markets were perfectly "healthy," Santelli became the go-to financial expert darling for conservatives overnight.

Regardless of Santelli's involvement or lack of involvement with right-wing operatives before his rant, the conservative machine kicked into high gear to make anti-Obama Tea Parties a reality. FreedomWorks registered several other Tea Party websites, like IAmWithRick.com, and revived the old 2002-era Citizens for a Sound Economy Tea Party website USTeaParty.com. Odom, working with a variety of other bloggers and popular Twitter users, formed the Nationwide Tea Party Coalition the day after Santelli's rant to coordinate messaging. Americans for Prosperity, with over fifty staffers operating across the country, began producing press releases and scheduling rallies in Arizona, Missouri, Kansas, New Hampshire, New Jersey, North Carolina, and other states. Many of the libertarian activists who received Tea Party awards in 2007 and 2008 from the Sam Adams Alliance began mobilizing anti-Obama Tea Parties in their respective states. Other groups from across the conservative movement got involved. The American Future Fund, a shadowy front used to run attack ads against Democrats, launched a Tea Party petition on the same day as Santelli's screed.

On February 27, the first official Tea Parties were held in several cities. Some of the original plotters of the Tea Party idea, including staffers from the Sam Adams Alliance and Illinois Policy Institute, spoke at the protest in Chicago. Many of the activists recruited to stage "Porkulus" rallies were asked to rebrand as Tea Parties. Tom Gaitens, the Florida coordinator for FreedomWorks, contacted conservative activist John Hendrix to host the February 27th Tea Party in Tampa. In an interview with a conservative blogger, FreedomWorks' Brendan Steinhauser admitted that

FreedomWorks provided a list of contacts and paid for much of Hendrix's event.[25]

In March, populist sentiment exploded with the news that executives at AIG, the insurance giant at the center for the financial collapse, were preparing to reward themselves with $165 million in taxpayer-subsidized bonuses. Largely left-wing protesters picketed the home of AIG executive Douglas Poling and AIG's headquarters in New York. Harnessing outrage at the bonuses, union organizers from the SEIU and other labor groups mobilized demonstrations. Conservatives quickly latched on to the Tea Parties to divert populist anger from corporate America to President Obama. "These tea parties are blossoming and growing all over the fruited plain. People are fed up, and I'll tell you what, it's not about bonuses to AIG people," barked Rush Limbaugh on his program. An Americans for Prosperity set of talking points told activists to direct their anger related to the AIG bonuses to the Obama administration for supporting the bailout.

A Cincinnati Tea Party protest in March, one of the biggest at the time with nearly 5,000 people, rallied angry conservatives against Obama.[26] They claimed that his stimulus program was the cause of unemployment—which reached 8.5 percent that month, the highest since 1983.

The success of the Cincinnati protest encouraged the broader conservative movement to fully endorse the Tea Party idea. Earlier in March, Fox News hate television star Glenn Beck announced his 9/12 Project to organize his own Tea Parties and rallies, somehow combining the concept that the Founding Fathers would oppose Obama with the claim that his movement would bring the country together in a way that the September 11th terrorist attacks had. Newt Gingrich's attack group, American Solutions for Winning the Future, endorsed the Tea Parties and became a sponsor of several Tea Party groups. It also sponsored Grover Norquist's Americans for Tax Reform and National Taxpayers' Union, which had mobilized the Tea Party–themed protests against the congressional pay increases in 1988. Behind the scenes, FreedomWorks staffers helped launch Tea Party Patriots and its affiliated listserv to coordinate national Tea Party events. Armey, as the leader of FreedomWorks, began appearing on cable television to speak on behalf of the protests his organization had put together. Let Freedom Ring, the front funded by John Templeton Jr., an heir of his billionaire father's investor fortune, became a prime sponsor of the Tea Party Patriots' venture. Fox News host and popular radio talker Sean Hannity began promoting the Tea Party on a daily basis. By the end of March, virtually all of the major organs of the right-wing infrastructure began publicizing a massive series of tax day protests on April 15, 2009.

Certainly not all of the Tea Party organizing was top-down. Conservative activist Michael Patrick Leahy efficiently organized hundreds of smaller Tea Party rallies using a website called TCOT (Top Conservatives on Twitter) and a new unified Twitter feed of top right-wing bloggers. However, Leahy also relied heavily on petitions and online forums created by Odom and FreedomWorks. But with experienced front groups leading the way, activists replicated the strategy and designed their own relatively independent Tea Parties as well.

Mindful of their association with the discredited and unpopular Republican Party, right-wing operatives courted Ron Paul types with constant promises that the new movement would be strictly nonpartisan. In an interview with the *Washington Independent*, Tea Party organizer and Ron Paul activist Jason Pye attacked the involvement of Republicans like Newt Gingrich, who he said "enabled George W. Bush" and the "big spending" and "bailouts."

While front groups did the legwork of contacting local activists, securing permits, and handing out talking points and template press releases, the right-wing propaganda megaphone went into full battle mode to boost attendance of the April 15th Tea Parties. Fox News hosts Glenn Beck, Neil Cavuto, Greta Van Susteren, and Sean Hannity aired their shows live at rallies, termed "FNC Tax Day Tea Parties," in different cities across the country.[27] Fox Nation, the network's imitation of the Drudge Report website, created a special "virtual Tea Party" for its online audience. Media Matters for America found that in the ten days leading up to the tax-day protests, Fox News aired 107 segments and commercial break advertisements promoting the Tea Parties. Many of the Fox News announcements didn't bother to hide the network's bias. Fox's Bill Hemmer, a daytime news anchor, instructed viewers: "If you go to our website, you will find a growing list of these events, hundreds of photos, and a new tea-party anthem that you will hear from the man who wrote it and recorded it next hour." He helpfully added, "And there's a list of the nationwide Tax Day tea-party events coming up on the 15th of April, which will be a huge deal for those organizations. So check it out online right now." Virtually all of conservative talk radio fell into line to promote the Tea Parties as well.

It wasn't just ideological media, however. The novelty of a conservative street protest movement struck many in the press as the perfect man-bites-dog story. According to a search of Nexis, between inauguration and April 15, 2009, there were at least 839 print news mentions of the Tea Party, and over 632 mentions on nationally syndicated radio and television.[28] The seemingly spontaneous, grassroots feel of the Tea Party, coupled with its perception as being independent of any recognized political group, also intrigued journalists. "Democrats, Republicans, national debt and assorted other pet peeves about the government and you have tax day tea parties," remarked a clearly amused Melissa Block, a reporter for NPR, on the morning of the national anti-Obama protests of April 15.

While the general message of the Tea Party was "taxed enough already," the movement invited conservatives of every stripe to join as long they opposed Obama and his reforms. The Tea Party was a catchall opportunity to vent rage at the new president. "To the far right, everything about Barack Obama and his administration seemed somehow alarming, as if his election had ripped a tear in the fabric of time," noted Jill Lepore. Regardless of the true history of the Boston Tea Party, it reminded even law-and-order conservatives that one could be patriotic yet violently subversive. The far right militia group Gun Owners of America mobilized Tea Parties under the false claim that Obama planned to confiscate firearms. Neo-Nazi websites like Stormfront immediately seized upon the Tea Parties as recruiting tools. ResistNet, which had led anti-immigrant protests for years, quickly converted itself into a Tea Party organization. Despite the libertarian bent of the Tea Parties, pro-life activists attended Tea Parties en masse to protest Obama's pro-choice beliefs. Local Republican volunteer groups, the State Policy Network of state-based conservative think tanks, and of course various strands of the libertarian movement found a big tent in the Tea Party movement. Barely two months into Obama's presidency, a March 2009 Tea Party protest featured dozens of signs calling for Obama's impeachment ("Obama Bin Lyin' IMPEACH NOW").

Fearing that Obama's then-sky-high approval ratings would translate into sweeping reforms, corporate lobbyists discovered that Tea Party enthusiasm could be easily harnessed to beat back legislation. A front created by Porter Novelli, a drug company lobbying and public relations firm, began sponsoring Tea Parties to encourage participants to oppose health reforms related to the pharmaceutical industry. In 2009, as FreedomWorks channeled its Tea Party networks into opposing a climate change bill, the oil industry trade association American Petroleum Institute handed the group at least $100,000 in extra funds.[29] And returning to the roots of the Tea Party idea, tobacco industry lobbyists seized upon the rallies to push back against taxes on cigarettes. When legislators in Georgia considered a dollar-a-pack cigarette tax to close the budget deficit, Philip Morris paid Americans for Tax Reform to promote a Tea Party protest to oppose the tax.

The Tea Party provided a direct path to political revival for the Republican Party. Shortly after Obama's election victory, Republican leaders in Congress determined that they would create a contrast with the president by unanimously opposing every major agenda item that he supported. A few GOP lawmakers weren't initially sold on the idea, like South Carolina representative Bob Inglis, who privately worried that simply being a "party of 'no'" would be irresponsible. But Inglis became an outlier in the Republican Party. A groundswell of protests against Obama, against spending, against government, and against taxation provided the perfect cover for the Republican agenda of blanket obstruction.

On the first national Tea Party on April 15, 2009, at least 35 Republican members of Congress spoke at rallies in their home districts. Grandstanding Republican governors, like

Rick Perry of Texas and Mark Sanford of South Carolina, addressed Tea Parties and declared they would block stimulus aid to their state (both later backtracked and accepted the money). Senator David Vitter (R-LA) introduced legislation formally honoring April 15 as "National Tea Party Day." The frenzy to oppose Obama sucked once moderate Republicans into populist absurdity. Republican representative Mark Kirk, a leader of the middle-of-the-road Republican Main Street Partnership, suggested that the Democratic governor of Illinois ought to be assassinated over proposed tax increases.

Most important, the Tea Party focused attention on things that caused great anxiety for many Americans—high unemployment, a weak economy, and uncertainty about the future—and channeled the blame to Obama, while causing amnesia about the failures of politicians of the past, namely President Bush, and the corporations at the heart of the recession. Quietly, the former president sold his Crawford ranch and moved to a well-to-do neighborhood of Dallas. As protests against Obama raged across the country in April 2009, Bush watched on the sidelines without making any public appearances. Privately, though, he had kind words for this new rebellion. Michael Burgess, the Texas representative for the northern Dallas suburbs, arrived at the April 15 Tea Party at the Denton courthouse bearing a message. "Let me just tell you something that happened to me today. I had occasion to sit down with my president, that's George W. Bush," he announced. Bush, Burgess said, had told him to bring the Tea Party his "best wishes."

2

COORDINATING THE MESSAGE

The modern conservative movement has always been advanced by close coordination among its leaders. Although the right is not monolithic, the strategies and campaigns used to advance conservatism and its goals are often organized by small groups of highly ideological partisans, businessmen, and lobbyists. Many of the calls to oppose President Obama can be traced back to at least one of these powerful, often secretive, committees. With Bush and his political deputies out of office, and the Republican National Committee hampered by distrust of its gaffe-prone chairman, Michael Steele, coordinating committees have gained more and more authority within the movement. Some strategic conservative planning committees have become more influential in directing the Republican Party than the Republican Party committees, dictating the agenda, the candidates, and even controlling the right-wing fund-raising to a greater degree. The rightward veer of the conservative movement—from the Tea Parties to the historic level of ugly Republican

partisanship—is also a result of the rise of particularly ideological strategy committees.

Republicans suffered the worst defeat in over a generation
to Democrats on the first Tuesday of November 2008. Just 48
hours later a major meeting of conservatives was convened.
L. Brent Bozell III, a career conservative activist, director of
the Media Research Center, and son of Barry Goldwater's
ghostwriter, organized the meeting in his Shenandoah Valley
country home in Stanley, Virginia, to plot the future of the
American right-wing movement. Several people joined the
discussion by conference call, but twenty other top conservative leaders—including Grover Norquist; Richard Viguerie;
Greg Mueller, the head of the right-wing PR firm Creative
Response Concepts; Tony Perkins of the Family Research
Council; Leonard Leo, an executive member of the Federalist
Society; the Leadership Institute's Morton Blackwell; poll-
ster Kellyanne Conway; and conservative publisher Al
Regnery—were present at Bozell's house in the Blue Ridge
Mountains.[1]

According to the *Washington Times*, most of the attendees expressed relief at the prospect of not having to defend
George Bush and John McCain any longer, and were eager to
mull over plans for the 2010 midterm elections and for taking
back the White House in 2012. Bozell reportedly urged conservatives to dramatically increase their investments in communications technology and grassroots organizing. During
the six-hour meeting, several potential strategies for reviving conservative ideas were discussed, especially the need
for more rigid ideologues and populists like Sarah Palin. "As
the afternoon went on, it didn't take long for attendees to
become resolute in their resistance to moderates and to the
opinion that the conservative movement will become the

opposition to Obama," noted R. Emmett Tyrrell, editor of the *American Spectator*, who attended the meeting.[2] Other attendees attacked conservative *New York Times* columnist David Brooks for endorsing Obama, and called for evicting centrists from the GOP. Viguerie in particular stressed an outside approach of building up the conservative infrastructure and not relying on the Republican Party apparatus. "We will march to our own drummer," said Viguerie.[3] "The GOP leaders can join us whenever they feel like joining us." While not everyone coalesced around the exact strategy, the goals were clear. "The conservative movement is going to retake America," predicted Bozell to the *Washington Times* after the meeting.

The people in Bozell's living room who pledged to rebuild the movement were the same people who laid the foundation for the post-Nixon so-called New Right. Bozell and his associates were almost all over the age of fifty, so it might have seemed ironic that they were the ones plotting the fresh tactics for reviving the twenty-first-century right. But, on the other hand, they were uniquely positioned as the visionaries who had built the modern interlocking network of think thanks, ideological foundations, front groups, media outlets, and training institutes. They had worked for over thirty years to build the Reagan, Gingrich, and Bush eras of power through a powerful coalition combining the religious right, jingoistic populists, the business lobby, and economic libertarians. While they preached capitalism's gospel of self-interest, they had worked carefully behind the scenes to discipline the members of their coalition to promote each other's issues in the interest of advancing the wider conservative movement. In short, Bozell and his group were the ones most capable of leading a new resurgence.

Each member of the Bozell group soon made important contributions to the attacks on Obama and his agenda. In the first few months of the Obama presidency, Greg Mueller worked with former hospital executive Rick Scott to set up a front group called Conservatives for Patients' Rights to mobilize early opposition to health reform. Bozell, through his Media Research Center, a think tank with an $11 million per year budget dedicated to moving the establishment media culture to the right, fired off a round of reports criticizing the media for being too friendly to Obama during the campaign and challenging the major media outlets to report on the administration's "socialist agenda." To the outside observer, the various threads of the conservative infrastructure were simply fulfilling their respective duties. Beneath the surface, however, conservatives began coordinating their efforts—and rivalries broke out to determine the direction of the movement, and who would control it.

Bozell and his colleagues were not the only movement conservatives who tried to fill the vacuum left by the end of the Bush administration. In March of 2009, Newt Gingrich tried to assemble a grand coalition of Republican activists and social conservatives, with himself at the center, through an organization called Renewing American Leadership. In a meeting unveiling his group, Gingrich made a PowerPoint presentation arguing that he could position antitax fiscal conservatives best with social conservatives. His presentation named the U.S. Chamber of Commerce as an example of a natural ally to the Christian right, and suggested that conservatives unite to criticize President Obama's stimulus plan for prohibiting colleges from using federal funds to build or repair religious facilities.[4] Gingrich, seen by many even within Republican circles as a self-interested opportunist, did not gain traction with his group. However, he did sign up the American Family Association, an aggressive network of evangelicals best known for their hatred of gays and Muslims and their annual boycotts of retailers that greet customers with "Happy Holidays" instead of "Merry Christmas."

Republican congressman Eric Cantor quickly flamed out in his own early attempt to establish an organization of conservative leaders. Dubbed the National Council for a New America, Cantor's group recruited several GOP governors, like Louisiana's Bobby Jindal, and lawmakers who would supposedly rebrand what it meant to be conservative and drop the "nostalgia" for old, failed policies.[5] Social conservatives, including former Arkansas governor Mike Huckabee and former Ohio secretary of state Ken Blackwell, sharply rebuked Cantor for excluding topics like gay marriage or abortion from the National Council website issue page.[6] Conservative leaders involved in their own conservative movement leadership committees, such as Newt Gingrich and Family Research Council's Tony Perkins, were not initially invited to Cantor's group. Perkins attacked Cantor for "running scared on the claims of the left and the media that social conservatism is a dead-end for the GOP." But the true death knell for Cantor's National Council came when Rush Limbaugh called it a "scam" and a backdoor attempt by "people who don't believe in conservatism" to "leave Reagan behind."[7] Cantor mustered only a single public event for his group, a town hall session with former governors Mitt Romney and Jeb Bush at a pizza parlor in suburban Virginia. Shortly after Limbaugh's comments, Cantor quietly abandoned his effort, which only lasted about a month after it began in the early stages of the Obama presidency. Cantor's effort at moderation was the only organized attempt for the right to move toward the center after Bush. Its quick death sent a signal that conservative power would remain with activists on the far right.

During much of the Bush administration, Grover Norquist's Americans for Tax Reform held court as the main group coordinating the day-to-day messaging for the movement.[8] Norquist's Wednesday Meeting, a weekly invite-only, off-the-record event, became famous for its role in setting the agenda for conservatives. The meetings, which began in 1993 to coordinate the Republican response to Clinton's health reform plan, were typically a collection of reporters from conservative media outlets, corporate lobbyists, Republican congressional staffers, political strategists, and representatives from various right-wing groups, from the National Rifle Association to the Club for Growth. Norquist provided opportunities for new organizations, young leaders, and groups traditionally outside the conservative sphere—like gay Republicans and single mothers—to present themselves to the establishment.[9] Starting early in Bush's first term, Norquist began exporting his Wednesday Meeting model to state-level groups, as well as to countries like Canada and Japan. In 2010, there were sixty-one Norquist-inspired regular meetings in forty-six states.[10]

Networking the various elements of the conservative movement brought many successes for Norquist. Chief among them were the passage of the estimated $2.5 trillion Bush tax cuts and the administration's rollback of environmental regulations, labor protections, and some social programs. Ken Mehlman, the Republican National Committee chairman during several years of Bush's tenure, leaned heavily on Norquist and his meetings to reelect Bush as well as

Republicans around the country. However, the failure of Bush's drive to privatize Social Security, long prioritized by Norquist and often discussed at his meetings, may have tested the limits of even the combined efforts of nearly every conservative group.

Norquist's role as the conduit for corporate lobbyists and the right mired him in several controversies. *Mother Jones* reported, "Oregon Department of Justice investigators found [Norquist's Americans for Tax Reform] had served as a conduit in what authorities said was a 'laundering scheme,' through which Norquist collected money from Oregon business leaders and trade groups that was then rerouted into the coffers of Oregon Taxpayers United, an anti-tax organization working to limit state spending." He frequently funneled money from Republican Party committees into attack ads, despite his group's nonpartisan tax-exempt status. During the Jack Abramoff investigation, Norquist was exposed for selling support from his front groups to corporations. In one damning e-mail, Abramoff promised Norquist $50,000 dollars in exchange for providing his Americans for Tax Reform support to one of Abramoff's clients.[11] Unlike most front groups serving as the nexus between supposedly ideological entities and corporate lobbying, however, Norquist has been fairly honest about his behavior. "I am aggressively letting people who might want to be involved in soft-money contributions know what we do," he once commented.[12]

But Norquist's greatest conflict with the movement has had nothing to do with his alleged money laundering or association with Abramoff—it has been his adamant inclusion of right-wing minority and gay groups. Center for Security Policy president Frank Gaffney spread smears against

Norquist, claiming that he was attempting to bring known terrorists into the conservative movement. Gaffney, writing several documents connecting Norquist with al Qaeda figures, repeatedly tried to purge Norquist for his outreach to Muslim Americans.[13] Gaffney, a well-funded racist, has written multiple articles accusing President Obama of being the "first Muslim President" and claims that Obama is a member of the "Muslim Brotherhood," which Gaffney says is trying "to destroy Western civilization from within by its own miserable hand."[14] While Gaffney's purge was ultimately unsuccessful, it tarnished Norquist's reputation with much of the right. Norquist's policy positions alienated him from the movement too. Norquist's support for Bush's failed attempt at immigration reform and many other minority-friendly positions placed him even further at odds with the larger right-wing community. He has also caught flak from the Christian right for his outspoken support for gay rights groups, but still joined the board of GOProud, an organization developed for gay Republicans.[15] Because of his outreach, he has been lampooned by several anonymous conservatives as a "freak show."

In the Obama era, Norquist has taken a far more subdued position as other groups and meetings have largely displaced him. However, he still maintained his meetings, which continued to draw 150 a week in June 2010, according to a *Washington Post* blog. He also continued to connect key elements of the right for corporate interests. I reported in March 2010 about a Tea Party rally in Georgia against a proposal to levy a dollar-a-pack cigarette tax increase to close the budget deficit. The rally, it turned out, was organized in part by Norquist with funds from tobacco giant Philip Morris.[16] Two months later, I exposed a new anti–

Net Neutrality front called No Net Brutality which presented at Norquist's Wednesday Meeting. This new front was created by David MacLean, a Canadian staffer at the Alberta Enterprise Group, working with a team through a "think tank MBA" program at the Atlas Economic Research Foundation—an international think tank that primarily helps new front groups and libertarian think tanks get off the ground all over the world, including in the United States. Together they smeared Net Neutrality, a regulation permitting an open and free Internet, by claiming it was somehow equivalent to Chinese government censorship. A month after MacLean's presentation, which used information supplied by the telecommunications industry, Norquist organized a multifaceted campaign to kill Net Neutrality. He brought several groups to Capitol Hill, including minority organizations like the Hispanic Leadership Fund, to denounce the regulation alongside Florida Republican Cliff Stearns, who used the press event to announce new legislation to ban the FCC from enforcing Net Neutrality. Norquist gave brief remarks, in which he used several talking points from MacLean's presentation, then unveiled a $1.4 million ad campaign attacking Net Neutrality under the Americans for Prosperity brand.[17] It was classic Norquist, and a textbook example of how he leverages the power and ideas of various groups to advance a corporate mission.

As Norquist has faded somewhat from his position organizing broad national campaigns across the conservative movement, other groups have stepped up to fill the void. A weekly, invite-only meeting called the Weyrich Lunch, named after Heritage Foundation and American Legislative Exchange Council founder Paul Weyrich, who died in

2008, connects Republican politicians and congressional Republican staffers with key movers and shakers of the right.[18] Founded in 1983 and also meeting on Wednesdays, the Weyrich Lunch is similar to Norquist's breakfast in that it serves as a venue for conservative strategists to meet and make certain their lobbying and messaging campaigns. At a lunch in the summer of 2009, Republican Senator John Thune presented his proposal to allow concealed weapons across state lines. Thune, who had long postured as an advocate for states' rights, would have eviscerated state gun laws with his amendment.[19] Regardless, his presentation at the Weyrich Lunch reportedly galvanized support and motivated bloggers like Redstates' Erick Erickson into promoting the measure, which ultimately failed by a narrow margin.[20]

But unlike Norquist's breakfast meeting, the Weyrich Lunch is dominated by social conservatives and fire-breathing reactionaries who place ideological purity over making the conservative "team bigger," as Norquist would say.[21] The lunch mirrors the sensibilities of its namesake, who was known as "the Robespierre of the right" for his eager purges of moderate Republicans. Sponsors of the lunch include the rabidly conservative 60 Plus Association, a front group posturing as a right-wing alternative to the AARP; Let Freedom Ring, a group funded partially by John Templeton Jr., a billionaire heir and promoter of evangelical causes; the American Society for the Defense of Tradition, Family and Property, an extremist Catholic organization; Judicial Watch, the Right to Work Committee, the powerful evangelical lobby; the Family Research Council, James Dobson's political organization; and several other groups forming the traditional right-wing coalition. Republican lawmakers giving speeches at the Lunch have been dressed down and forced to explain any bipartisan votes or other moves perceived as violating right-wing values. A 2004 *National Review* article about the general atmosphere of the lunch described it as "more inquisitorial that at Norquist's meeting":

> A congressman is hauled over the coals for pondering a run for the Senate and thereby losing a place on a key committee. Bullied about an upcoming vote on school vouchers in the District of Columbia, a senator promises to provide the names of his colleagues who might be "a little wobbly.". . . Every piece of paper at the Weyrich meeting is also a call to arms. Two-thirds of all partial-birth abortions are committed in New Jersey! Half of all marriages end in divorce! Girls Gone Wild videos are for sale in supermarkets![22]

The lunch may seem like a throwback to the culture wars of the nineties, or for that matter, the sixties, but post-Bush, it has reemerged as the main get-together for crafting the conservative agenda.

After Weyrich's death on December 18, 2008, the Leadership Institute's Morton Blackwell and Let Freedom Ring leader Colin Hanna took over as the chairmen of the lunch. Before, Norquist commanded power because of his close relationship with Karl Rove and other key Bush administration political figures. During that period, operatives would focus on attending the Norquist breakfast and only later that day attend the Weyrich Lunch if they needed to work on an issue related to conservative social values, like marriage or abortion. However, more and more conservatives now flock every Wednesday to a small D.C. Christian coffeehouse called Ebeneezer's, the venue for the Weyrich Lunch, as the prime destination for organizing opposition to Obama.

The growing prominence of the Weyrich Lunch has affected crucial political developments in the Obama era. Several groups closely associated with the lunch, including the 60 Plus Association, the Family Research Council, and the Susan B. Anthony List, ran millions of dollars' worth of ads during the health reform fight—using donor money that might have otherwise gone to Norquist-related organizations in the Bush era.[23]

Republican elected leaders have also gravitated more and more to the lunch. During the first two years of the Obama administration, Representative Mike Pence (R-IN), then the third most powerful Republican in the House, promised to attend every single meeting of the lunch to update the members about the activity in the GOP caucus, legislative fights, and what to expect that week. If he could not attend, he also pledged that he would send either Representative John Boehner (R-OH), then the minority leader, or Representative Eric Cantor (R-VA), the Republican whip, as his replacement. Indeed, after Republicans seized the House in 2010, GOP leadership sent a representative—often a freshman lawmaker—to the meeting every week.[24]

Starting in 2009, Weyrich Lunch supporters expanded by setting up their own Wednesday morning breakfast—a special meeting time for the Conservative Action Project—at the offices of the Family Research Council. The new breakfast, according to Weyrich Lunch supporters, was not an effort to force conservatives to choose between Norquist's

Wednesday morning meeting or their own. Although the timing of the new Family Research Council breakfast comes close to overlapping with Norquist's, it was scheduled so that conservatives could attend both. Even though Norquist was among the members of the post-2009 election meeting at Brent Bozell's house, most of the attendees, including Bozell, R. Emmett Tyrrell, Alfred Regnery, Richard Viguerie, and of course Tony Perkins, chose the Weyrich Lunch and Family Research Council Wednesday breakfast as their new Wednesday morning haunt.

The influence of the Lunch has played out behind the scenes in Republican primary battles. When Congressman Pete Sessions, chairman of the National Republican Campaign Committee (NRCC), came to the Weyrich Lunch, Politico reported that he was angrily confronted by attendees for supporting Dede Scozzafava, a moderate Republican running in a special election in upstate New York. Sessions's NRCC had donated well over $1 million to Scozzafava, a popular upstate New York assemblywoman.[25] "There were some raised voices," observed an anonymous source at the lunch. But unlike any ordinary band of hard right activists upset with the Republican establishment, the Weyrich Lunch members were prepared to back up their words with action. Groups associated with the lunch threatened to withhold money from the NRCC, and several of the regular lunch attendees launched a smear campaign attacking Scozzafava with an avalanche of ads and robo-calls in the district.[26] The Susan B. Anthony List, for instance, sent staffers into the district and attacked Scozzafava as an "abortion radical" and claimed her candidacy jeopardized the "lives of women and their unborn babies." Scozzafava eventually suspended her campaign the weekend before the election and endorsed her opponent, Democrat Bill Owens. On election day, the longtime Republican district fell to Owens over the Weyrich Lunch and Tea Party favorite in the race, New York Conservative Party candidate Doug Hoffman.

Nonetheless, Weyrich Lunch attendees celebrated the electoral defeat as a success. Scozzafava favored some abortion rights and was less antiunion than most Republicans. The election of a Democrat over such a moderate Republican kept the party, and the movement, more ideologically pure. A *Washington Post* account of the Conservative Action Project and the Weyrich Lunch noted that at the Redstate morning briefing, blogger Erick Erickson's widely distributed daily e-mail newsletter of talking points helped ensure that the wider right-wing movement stuck to the argument that Scozzafava's loss was actually a good thing for conservatives.[27]

Before the Scozzafava campaign fiasco, Republican Party planners had pinned their 2010 midterm election prospects on a cadre of moderate, even liberal, Republicans who could appeal to independent voters and disaffected Democrats. Republican strategists for the Senate organized endorsements and support for Republican Governor Charlie Crist of Florida, the only Republican governor to openly embrace President Obama's stimulus, for his bid to the Senate. Similarly, the same establishment party strategists were openly building the campaign infrastructure for former Lieutenant Governor Jane Norton, another moderate, to run for Senate.[28] The planners, more focused on electoral victory than conservative purity, ignored non-mainstream candidates like Tea Party–backed Republican Marco Rubio, who vied for the Republican nomination in Florida, and Ken

Buck, another far-right primary candidate in Colorado. But the Scozzafava effect sent shock waves through the GOP, and shortly after November 2009, Republican Party candidate committees pledged to stay neutral.

Rubio gained steam by directly addressing many of the Weyrich Lunch sponsors at a Council for National Policy summit in Naples, Florida, in March 2010. Maggie Gallagher, an audience member for Rubio's speech and former president of the antigay National Organization for Marriage, gushed "when Rubio speaks, he is not spinning—he is weaving together from his life story, in his person as well as his words, the frayed threads of the old Reagan coalition."[29] Gallagher had been active in purging Scozzafava, and called for conservatives to rebuke the moderate Crist.[30] Norton and dozens of other moderate GOP nominees for Congress would later go down in crushing primary election defeats to far more radical Republican candidates. Crist avoided the embarrassment of a loss to Rubio by bolting the party altogether and running as an independent. In the end, Rubio easily won his election. While many forces—especially the influence of talk radio and Fox News—affected the outcome of Republican primaries, the Weyrich Lunch–drawn line in the sand against moderate Republicans reverberated in campaigns across the country.

The most prominent, and underreported, example of Weyrich Lunch influence was its role in elevating radical right Senate candidates in Delaware and Alaska. Early in 2010, a parade of far-right challengers hoping to upset Republican establishment-ordained candidates for Senate visited D.C.—and specifically the Weyrich Lunch—to find support. In Delaware, the Republican establishment sought Representative Mike Castle (R-DE), one of the most moderate members of the entire Republican caucus, to run for Senate. Every poll showed him beating any leading Democrat in the state, including New Castle County Executive Chris Coons and Delaware Attorney General Beau Biden, the son of the vice president. However, a local antiabortion activist named Christine O'Donnell—known primarily for her status as a perennial fringe candidate— went to the Weyrich Lunch for support.

O'Donnell had known the Weyrich Lunch leaders through her work leading the abstinence group The Savior's Alliance for Lifting the Truth, and the Weyrich Lunch supporters admired her staunch right-wing positions, particularly in contrast to Castle. Quietly, before any other national groups entered the race, the Family Research Council sent organizers into Delaware to reach out to local Tea Party groups and to build O'Donnell's candidacy. In August of 2010, the bombastic Tea Party organizing group Tea Party Express endorsed O'Donnell and led a highly publicized primary effort to help her win the nomination. Similarly, attorney Joe Miller, a friend of Sarah Palin, visited the Weyrich Lunch early in 2010 to lock up support in his primary campaign against incumbent Senator Lisa Murkowski (R-AK). Again, after a friendly reception at the Weyrich Lunch, the Family Research Council dispatched organizers and resources to help Miller win his race. Family Research Council operatives worked with local evangelical groups to tie supporters of a ballot initiative requiring parent notification of teenage abortions to the candidate. Both O'Donnell and Miller won stunning upsets against their more moderate Republican primary opponents.

In both cases, the Tea Party Express claimed credit for the primary victories of newcomers like O'Donnell and Miller.

But the true initial support came from the Weyrich Lunch. When Weyrich Lunch chairman Colin Hanna explained his strategy in September of 2010, he believed that both O'Donnell and Miller could win their general elections.[31] He had personally recorded a radio ad mocking Murkowski as a "Queen" for not bowing out of the race after her primary loss (she continued to run as a write-in candidate). However, in the end both Miller and O'Donnell went down in spectacularly crushing defeats—Murkowski won a historic write-in campaign, and Democrat Chris Coons sailed to victory in Delaware. The Weyrich Lunch could flex its muscle, but its strength also undermined Republican efforts to regain control of the Senate in 2010.

Extremely conservative Republican politicians, like Senator Jim Inhofe, Congressman Louie Gohmert, and Virginia attorney general Ken Cuccinelli, are reportedly close to the Weyrich Lunch and the Conservative Action Project. Inhofe, on several occasions, has addressed the Weyrich meeting to explain issues ranging from judicial appointments to environmental issues.[32] Inhofe takes a particularly hard-line conservative position on both subject areas. He announced that he would oppose Supreme Court nominees Sonia Sotomayor and Elena Kagan before hearings were even scheduled, and has earned a reputation for fighting tooth and nail against every attempt to address climate change. Several years before Obama's presidency, Inhofe was alone in the Senate in asserting that climate change is a complete "hoax." However, Inhofe's views had become the conservative status quo by the end of 2009. A study compiled by climate activist and blogger Brad Johnson found that over half of the Republican class of 2010 did not believe in climate science.

The Weyrich Lunch and its affiliated meetings and groups provided a nexus for right-wing front groups organizing the Tea Parties to collaborate with other conservative groups and corporate fronts. FreedomWorks, one of the premier groups organizing Tea Parties, sent its vice president Matt Kibbe, campaign director Brendan Steinhauser, and New Media Director Tabitha Hale to different Weyrich Lunch meetings. Americans for Prosperity, the other major group dedicated to mobilizing Tea Party protests, had its director Tim Phillips attend many Conservative Action Project strategy breakfasts. Several other Tea Party groups, like Liberty Central, the "grassroots" conservative group founded by Supreme Court Justice Clarence Thomas's wife Ginni Thomas, were regular participants in the Weyrich-related sessions. Essentially every new conservative advocacy group relied on the Weyrich Lunch membership to branch out and coordinate its efforts.

The rise of religious intolerance within the conservative movement is also a reflection of the growing prominence of the Weyrich Lunch and its members. Muslim-haters like Frank Gaffney, Norquist's tormenter, were regular faces at Weyrich Lunches in 2009 and 2010. Starting in the summer of 2010, Gaffney started a coalition website called StopThe911Mosque.com to mobilize opposition to the Cordoba House, a proposed Islamic community center and mosque a few blocks from Ground Zero.[33] Through Liz Cheney's neoconservative group Keep America Safe, Gaffney's coalition ran ads against the Cordoba House and mobilized anti-Muslim rallies in lower Manhattan. He also brought in other Weyrich Lunch sponsors, like Liberty Central and the Traditional Values Coalition, to assist with the effort.

From the sidelines, Norquist was one of the few conservative leaders to speak out against the transparently anti-Muslim effort to prevent the construction of the Cordoba House. He called the Gaffney campaign a "distraction" that Republicans should not pursue.[34] But his voice was by then drowned out by the chorus of Republican and conservative movement leaders all marching to the Gaffney's Islamophobic tune. America's Future Fund, an establishment Republican front group, began running ads attacking Democrats for supporting the right of Muslims to build the Cordoba House, as did Roy Blunt in his campaign for Senate in Missouri. Sarah Palin, Newt Gingrich, and almost every prominent right-wing pundit chimed in with anti–Cordoba House rhetoric.

This rising tide of anti-Muslim zealotry cannot be viewed in a vacuum. William Murray, the leader of a right-wing Christian political action committee and longtime attendee of the Weyrich Lunch, explained that organized efforts to demonize the Cordoba House took shape at Weyrich Lunch meetings.[35] He also said he hoped to launch new anti-Muslim crusades in 2011 and 2012 to set the stage for the next election. "Where in America should Muslims be allowed to build mosques?" I asked. He replied that none should be constructed in America until every Christian church destroyed in a Muslim country is rebuilt. Gaffney had helped organize an effort to place a successful ballot initiative in Oklahoma to ban Sharia law in state courts. The initiative was arguably unconstitutional, but it served as a powerful wedge issue that could be exploited in swing states for future elections. Murray explained that more ballot initiatives like the Oklahoma example would be crucial for Republican efforts in 2012.

The prominence of the Weyrich Lunch ensured that once-fringe activists like Murray held a central role in the Obama-era conservative movement. And it wasn't just Murray's prejudice that gained such a wide audience. Extremist candidates such as Christine O'Donnell and Joe Miller became GOP stalwarts, at least for one election cycle. Far-right gun legislation and radical obstruction to anything Obama proposed became incorporated into the political machinery beyond the K Street–prescribed filibusters to economy reforms. And most of all, the Republican leadership began playing second fiddle to the organizing strength of Weyrich Lunch leaders.

THE HERITAGE FOUNDATION, STILL THE CENTER OF CONSERVATISM

The Heritage Foundation, founded in 1973 to lead the "New Right" revolution against liberalism, became the cornerstone of the conservative movement during the eighties when it structured many of President Reagan's policies and appointments. Heritage expanded through the years, but continued the core goal of assisting congressional Republicans and Republican administrations. A People for the American Way report noted that Heritage officials declared that much of the second President Bush's domestic policies were "straight out of the Heritage play book."[36] And indeed they were, from Bush's faith-based initiatives to endless orders to deregulate business. Top conservative talkers like Rush Limbaugh and Sean Hannity have long referred to Heritage as the source for their research. The idea factory model of Heritage is streamlined by a Heritage website called Policy Expert, which allows hundreds of conservative scholars to be dispatched for media appearances, conferences, or to town hall meetings hosted by Republican lawmakers, where they can provide academic cover for Republican policies. Additionally, Heritage's "Candidates Briefing Book" is widely used among almost all Republican candidates for Congress, providing them talking points and statistics to campaign on.[37] Heritage also maintains one of the largest job banks for the conservative movement, with full-time staffers organizing employment conferences for right-wing operatives at every stage of their careers. By supplying policy ideas, hosting an endless array of conservative experts to testify on behalf of legislation, as well as other services, Heritage has become what many correctly call the "most influential conservative think tank."

Much of Heritage's decisive influence, however, must be measured by its primary—if underrecognized—role in coordinating the conservative movement and thereby setting the strategy for advancing cohesive right-wing ideals. Heritage sets the agenda for state-level conservative think tanks through the State Policy Network umbrella group, and its affiliated "Resource Bank" conference, while also providing assistance for right-wing think tanks internationally through its partnership with the Atlas Economic Research Foundation. During the Obama presidency, Heritage took an even more aggressive stance, pulling together the key elements of the conservative coalition to fight progressives at every opportunity.

Starting in 2006, Heritage began holding a weekly meeting called the Blogger Briefing in its offices to allow conservative voices from the blogosphere to meet top Republican strategists and politicians and hash out framing advice. In early 2012, the American Legislative Exchange Council faced a growing corporate boycott over its role in crafting the "Stand Your Ground" law that permitted a boy in Florida to be shot by a vigilante neighborhood patrolman. The public relations strategy to combat the criticism was crafted at the Heritage Bloggers Briefing. Attendees were asked to help design a "Stand with ALEC" social media campaign.

Flaunting their disregard for their status as a nonpartisan tax-exempt nonprofit, Heritage hosted officers from Republican campaign committees at blogger meetings where the Republican campaign officers suggested strategies for defeating Democrats or promoting Republicans. However, most of the Blogger Briefings are policy related, and have ranged from how to defeat health reform to how to extend the Bush tax cuts. Heritage's Robert Bluey, the director for its Center for Media and Public Policy, worked to build a rapid response network of right-wing bloggers and journalists not just through the Blogger Briefing, but also through private listservs and collaborations with other online conservative news outlets. Townhall.com, an online portal to conservative opinion and radio-show hosts, was initially created by Heritage, but was later bought by Salem Communications. During the Obama presidency, Heritage spawned a new social networking website called Heritage for America. Organized under the 501c(4) tax code, which permits issue-based political advocacy, Heritage for America sought to connect grassroots activists with opportunities to campaign against Democrats.

To guide the movement, Heritage provides the practical service of connecting conservative scholars and strategists with active donors around the country. There are regional committee groups for Heritage in Atlanta, Chicago, San Francisco, New York City, Omaha, and several other cities. A typical regional committee event would bring a conservative celebrity such as Karl Rove or radio host Herman Cain for a short speech, and afterward a cocktail party would provide a chance for donors to mingle with local Republican staffers and local conservative activists. For higher-level donors, there are "President's Club" conferences, such as the President's Club meeting in the cavernous Reagan International Trade Center in Washington, D.C., on May 4, 2009. More of a pep rally than an ideas conference, the President's Club conference was essentially a day of speeches from right-wing Republicans on how the party would triumph over progressive reforms promised by Obama. At dinner, Rush Limbaugh regaled the crowd with a reprise of his radio routine, then began boasting about his $400 million contract with the radio conglomerate Clear Channel. "I've never had financially a down year. There's supposedly a recession," he said, grinning. He continued, "Back in February we already had 102% of 2008 overbooked for 2009. So I always believed that if we're going to have a recession, just don't participate!" The crowd of donors erupted in laughter. At the front-row dinner table, Thomas Saunders, a wealthy Wall Street investor and a top donor to Heritage and many other right-wing causes, was seated between Supreme Court Justice Clarence Thomas and South Carolina Senator Jim DeMint.*

---

* From my position on a balcony above, I couldn't tell if Saunders and his table were enjoying Limbaugh's joke about the suffering economy, but everyone seemed to be having a good time.

To coordinate messaging on some of the most important issues for the conservative movement, Heritage created a set of ad hoc organizations in 2009. Heritage partnered with the Acton Institute to launch "Seek Social Justice," an effort to guide the evangelical community toward the belief that the best way to help the poor was to slash government programs and welfare institutions.[38] Heritage initiated a site called "Fix Health Care Policy" to provide rapid response attacks on health reform legislation.[39] Many of the attacks leveled by Republican lawmakers on the floor of the House of Representatives came straight from Heritage's daily talking points about the legislation. Heritage focused its criticism on health care reform's individual mandate, denouncing it as "both unprecedented and unconstitutional," and on the reform's expansion of Medicaid, attacking the proposal as stretching a "broken entitlement program" that provides "low-quality" care. Ironically, in 2006, Heritage had worked with then-Governor Mitt Romney to help him formulate his health reform plan in Massachusetts to include both a Medicaid expansion and an individual mandate. At the time, Heritage hailed Romney's individual mandate as "clearly consistent with conservative values," and his plan to expand Medicaid coverage as an innovative way to reduce "the total cost to taxpayers" by taking people out of the "uncompensated care pool."[40] Big conservative "ideas" put forward by Heritage often amount to window dressing for GOP policy positions.

The Heritage Foundation's most audacious move to harness the conservative movement has been its role in crafting the Conservative Action Project—a strategy committee that meets at the Wednesday morning breakfast hosted by the Family Research Council. This is the same meeting that rivals Norquist's Wednesday morning planning meeting and is closely connected to the aggressively ideological Weyrich Lunch. The Conservative Action Project is actually part of a broader plan set forth by Heritage vice president Becky Norton Dunlop, a point person for Heritage's sprawling external affairs program. Throughout her career, Dunlop had spun through the revolving door of working in various Republican administrations on both the state and federal level, a corporate PR firm, and multiple conservative nonprofits, including Heritage, the Alexis de Tocqueville Institute, and the Virginia Institute for Public Policy. A committed conservative, Dunlop was once asked how to spread conservative ideas at a panel discussion hosted by the Atlas Economic Research Foundation. "How do you maintain liberty?" Dunlop replied, "Well, at the end it's at the cartridge box if you can't win at the ballot box."[41] She then smiled and said that her response was probably too "extreme" for her audience of international right-of-center donors.

As the Heritage Foundation's "chief ambassador" to the movement, Dunlop helps the American Conservative Union plan its annual CPAC convention, the largest annual gathering of conservatives.[42] As a former standing member of the Philanthropy Roundtable, Dunlop and her external affairs team also organize multiple events to bring corporate donors and conservative foundations together, and she organizes regional and President's Club events. Dunlop sits on the boards of over half a dozen other organizations, from the Phillips Foundation, which disburses grants to young right-wing journalists, to the Family Foundation of Virginia, a religious right powerhouse in the state, to the American Conservative Union itself.

Despite Dunlop's impressive set of official responsibilities, her most important duty is not revealed on her profile page on the Heritage Foundation website. Behind the scenes, Dunlop serves as the president of the Council for National Policy (CNP), a secretive right-wing committee that has brought together key Republican officials, Christian right leaders, and wealthy right-wing donors to set the conservative agenda since 1981. Although she had been a director for the CNP for many years, according to tax disclosures filed with the IRS, Dunlop appeared to take the reins of the organization in 2008. Called the "most powerful conservative group you've never heard of" by ABC News, the CNP is still critical to the conservative movement, and deeply entwined with Heritage and other prime players of the conservative movement.[43]

Initially organized by fundamentalist preacher Tim LaHaye, author of the Left Behind Rapture-genre series, the CNP is credited with cementing the role of the religious right within the modern Republican Party. The CNP initially hosted Pat Robertson, the televangelist owner of a network of different Christian media companies, Moral Majority Founder Jerry Falwell, LaHaye, and theologian Cleon Skousen, an influential thinker within the religious right who wrote that white slave masters were the real victims in the antebellum South. Some of the first wealthy businessmen included in CNP were Amway's Richard DeVos and oilman Charles Koch. Reagan Attorney General Ed Meese eagerly embraced the group and served as a direct link between the CNP and the Reagan White House. In addition to Republican Party officials, the religious right, and wealthy donors, CNP members include representatives from the conservative media infrastructure, libertarians, and many neoconservatives. Although the CNP has never allowed the press access to its events, it is widely known that the group hosts several meetings a year to allow Republican leaders to consult with movement conservative types. According to Bob Barr, the Republican lawmaker who spearheaded the impeachment proceedings against President Clinton, Barr met with the CNP to hone "our message and focus" around the impeachment effort at a CNP meeting in 1997, well before Clinton made his claim that he did not have "sexual relations" with Monica Lewinsky. In his memoirs, Barr said the CNP members were in "near universal agreement" that impeachment was necessary because of Clinton's "abuses of power" concerning "national security."[44] However, CNP continued to support the impeachment when it transformed into a crusade against Clinton's claims about his sexual improprieties.

In 1999, George W. Bush reportedly gave a speech to the CNP promising to only appoint pro-life judges, which in turn helped guarantee the support of CNP members and solidify Bush's nomination in the Republican primaries. Although little is known about the activities of CNP events, many have speculated about the degree to which CNP used its influence within the Bush administration. Salon's Ben Van Heuvelen has noted that the rise of the private military contractor Blackwater, now known as Academi, might have stemmed from the fact that Blackwater CEO Erik Prince's parents Edgar and Elsa Prince were prominent donors to the CNP and its affiliates, especially the Family Research Council. Prince family members met regularly with prominent Bush administration war planners, like Dick Cheney, Donald Rumsfeld, and Paul Bremer, through the CNP.

John McCain kowtowed to the CNP in a speech shortly

after locking up the GOP nomination in 2008, but still struggled to gain their trust. "I want to look you in the eye and tell you that I won't let you down," pledged McCain to the group of evangelicals and donors in his March 2008 address to the group.[45] According to the *New York Times*'s David Kirkpatrick, several audience members in the CNP crowd said that McCain made "little impression" despite his pandering. James Dobson, Tony Perkins, and many social conservatives simply did not trust McCain, and viewed his acclaimed "maverick" streak as a liability to the movement. According to the *New York Times* and the *Nation*'s Max Blumenthal, CNP officials finally pledged their support to the McCain campaign—and in turn the support of tens of thousands of evangelical churches organized by CNP members, various right-wing front groups owned by CNP members, and other conservative organizations—only after McCain selected Sarah Palin as his running mate.[46]

To make the CNP more proactive in the day-to-day political confrontations with Obama's agenda, Heritage's Becky Norton Dunlop created a CNP subsidiary called the Conservative Action Project (CAP). Dunlop financed the CAP project partially with a $50,000 grant from the Bradley Foundation, and with support from Heritage and the Free Congress Foundation. CAP organized a set of action alerts, simple memos outlining where conservatives should engage in political disputes or appointments. CAP's first major calls to action were to oppose President Obama's first budget proposal, the nomination of David Hamilton, who was Obama's first appellate judge appointment, and a piece of legislation aimed at expanding the definition of hate crimes to extend to attacks on members of the gay, lesbian, and transgender community. Hamilton was eventually confirmed, and Democrats prevailed in each of these initial battles, but each attempt at organizing opposition provided opportunities for conservatives to collaborate.

The right-wing movement's opposition to Hamilton conveyed a revitalized sense of cohesiveness. CAP distributed a scrub sheet on Judge Hamilton, alleging that he was a "liberal judicial activist who would impose his radical ACLU-inspired agenda from the bench" and also circulated a smear that Hamilton had ruled "that prayers to Jesus Christ offered at the beginning of legislative sessions violate the Constitution, but that prayers to Allah do not." As Ian Millhiser noted in the Huffington Post, Hamilton had simply struck down "sectarian" prayer in the Indiana legislature—not exclusively the words "Jesus Christ"—and in a postjudgment motion, clarified that prayers may include all "non-sectarian" general references to God in any language.[47] The CNP's Conservative Action Project compelled Senator Jeff Sessions, the ranking Republican on the Judiciary Committee, to denounce Hamilton and organize a filibuster, which was announced through a speech at Heritage. Senator James Inhofe, a Republican close to the Conservative Action Project, repeated the CNP-created myth that Hamilton favored Allah over Jesus Christ. Two dozen conservative organizations signed a letter under Conservative Action Project letterhead calling for a filibuster, blogger Erick Erickson mobilized conservative bloggers to demand that their readers call senators to oppose Hamilton, and the *Washington Times* and Fox News blared attacks incessantly against the judge. The right-wing coordination prompted traditional news outlets, like *Politico*, to frame Hamilton as "controversial," even though his nomination had previously been supported by Democrats and Republicans alike.[48] The *Hill* newspaper pointed out that nine of the twenty-two groups seeking a filibuster against Hamilton had signed another letter in 2005 calling for Republicans to abolish the filibuster for Bush's judicial nominees.

In late 2009, Heritage president Ed Feulner expressed his satisfaction with the work of the Conservative Action Project in a memo to movement leaders. *American Spectator* editor R. Emmett Tyrrell, a recipient of Feulner's memo, said that the Heritage chief noticed that "since the Conservative Action Project began its efforts conservatives are working together more and quarrelling less."[49] Feulner also outlined a plan to bring about six different "working groups" of members representing different conservative constituent organizations.

Consciously channeling the Sharon Statement—a 1960 agreement among conservatives to unite around common principles—Feulner drafted a memo called the "Mount Vernon Statement" for a widely publicized event in mid-February of 2010. The Mount Vernon Statement reaffirmed the position of a hawkish foreign policy, religious right values, free-market capitalism, and limited government. But more important, it served as a flashpoint for the Heritage Foundation to expand its Conservative Action Project coalition. Feulner worked closely with Becky Norton Dunlop and his other deputies to use the Mount Vernon Statement ceremony to sign up a much broader coalition of conservative groups—from the Gun Owners of America, a militia group supporting the "right" of Americans to take up arms against the government, to the Galen Institute, an industry-friendly health care think tank, to the Tea Party Patriots, the umbrella Tea Party organizing group supported by FreedomWorks. By early 2010, the expanded coalition included over 80 different conservative groups, all coordinating their attacks through the Conservative Action Project and its weekly action alert memos. Ned Ryun, who was the head of the American Majority and one of the signatories to the new coalition, explained the reasoning for the Conservative Action Project. He told the *Washington Post*, conservatives "have been stuck in the mind-set that good ideas win out simply because they're good ideas. Without proper organization, they don't."

The Conservative Action Project, under the auspices of Heritage Foundation leadership, organized broad right-wing opposition to health reform, the DISCLOSE Act, which was a campaign finance reform meant to increase transparency in campaign spending, Wall Street reform, and many other measures. The strategy used against judge David Hamilton was used against respected Berkeley law professor Goodwin Liu, Obama's pick for the Ninth U.S. Circuit Court of Appeals. His nomination had been first opposed by the *National Review*'s Ed Whelan, who wrote in February of 2010 that Liu's record "represents a volatile mix of aggressive left-wing ideology and raw inexperience." The Conservative Action Project took up the challenge of opposing Liu a month later and deployed an action alert with suggested weaknesses about Liu's nomination. The memo denounced him for opposing the Prop 8 ban on gay marriage in California and for once daring to write that the Constitution "assigns equal constitutional status to negative rights against government oppression and positive rights to government assistance on the ground that both are essential to liberty." The volley of attacks began on Heritage's blog and on the Morning Bell, Heritage's online newsletter, which deemed Liu as "Obama's most radical judicial nominee." Americans for Limited Government's Bill Wilson condemned Liu in a press release, stating, "Beneath the 'nice guy' exterior, Goodwin Liu, like Obama, is a radical redistributionist of the first order."[50] One Conservative Action Project memo fired off against Liu was literally reprinted as a news article in the publication *Human Events*.[51] Conservative blogs and talk radio again led the charge in organizing calls to Congress to oppose Liu.

The American Bar Association endorsed Liu, as did many legal scholars on both ends of the political spectrum. According to the *New York Times*, Kenneth Starr, the dean of Pepperdine's law school and former Whitewater prosecutor, co-wrote a letter praising Liu and stating that he should be confirmed because he "is a person of great intellect, accomplishment and integrity, and he is exceptionally well-qualified to serve on the court of appeals."[52] Nevertheless, the conservative movement, from social groups to fiscal conservative organizations to Tea Parties, had placed enough pressure to embolden a bloc of Republican senators to effectively kill Liu's nomination. The Conservative Action Project prevailed.

A FOUNTAIN OF CASH

In a drab office space at New York Avenue and 14th Street, just around the corner from the White House, elements of the Bush White House constructed a network of nonprofits dedicated to seizing power. This effort was not about restoring small government or changing America's cultural fabric. It was a cold, calculated project to seize tens of millions in anonymous corporate money and use it to clobber their enemies with deceptive advertisements. Unlike the ideological right, these men—some of them lobbyists, most of them experienced partisans—had one and only conviction: defeating Democrats.

The informal network, called the Weaver Terrace Group, named after the street where Karl Rove convened meetings at his home, came together because of the *Citizens United* ruling. On January 21, 2010, the Supreme Court, in a 5-4 decision, eliminated nearly a century of campaign finance law by allowing corporations and unions to spend unlimited amounts on electioneering. It was the second ruling in a row, after *F.E.C. v. Wisconsin Right to Life*, which allowed corporate-funded "issue-ads" to be run near election season, to open the floodgates to big business influence.

That spring, as Democrats toiled over health reform, jobs measures, and the financial overhaul known as Dodd-Frank, the Republican planners got to work. *Citizens United* provided an opportunity, but why would any corporation risk the public backlash of directly backing a candidate or cause? The idea, therefore, was floated to take advantage of the decision by developing a sprawling network of nonprofit organizations to funnel corporate cash into campaign commercials. The nonprofit organizations would simply be brands to conceal the true financiers of the advertisements. As Democrats continued their push for reforms, these GOP lobbyists and ad-makers would solicit funds from the companies that faced new regulations or taxes.

In February, only just short of a month after the *Citizens United* ruling, a group of Republicans, among them former Senator Norm Coleman, former Congressional Budget Office economist Doug Holtz-Eakin, and Karl Rove, Bush's right-hand political strategist, announced a new set of groups. The organizations, known collectively as American

Crossroads, American Action Network, American Action Forum, and American Crossroads GPS, would form a "think-and-do tank" of conservative ideas.[53] But policy announcements were little more than cover to maintain their preferred IRS tax status (politically active nonprofits must have a "primary purpose" of education, not advocacy). Some of these nonprofits would be so-called Super PACs—disclosed political entities capable of raising and spending unlimited amounts. Others, like Crossroads GPS, would simply be 501c4 nonprofits, which can conceal all of their donors while spending as much as they desire on political attacks.

On April 21, several corporate lobbyists joined the mix. Bill Miller, then the political director of the U.S. Chamber of Commerce, arrived at Rove's Weaver Terrace home to discuss plans to ramp up political spending ahead of the pivotal midterm elections. Steven Law, a former chief of staff to Senator Mitch McConnell, had recently left the chamber to join Rove as the president of American Crossroads GPS. The meeting established the ground rules that would ultimately tip the balance of power in the Obama presidency by remaking the composition of Congress. According to the *National Journal*, the operatives in attendance, including GOP fund-raiser Fred Malek, hashed out plans on how to coordinate their spending to keep Democrats permanently on the defensive in the election.[54] The fund-raising apparatus was also a long-term plan to overwhelm Democrats in 2012 and lay the groundwork for ousting Obama from the White House.

The groups would coordinate corporate donations to various Republican-leaning issue-ad groups to hammer every congressional Democrat perceived as vulnerable. For Reps.

Kathy Dahlkemper and Steve Driehaus, both pro-life fresh-man lawmakers, the Weaver Terrace group assigned the Susan B. Anthony List, a pro-life group, to run attack ads accusing them of violating their principles. For Reps. Paul Kanjorski and Chris Carney, two Democrats in districts with a large number of senior citizens, the Weaver Terrace Group commissioned the 60 Plus Association, which purports to be a seniors' advocacy organization akin to the AARP, to run ads accusing them of killing Medicare.[55] The pot of money used to run the ads would be the same, but the public would only see the short tagline at the end of each ad.[56] Since none of the issues and groups behind the plan faced disclosure re-quirements the plan went forward without contention.

The money was a source of mystery the entire election. Some congressional Democrats, like the late John Adler, raised about as much or more than their Republican challengers—only to see an unrestricted fusillade of ads appear almost every day, from August until Election Day, from outside groups. No matter how much these incumbent Democrats raised, the issue ads from random groups—the Commission on Hope, Growth and Opportunity or Americans for Job Security—would keep coming.[57]

The election demonstrated the brute power of the U.S. Chamber of Commerce. When any issue-ad group would go dark, meaning their ads stopped, the chamber's ads would turn on. And the ads were merciless. One chamber ad against Paul Hodes, a U.S. Representative running for Senate in New Hampshire, skewered him for voting for President Obama's stimulus. The chamber had publicly lobbied members like Hodes to vote for the stimulus—now they were telling his voters that he was burying them in debt by voting for it.[58] The chamber raised $75 million alone for its electioneering campaign in 2010, bringing itself close to the size of the political parties.[59]

"*Citizens United* opened the door for the unparalleled participation by corporations at the financial level," said Scott Reed, speaking to veteran reporter Peter Stone.* "But it took the combination of the RNC being inept and the Obama administration's political agenda to bring it all together."[60]

Some suspect that the reason so much money was raised by outside groups rather than the Republican Party itself related to conservative mistrust of an Michael Steele, the chairman of the party during Obama's first two years.** But a more likely scenario is that corporate money could be better concealed using outside groups. Although *Citizens United* struck down limits on corporate electioneering, the ban against direct corporate contributions to parties and candidate committees remained. Parties and candidate committees are also transparent, meaning that any average citizen could pull up the Federal Elections Commission website and figure out the donors. Corporations wanting reprisals against Democrats preferred anonymity.

Well after the election, questions still lingered about who truly financed the onslaught of advertising. An accidental regulatory filing revealed, two years after the election, that the health insurance company Aetna gave $3 million to Rove's American Action Network. The money helped finance a wave of inflammatory ads, including one showing an

---

* Reed's Super PAC raised millions from the oil, health insurance, and banking sectors to run ads against Democrats in 2010. He was hired as a political director for the U.S. Chamber of Commerce in 2012.

** Ed Gillespie, the former chair of the Republican National Committee, owned the deed to the building during Steele's tenure. Gillespie helped Rove develop efforts to elect state-level Republicans during the midterm election.

actor playing Senator Patty Murray stomping a child into the mud, and another making the false claim that Democrats had voted to give Viagra to rapists (PolitiFact.com rated this ad "Pants on Fire" for its level of deceit).[61]

Charles and David Koch, among other wealthy billionaires, had a seat at the Weaver Terrace Group table. Among the corporate lobbyists and GOP operatives, the Koch network sent its political representative, a Republican consultant named Sean Noble, to participate in the strategy sessions. Disclosures revealed after the midterm election that Noble had helped channel some $55 million into an array of attack ad groups, from the 60 Plus Association to the American Future Fund and even pro-life groups, like the Susan B. Anthony List.[62]

The success of the Weaver Terrace Group at vaporizing the Democrats' numbers in 2010 only led to talk of more collaboration. Shortly after the Republican primaries settled down and Mitt Romney was all but chosen as the party's standard-bearer, the GOP planners set about finishing off the Obama presidency. While tens of millions of shadowy corporate cash was needed to win in the midterms, hundreds would be necessary to take down a sitting president and his party. A group of strategists consisting of the original Weaver Terrace club, representatives from the Koch brothers, lobbyists from the chamber, and several consultants working for Romney's Super PAC came to a conclusion—they would raise over $1 billion in third-party campaign cash to win.[63]

SHADOW PARTY, REAL POWER

In the background of the large political battles of the Obama era, the organizing strength of the opposition is not situated at the Republican Party headquarters, as conventional wisdom might suggest. Conservative coordinating committees have always played a vital role in managing the agenda of the right; however, in the absence of a national political leader and facing a wave of reforms promised by Obama, centralized strategy committees like the newly formed Conservative Action Project and older groups like Heritage have assumed leadership of the movement. Notably, the people commanding the most powerful coordinating committees are right-wing ideologues with little interest in moderating conservative policies.

On election night 2010, the original set of conservative activists who had met in November 2008 at Brent Bozell's home in Stanley, Virginia, held a large party in suburban Virginia as they watched the results roll in. Many of the far-right candidates they had guided through the primaries, like Christine O'Donnell, would ultimately lose. But it was a night worth celebrating. It was one of the largest Republican sweeps in history, and, most important, the vast majority of the candidates had pledged far more conservative views than Republicans had in 1994, 1966, or 1946. O'Donnell and Miller lost largely because statewide races attract far more media scrutiny than House or lower-level elections. The political dynamic created by groups like the Weyrich Lunch ensured dozens of hard-right candidates not only won their primary, but became new members of elected office in 2010.

Two days later, on Friday, November 5, 2010, the original band of right-wing leaders from 2008 met again at Bozell's home in Virginia with the leaders of the Conservative Action Project and the Weyrich Lunch. Taking credit for the election, one attendee told ABC News, "Conservatives and the Tea Partiers nationalized this election as a referendum against big government." Looking back on the 2010 results, Bozell proudly declared, "the moderate wing of the Republican Party is dead." But the goal of the meeting was not celebratory—they had work to do to plan 2012. The slate of candidates for the next election must be "full-throttle, across-the-board conservatives," they said.

3

THE KOCH-FUELED WAR ON OBAMA

Democratic presidents promising bold, progressive change have faced orchestrated attacks from the titans of industry since President Franklin Roosevelt. Irénée Du Pont, the executive and heir to the Du Pont chemical and munitions industry fortune, formed the Liberty League along with the nation's leading bankers, manufacturers, and wealthy families to repeal Social Security and to mobilize public opposition to other aspects of the New Deal. He tried desperately to cloak his campaign in the veneer of a principled, ideological cause of protecting the Constitution and the value of limited government. Along with executives from General Motors and Eastman Kodak, Du Pont, through his Liberty League group, created fronts with names like the New York State Economic Council, the Southern Committee to Uphold the Constitution, and Minute Men and Women of Today. One Liberty League–affiliated front opposing the New Deal, the Farmers' Independence Council, did not have a single family farmer as a member, but did count executive Lammont Du Pont as a main contributor. Irénée Du Pont needed popular support for his opposition to Roosevelt's reforms and sought to form a coalition with nationalist groups like the American Legion. In one letter to another executive, he contemplated forming an alliance with "even the Ku Klux Klan."

Unfortunately for the corporate leaders of the thirties, the front groups didn't work. In the 1936 election, Democrats portrayed the Republican nominee Alf Landon, who was bankrolled by Liberty League members, as a pawn of the Du Pont family and the "economic royalists" who had caused the Great Depression. James Farley, then the chairman of the Democratic Party, said the Liberty League "ought to be called the American Cellophane League" because "first it's a Du Pont product and second, you can see right through it!"[1] Democrats roundly mocked the "Millionaires' League" and its attempts to drag down the New Deal, and Roosevelt easily swept the election. The story of the vigorous class war waged by Du Pont and his contemporaries against Roosevelt is chronicled in the underrated *Invisible Hands*, a book by Kim Phillips-Fein examining the conservative movement from the New Deal to Reagan.

But at the time of Du Pont's failure, the corporate interests lacked a coherent intellectual framework, and their forays into politics were perceived as motivated largely by greed. Generations of wealthy businessmen repeated the Du Pont family's attempt to forge a political force capable of fighting progressive administrations tooth and nail. Joseph Coors of the Coors beer fortune dedicated his wealth to building a bulwark of conservative institutions, starting with the Heritage Foundation. Richard Mellon Scaife famously devoted much of his inherited wealth to financing opposition to President Clinton. The investments of conservative scions were important in their own right, but never did a single wealthy

American family directly challenge an American president and his policies until the Koch brothers decided to take on President Obama.

Looming large against Obama and his plans, two billionaire brothers—David and Charles Koch—adamantly fought every progressive policy he proposed. Before Obama even officially assumed office, the pair made it their goal to neuter the young president and remove him from the White House in four short years. The brothers organized members of their class, fellow corporate executives and oil barons, to aid them in their steadfast opposition. They funded fronts to fool working-class Americans into joining their cause. They funneled large sums into dummy organizations to win campaigns. Their money went to propaganda, in schools and the media, to candidates, and to extremists—so long as the recipients of Koch money furthered the Koch cause. Perhaps the similarities between the pitched battles of the Du Ponts and Roosevelt were a coincidence. But unlike the New Deal era, when a popular progressive president outflanked the small clique of elite businessmen trying to obstruct his reform, the Koch brothers have triumphed over Obama in many significant ways.

Koch-funded groups decimated Democratic majorities in Congress in Obama's first midterm election, crushed legislative efforts to address climate change, nearly killed health reform, swept labor reforms like the Employee Free Choice Act off the table, and, perhaps most important, orchestrated the rise of the so-called Tea Party movement. Two years into his term, Obama had been pinned down by only two men with very narrow conservative interests. After a "shellacking" in the midterm elections, Obama offered to extend billions in Bush tax cuts to the very rich and retreated on reinstating a higher estate tax, two priorities of the Koch brothers. How did this happen?

Obama, unlike Roosevelt with Du Pont, waited years before confronting the Koch brothers in the public arena. Rather than taking them on directly, Obama, for a short period during the midterm elections, mocked the Koch-financed group called Americans for Prosperity, saying the name was misleading. The Koch brothers were accused of rampant oil speculation, driving the price of gasoline up for consumers, and their allies in the banking sector of crashing the economy. However, Obama and the Democrats were slow to recognize the political threat, and for some reason, were too timid to explicitly denounce the Koch brothers. The circumstances, of course, were also different. America suffered through a housing market collapse, a financial crisis, and perpetual unemployment as Obama took office, but not an earth-shattering event like the Great Depression. Backlash against the rich never materialized in the same way as it had under Roosevelt, and Obama suffered from the right-wing charge, amplified on Fox News and talk radio, that he was a "socialist." Maybe Obama thought a confrontation with the Koch brothers would only lend credibility to the belief that he practiced left-wing "class warfare." In any event, the calculation to largely ignore the Koch brothers only helped them lurk in the shadows, exercising even greater influence.

And the Koch brothers were prepared for battle with Obama unlike any plutocrats of the past. The Du Ponts stumbled awkwardly into forays with Roosevelt and never learned to avoid the press and public scrutiny into their lobbying. More profoundly, the Koch brothers had developed a political strategy perfected by generations of right-wing tycoons—including their father, the founder of the Koch family conglomerate, Koch Industries. For fifty years, the Koch family plotted, experimented, and financed groups to advance a very right-wing form of conservatism. The tactics employed against Obama had been concocted for many years prior.

The Koch brothers surpassed the influence of any other single wealthy individual or business group because of their holistic approach to, as Charles would say, "advancing liberty." Organizations like the U.S. Chamber of Commerce would fund advertisements and pay insider lobbyists. The Coors family funded conservative think tanks and cultural institutions. John Allison, former CEO of BB&T bank, singlehandedly financed an array of professors dedicated to the beliefs of Ayn Rand at major universities. Conservative activists like Grover Norquist convened regular meetings for ideological peers to collaborate. The Koch brothers incorporated all of these tactics, and more. They funded talent to come up with even better strategies and offered to lend money to anything—movies, internships, ad campaigns, books, social networking websites—that would "create value" to further the cause.

A longtime political deputy, Richard Fink, in a presentation to the Philanthropy Roundtable in 1995, laid out the strategy for the Koch brothers. Fink said that investors should follow Friedrich Hayek's model of the production process as a concept for social grant making. Fink believed that social and political change required the "development of intellectual raw materials, their conversion into specific policy products, and the marketing and distribution of these products to citizen-consumers."[2] Donors, therefore, could succeed by financing every step along the way, from education, to policy groups, to cultural institutions, communication efforts to market ideas.

A report by Greenpeace provides a snapshot of the Koch approach to politics. The report, which only covers Koch efforts in the realm of climate science, details over $50 million the Koch brothers used to spread propaganda against the belief in anthropogenic climate change. Koch foundation money flowed to the Media Research Center, a group that scrutinizes press outlets which report on climate change science; the Hot Air Tour, a roving circuslike act casting doubt on clean energy solutions; a junket program called the Foundation for Research on Economics and the Environment, where federal judges are treated with vacations to Montana and lectures from climate change skeptics; as well as fellowships for dozens of academics at the Cato Institute and George Mason University, who in turn produced studies challenging the global consensus that temperatures are rising. All told, Koch financed over thirty-five groups, as well as scores of lobbyists and politicians, all opposed to regulating carbon pollution. As a Koch political deputy later explained his strategy in defeating clean energy legislation to a gathering of conservative bloggers, "if we win the science argument, it's game, set, and match."[3]

The Koch brothers have applied the same strategy to broad deregulation efforts, school and Social Security privatization, and other policy goals. And it was applied, on a broad scale, to obstructing Obama's policy goals for reviving the economy, fixing America's health reform crisis, reforming the tax code, and giving workers more power in the workplace.

Many political donors, on both the right and left, allow some distance between themselves and the organizations they finance; but not the Koch brothers. "If he doesn't like the program, if he doesn't think the program is creating value, he'll cut that program," explained Claire Kittle, who spoke to a group of conservative activists while working as a grant director at the Charles Koch Charitable Foundation. Although some donors allow their nonprofits to drift, Kittle said the Koch family is sure to place their children on the boards of organizations they invest in, and the family literally shows up at board meetings to question "everything that happens."[4]

To ensure that the Koch brothers' financial interests are constantly being advanced by their political and nonprofit investments, a top Koch lobbyist named Kevin Gentry holds the dual role of "director of strategic development for Koch Industries" and "vice president of the Charles Koch Charitable Foundation." On a monthly basis, Gentry convenes a meet-and-greet for operatives working in Koch-funded conservative groups to teach them better fund-raising techniques so they may expand without being fully reliant on Koch money. On any other given day, he works with corporate allies to see where their lobbying campaigns can sync with the interests of Koch Industries or one of its subsidiaries.

To amplify their influence, since 2003, the Koch brothers convened twice annual fund-raising retreats among other corporate donors to give to Koch-supported conservatives and conservative institutions. I was helped in revealing the attendance list of these retreats when an anonymous source leaked a letter from Charles Koch to me and a reporter from the *New York Times*. Richard DeVos, founder of Amway; Steve Schwarzman, the chairman of the investment firm Blackstone Group; billionaire heiress Diane Hendricks; and oil billionaire Phil Anschutz have been regular attendees of the event. At these retreats, journalists who work at Koch nonprofits, political operatives long employed by Koch fronts, and lobbyists working for Koch Industries wine and dine crowds of upward of two hundred wealthy donors at resorts in Aspen and Palm Springs. At Koch-convened meetings in the summer

KOCH INDUSTRIES INC

CHARLES G. KOCH
CHAIRMAN AND
CHIEF EXECUTIVE OFFICER

September 24, 2010

"If not us, who? If not now, when?"

That question was posed by a member of our network of business and philanthropic leaders, who are dedicated to defending our free society. We cannot rely on politicians to do so, so it is up to us to combat what is now the greatest assault on American freedom and prosperity in our lifetimes.

Twice a year our network meets to review strategies for combating the multitude of public policies that threaten to destroy America as we know it. These meetings have been critical in improving and expanding our efforts.

Our next meeting will be held January 30-31, 2011, at the Rancho Las Palmas Resort in Rancho Mirage, California. You would be a valuable addition to our gathering, and we hope you can join us.

In Palm Springs, we will assemble an exceptional group of leaders along with a strong line-up of speakers. Together, we will develop strategies to counter the most severe threats facing our free society and outline a vision of how we can foster a renewal of American free enterprise and prosperity.

At our most recent meeting in Aspen, our group heard plans to activate citizens against the threat of government over-spending and to change the balance of power in Congress this November. In response, participants committed to an unprecedented level of support. The important work being done with these initiatives continues. However, even if these efforts succeed, other serious threats demand action.

Everyone benefits from the prosperity that emerges from free societies. But that prosperity is under attack by the current Administration and many of our elected officials. Their policies threaten to erode our economic freedom and transfer vast sums of power to the state. We must stop – and reverse – this internal assault on our founding principles.

316.828.5201 Tel

P.O. Box 2256
Wichita, Kansas 67201

Invitation letter to Koch-sponsored strategy meeting

of 2010 and in January 2011, Charles promised to match every dollar raised with a dollar of his own for the conservative movement. At the following fundraiser, held at a private resort in Vail, Colorado, in June 2011, Charles promised to make the 2012 election the "mother of all wars" against "Saddam Hussein," his nickname for President Obama.[5]

Perhaps the most insidious strategy of the Koch brothers has been their ability to co-opt social liberals. The Cato Institute is known for its promotion of gay marriage and support for immigrant rights. In fact, a small number of libertarian fronts that receive funding from Koch charitable foundations do not toe the orthodox conservative line when it comes to issues like evolution or even drug policy. But these otherwise laudable causes are mostly a ruse. While the Koch brothers fund seemingly reasonable social libertarians with one hand, they finance a set of vicious social conservatives with the other. Peggy Venable, a longtime Koch operative, helped mastermind the crusade to rewrite the history textbooks in Texas to promote antigay bigots and to censor references to immigrant civil rights leaders like Cesar Chavez.[6] Americans for Prosperity spent considerable resources promoting Arizona State Sen. Russell Pearce and Colorado's Tom Tancredo, two of the leading anti-immigrant politicians in America. Koch also gives heavily to antigay groups like the Heritage Foundation. In fact, Charles attends meetings of the Council for National Policy, the nation's largest meeting group for far right social conservative donors, and in a speech posted on the group's website, pledged an "alliance" with the social right to change American society. Essentially, Koch will fund both conservatives and liberals when it comes to social policy. Because for them, social initiatives are more often a Trojan horse for imposing their radical economic views.

Every group in the Koch network is adamantly opposed to addressing climate change as well as other forms of environmental pollution, and is committed to weakening worker rights, sharply reducing regulations and social welfare programs, and cutting taxes for the wealthy. These policies are the defining aspects of Koch's philanthropy. The outreach to social liberals, in the case of the Cato Institute, or to social conservatives, through outfits like Americans for Prosperity, is part of a larger strategy to spread the antigovernment gospel to the largest audience possible. Koch-funded political groups have never, for example, expended serious resources or purchased television ads defending gay marriage, though David Koch reputedly favors marriage equality.

Moreover, the diversity of the types of conservative groups funded by the Koch network is what distinguishes the Koch network. For example, Koch doesn't simply fund scholars who would be sympathetic to their agenda. Ordinarily, businesses or lobbyists will hire a professor on a case-by-case basis if they need a study to support their cause. The consulting firm Charles Rives Associates, for instance, specializes in this sort of pay-to-play academia, and for a fee will help firms like ExxonMobil find the right academic to write a useful study or report. Instead, the Koch brothers fund entire academic programs at reputable universities as a long-term strategy of cultivating friendly sources and antigovernment fields of study. Working with the Manhattan Institute, a conservative think tank funded largely by the financial industry in New York, Koch grants have gone out to a variety of colleges for permanent departments devoted to ideas shared by the Koch brothers. At Florida State University, Koch underwrites the Program for the Study of Political Economy and Free Enterprise, a division of the economics department, as well as the Political Theory Project at Brown University, a special program offering supply-side speakers and opportunities for postdoctoral research. In 2004, the *Wall Street Journal* revealed that the Mercatus Center at George Mason University, a mini–think tank funded almost exclusively by Koch Industries, had set most of the Bush administration's environmental regulatory policies. Among twenty-three regulations eventually axed by the Bush administration, Mercatus proscribed fourteen. In addition, Mercatus fellows, like "anti-regulatory zealot" Susan Dudley, moved in and out of key regulatory posts within the Bush administration. It could be argued that the Koch academics at Mercatus wielded more power than any single K Street lobbying firm.[7]

The Koch approach to politics has been obscured from the public for years. Behind closed doors, it has evolved and grown. The Koch political strategy has been developed incrementally since the Koch brothers' father first entered politics in the late fifties. It's worth noting, the Koch brothers not only inherited a vast oil and cattle company from their father, but more important, they inherited a political philosophy.

The true story of the Koch family's dedication to right-wing politics begins back one generation with the father. Fred C. Koch, a hardscrabble Texan of Dutch ancestry, founded the Koch Industries empire and pioneered a strategy for advancing conservatism that was pivotal in shaping the modern American right. He unapologetically attacked his enemies, branding them communists, or worse. He paid for groups to help whip up a grassroots army filled with populist rage against the United Nations, Justice Earl Warren, and President Kennedy. He helped begin the process of evicting moderates from the Republican Party. And he instilled in his sons a philosophy that a proper "American businessman" should "fight like a tiger" when someone tries to "take a few thousand dollars away from him."

Fred, a racist who detested the civil rights movement, probably could have never imagined a black president of the United States. But Fred laid the groundwork for his sons to try to tear the first one down.

JOHN BIRCH SOCIETY BEGINNINGS

Although Fred's father, Harry Koch, struggled when he first immigrated to the United States, he eventually succeeded in purchasing the local newspaper, the *Tribune-Chief*, of Quanah, Texas. Harry saved enough for Fred to attend private primary school before going to Rice University and then out east to MIT.

After graduating from MIT, Fred invented a more efficient process for converting crude oil into gasoline. His innovation quickly earned him powerful enemies in eastern oil companies, which harassed him with a barrage of patent lawsuits. Seeking greater business opportunities elsewhere, in the 1920s and 1930s, Fred embarked for the Soviet Union, where he contracted to help erect fifteen oil stills in Grozny, Tuape, Batoum, Baku, and Yaroslav. There, he said he witnessed Stalin's purges and learned firsthand about the communist plot to take over America. "One of the old Bolsheviks," Fred recalled, "told me how the Communists were going to infiltrate the U.S.A. in the schools, universities, churches, labor unions, government, armed forces, and to use his words, 'Make you rotten to the core.'" However, it should be noted that Fred traveled throughout the Soviet empire doing business with a large cast of characters, and for two decades never saw any problem with accepting their money. His sudden hatred for his business partners, which did not become public until the 1950s, was never fully explained.

Returning to the United States, Fred prospered during the postwar boom. His Wood River Oil and Refining Company gobbled up several more refineries and eventually changed its name to Rock Island Oil and Refining. But as the Cold War intensified, Fred grew dissatisfied with President Eisenhower. He seemed enthralled by fears that the Eisenhower administration was capitulating to the communists, whom he now saw as a threat.

Because Eisenhower allowed the Panamanian flag to fly over the Panama Canal, Fred surmised that the president was "beginning to surrender" to the "Communist conspiracy." Fred wrote that "a former Assistant Secretary of State for Latin American affairs told me that certain members of the State Department helped put Castro in power and guide his every move." Fred believed Democrats, as well as moderate Republicans, were actively enabling Castro, who he called the "Mao Tze-tung of the Western Hemisphere."

In December of 1958, in the living room of a brick Tudor house in a quiet Indianapolis neighborhood, Fred was summoned for a meeting with eleven other staunch anticommunists who shared his fervent belief that Christian society and free markets were at grave risk of slipping away. Robert Welch, a candy manufacturer who had been financing and authoring a series of pamphlets articulating his anticommunist ideas for half a decade, presided over the special gathering. Welch bellowed that there had been an "800% expansion of Communist membership in [the] last 20 years" and that the recent surge in inflation and "collectivism" was part of a red plot to destroy American civilization. After two full days of nearly uninterrupted lecture, Welch presented his solution: a new organization to fight the left in every corner of America. Named after a Baptist missionary serving as an American soldier, who was reportedly killed by the Chinese in 1946, the John Birch Society was born. Welch wanted to make Birch a martyr and proclaimed him the first American death in the war against communism. The men at the meeting, many of them leaders of the powerful National Association of Manufacturers, agreed they would level the playing field with the communists and commit to "fight dirty."[8]

Welch parlayed his expertise in marketing candy into a multifaceted strategy for advancing his paranoid anticommunist beliefs. He recorded simple how-to videos, developed a door-to-door strategy for his organizers, and stressed the importance of advertising to his allies. Fred's wife Mary later remarked that she had always been impressed with Welch and his approach to politics. Welch was a "very intelligent, sharp man, quite an intellectual," she told the *Wichita Eagle*.

The Birchers, with plenty of seed money from Fred and his cohorts, spread quickly throughout the nation, hiring field operatives, hosting training sessions, and publishing hundreds of thousands of Welch's *Blue Book* of anticommunist theory and monthly newsletters proclaiming new examples of communist infiltration. The Belmont, Massachusetts, headquarters of the Birchers initially hired twenty-eight employees, in addition to many volunteers who labored to fire off $4,000 worth of mail every week. As a founding member of the national John Birch Society Council, Fred served as a liaison to paid coordinators, who in turn worked with volunteer chapter leaders and ordinary members. Under the seemingly benign motto of "Less government, more responsibility," the Birchers recruited upward of 50,000 people in a massive roll-out campaign during the spring of 1961. In the wake of the Kennedy victory and a relatively liberal Republican Party, the Birchers filled a vacuum of conservative leadership.

Through monthly bulletins and taped lectures from Welch, individual members were asked to advance the cause in their local communities. Goals would include tasks such as attending meetings of "Communist fronts" like the ACLU to shout down "disloyal" speakers or to organize "spontaneous" petition gatherings to impeach Earl Warren. Despite their belief that every liberal group in America was truly a front group for communists, the Birchers themselves were obsessed with using dummy organizations to better achieve their agenda. Welch recommended that members assemble various fronts like: TACT (Truth About Civil Turmoil), which connected civil rights groups and African American organizations with communists; TRAIN (To Restore American Independence), a group to mock the United Nations and pacifists; SYLP (Support Your Local Police), a particularly effective recruiting tool after the Watts riots; and MOTOREDE (The Movement to Restore Decency), which lobbied against sex education, birth control, and abortion.

A Bircher-led red scare rekindled McCarthyism in towns across the country. In Amarillo, Texas, the local Bircher leaders, including the mayor and a retired brigadier general, led a campaign to purge a clergyman accused of being a communist sympathizer. They also rid the libraries of "communist" books, which included Pulitzer Prize–winning literature, and punished teachers who had been accused of disloyalty. According to historian Rick Perlstein, Centralia, Missouri, became a "virtual Birch fiefdom; the owner of the factory that employed half the town's workforce made membership practically a condition for advancement." In Fred's hometown Wichita chapter, which included its own paid Birch Society organizer, *Time* observed that "student members of the society are trained to tell their cell leader of any 'Communist' influence noted in classroom lectures; by phone, parents belabor the offending teacher and his principal for apologies and admissions of guilt."

The rapid rise of the Bircher movement sharply divided the GOP. In early 1961, the national press reported on Welch's view that Dwight Eisenhower was guilty of "treason," and that his brother Milton Eisenhower was probably his "boss within the Communist party." This prompted a harsh rebuke from a group of Republican elders. "It is unbelievable that any sane person would make such accusations," said North Dakota Republican Milton Young during a speech on the Senate floor. Liberal Republican Senator Thomas Kuchel complained he was being targeted by Birchers in his reelection bid.

However, a faction of Southern lawmakers and Republican politicians found strength in the Bircher brand of conservative populism. Dixiecrat Congressman L. Mendel Rivers of South Carolina extolled the Birchers as a "nation-wide organization of patriotic Americans." Congressmen John Rousselot and Edgar Hiestand, both California Republicans, were card-carrying Birch Society members. *Life* reported that Republican defenders of the group believed that the Birchers would serve as a vanguard for the "conservative renaissance in America whose main respectable apostle is Arizona Senator Barry Goldwater."

Indeed, Goldwater's rise can be traced to Bircher operatives and Fred's deep pockets. Goldwater ghostwriter Brent

Bozell sat in on an executive board meeting of the John Birch Society to pitch Goldwater's "Conscience of a Conservative" shortly after a manuscript had been approved by the senator himself. Fred declared on the spot that he would pay for 2,500 copies. He reportedly then turned around and ordered his colleague and friend from Kansas, Bob Love, "You send it out." Clandestine bulk purchases from Birch members helped Goldwater's book to debut at number ten on *Time*'s bestseller list.[9]

Fred had served with Roger Milliken, a textile magnate in the South who also funded many right-wing causes, on the Committee of One Hundred to draft Goldwater to challenge Nixon for the 1960 Republican nomination.[10] Goldwater demurred in 1960, and later had to publicly distance himself from the extremism of the Birchers. But with their support, the groundwork was laid for Goldwater's triumphant victory over Nelson Rockefeller in 1964 for the Republican nomination to challenge President Johnson.

In the early sixties, Fred decided to pen his own Bircher-style pamphlet examining the communist scheme to destroy America. It provided a rare window into his beliefs and motivations. Titled "A Businessman Looks at Communism," Fred layered conspiracy upon conspiracy in thirty pages, finding communism festering in everything from the United Nations to Protestant churches to modern art (which had its "origin with Picasso, an admitted Communist"). Noting that "the colored man looms large in the Communist plan to take over America," Fred was suspicious of racial integration. He believed communists were luring "rural Southern Negroes and Puerto Ricans" to northern urban centers to "swing the balance in these populous states." Then, "when the Party is ready to take over," they would "use the colored people" to incite a "vicious race war." The communists pushed to end segregation, Fred concluded, "to stir up racial hatred in order to enslave both the white and black man."

Fred's wealth ensured that his ideas reached the public. In February of 1964, in a letter to the editor, Fred boasted that "over two and a half million" copies of his "little booklet" had been printed and distributed. He would promise that anyone who wanted a copy could simply write to him and be shipped one.

He also went on a speaking tour to spread his cause. "Maybe you don't want to be controversial by getting mixed up in this anti-communist battle," Fred said before a Kansas club for Republican women in 1961. "But you won't be very controversial lying in a ditch with a bullet in your brain." According to the Associated Press, Fred's speech meandered through the communist involvement in American universities, churches, political parties, the media, the State Department, and the United Nations, to an assembly of a thousand people.

According to Ernie Lazar, a researcher who has documented much of the government's knowledge of the John Birch Society using Freedom of Information Act requests, some of Fred's inflammatory rhetoric placed him on the FBI's radar. The FBI had taken note that Fred would regularly tell his audiences that Francis Gary Powers, a U-2 pilot who had been shot down but landed safely in Russia, was in collusion with the Soviets. An FBI memo stated that Fred had told crowds that Powers was paid by the communists to gather information about America. A memo addressed to Assistant FBI Director C.D. DeLoach noted that Fred's "utterly absurd viewpoints . . . typify the absolute confusion" promoted by the Birchers.

OPTIONAL FORM NO. 10

UNITED STATES GOV   MENT

Memorandum

TO   : Mr. DeLoach   DATE: 3-15-61

FROM   : D. C. Morrell

SUBJECT: THE JOHN BIRCH SOCIETY

The Bureau has, of course, been cognizant over a period of time of the many fanatical right-wing anticommunist organizations which are presently spreading widely throughout the country and of their utterly absurd viewpoints. For your information, I am attaching copies of letters dated March 6 and 8, 1961, from ██ which typify the absolute confusion and lack of confidence in American institutions and one's fellow man being caused by representatives of such organizations.

Both ████████████████████ inquire concerning the John Birch Society (JBS). The former makes wild allegations re Francis Gary Powers, the convicted U.S. "spy" now in Russia, being in collusion with Russia which reports are being disseminated by one Fred Koch representing the JBS.

████████████ mentions one General William Lee, a retired Air Force general, who recently spoke at a Parent-Teacher Association in his area (and possibly represented the JBS), at which time General Lee allegedly stated "we were not to trust anyone for he might be a communist--not our teachers, the textbooks, the minister, Sunday School teachers, not our neighbor, not even our mate." ████████████ informs "Tensions have built within the community and some churches until one might believe the communist were the winners of 'round one' in our city. Smear-gossip has run rampant until it is not safe to speak, teach or even talk with 'friends'."

General William Lee is not identifiable in Bufiles. Fred Koch, who is speaking for the JBS, may refer to Fred C. Koch, author of "A Businessman Looks at Communism" and   President of the Rock Island Oil and Refining Company, Inc., Wichita Kansas. The Manion Forum Network disseminates material presented by Koch.

REC- 85

RECOMMENDATION:

None. For information. Attached two letters have been acknowleged by forwarding to both ████████████ various publications on the subject of communism from the Bureau and informing them we could furnish no information concerning the John Birch Society.

Enclosures (2) DCL:mb (2)

66 MAR 27 1961

FBI memo regarding the John Birch Society

The Kennedy administration, after first dismissing the Bircher phenomenon as nothing more than a group of right-wing blowhards, became concerned once reports emerged of widespread indoctrination within the military. Birch Society board member A.C. Wedemeyer, a former general, hosted a two-day rally with the Fourth U.S. Army in San Antonio in September of 1961. He denounced Kennedy for "appeasing" the Soviet Union and the Episcopal Church for supporting the civil rights activists. Defense Secretary Robert McNamara moved to relieve Major General Edwin Walker, head of an infantry division in Europe, of command for inundating his troops with Birch Society propaganda.

Eventually, Kennedy decided to strike back directly. In a speech to 2,500 Los Angeles Democrats, Kennedy tore into the Birchers' "crusades of suspicion" and other "discordant voices of extremism." "They find treason in our churches, in our highest court, and even in the treatment of our water." That last line was a swipe at the Bircher-inspired hysteria that water fluoridation was a communist plot.

Regardless of the speech, the Birchers continued to press forward, launching a campaign to impeach Kennedy. They picketed in front of the White House, mobilized massive letter-writing campaigns, and spread the politics of paranoia throughout his presidency. Bircher businessmen sponsored ads and billboards across the country accusing Kennedy of being in league with communists.

Using a front group called the American Fact-Finding Committee, several wealthy Texas Bircher leaders paid for a full-page newspaper ad "welcoming" Kennedy to Dallas in 1963. "Why have you scrapped the Monroe Doctrine in favor of the 'Spirit of Moscow'?" howled the ad, which ran the morning of Kennedy's assassination.

Kennedy's death did not dissipate any of the Birchers' vitriol. In what columnist Drew Pearson called a "gimmick to recruit new John Birch members," Fred placed a full-page ad in the *New York Times* and the *Washington Post* after the assassination casting the fallen president as a casualty of the communist threat. The ad reminded readers that Lee Harvey Oswald was a communist, and that the communists will not "rest on this success." They will "use the shock, grief, and confusion of the American people, resulting from the assassination of our President, as an opportunity for pushing their own plans faster." On the bottom of the page, under Fred's name and the names of four other executive board members, there was a clip-out order form to request John Birch Society materials.[11] "When Kennedy was alive, they accused him of consorting with communists," Pearson wrote. "After he died, they claimed in the ad that he was a martyr to communism."

Pearson also mocked Fred as a hypocrite for once profiting off the construction of refineries in communist Russia. Pearson was one of the few to publicly denounce Koch for his anticommunist hypocrisy, and moreover, his delusional beliefs. Pearson's critique of Fred's hypocrisy could be extended to the modern Koch family.

Despite their rhetoric about the "free market," Fred's sons David and Charles Koch ruthlessly exploited federal contracts, including a lucrative deal from the Bush administration to expand the nation's Strategic Petroleum Reserve. It is perhaps the greatest of ironies of the Koch family that its fortune was created by communism and maintained by centralized government planning.

Almost until his death in 1967, Fred continued to finance candidates to make the Republican Party much more conservative. Working with a group of fellow industrialists (many of them John Birch Society Council members), former American Bar Association president Lloyd Wright, and Admiral Ben Moreell, Fred launched a political organization called the 1976 Committee to steer hard-right candidates for the 1968 Republican primary. Bircher Ezra Taft Benson, who was a fierce proponent of a constitutional amendment repealing the income tax, was chosen to lead the presidential ticket, with segregationist Senator Strom Thurmond as his running mate. The effort, first reported on September of 1966, used "1976" to refer to the target date the group set for when a "restoration of the Republic" should be complete. However, the overpowering campaign of Richard Nixon, coupled with the insurgent right-wing populism of George Wallace, eventually snuffed out any energy behind the 1976 Committee.

Fred bequeathed his vast wealth and his Rock Island Oil company to his four sons, Fred Jr., Charles, David, and Bill. Charles, who became president of the company in 1966, became chief executive of Rock Island Oil when Fred died the following year. As soon as he assumed the top position at the company, Charles renamed it Koch Industries after his father. However, a legal battle later ensued for over two decades in the eighties and nineties for control of the company. Fred Jr., a collector of the type of modern art his father abhorred, never had much of an interest in running the company, and, according to sources, was seen by his father as too effeminate to ever be a businessman. Bill, however, clashed with Charles and David, alleging that he and Fred Jr. had been forced out of the company by Charles and had been deceived into selling his share of the company at an undervalued price.

Although Charles and David eventually succeeded in wrangling control of the company, the feud was particularly nasty, with each side hiring private detectives to smear one another. A scandal showing that the company had stolen over 300 million gallons of oil from Native American reservations and federal land was a result of a whistleblower tip from Bill. In 2001, the federal government reached a settlement with Koch Industries to pay $25 million in penalties to the government for stealing oil from federal and Native American lands. For initiating the lawsuit, Bill received about a third of the $25 million in penalties. Years later, the brothers reportedly reconciled their differences.

Although Charles and David drifted from the John Birch Society roots of their father, they adored his political and business leadership. In the sixties, Charles hung out at Birch Society–funded bookstores in Wichita, but gravitated to the nascent libertarian movement and thinkers like Austrian economics radical Ludwig von Mises. By the midseventies, Charles and David began founding their own conservative organizations, starting with the Cato Institute and in 1984 a grassroots group called Citizens for a Sound Economy (later renamed Americans for Prosperity). Although they did not necessarily believe in the same conspiracy theories espoused regularly by Fred, the brothers worked tirelessly to honor their father. In his book *Market-Based Management*, Charles explains that Fred—a "John Wayne-type figure, charismatic and forceful, with great integrity and humility"—was his greatest influence in life. Perhaps in a bid to improve the family name, the brothers created the Fred C. and Mary R. Koch Foundation to fund local Kansas charities.

Every September 23rd, Fred's birthday, is "Founder's Day" at Koch Industries. Celebrations have featured barbecues and instructions on the importance of political engagement. The

2008 Founder's Day announcement included a stern reminder that employees need to "be educated and active citizens," particularly with regards to "government issues that shape our societies and the markets in which we operate." Pictures and anecdotes from Fred's life adorn Koch Industries office buildings, newsletters, and websites.[12]

Although Fred amassed an enormous political and business empire in his life, his sons were even more successful. Pursuing an aggressive strategy of buyouts, Charles estimated that he grew the company over two thousand percent. What started as a cattle, trucking, and oil refining company expanded into timber, oil pipelines, paper products, coal power plants, a global shipping company, chemical manufacturing, ethanol plants, and a vast financial products conglomerate. By 2009, the company boasted over $110 billion in annual revenues, making it the second-largest privately held company in America. In 2010, *Forbes* proclaimed David and Charles among the top ten richest men in America, each worth an estimated $21 billion.

The Koch business acumen is only matched by their political prowess. In the first two years of the Obama administration, few had heard of the Koch name. Using their network of front groups and lobbyists, the Koch brothers orchestrated a massive political assault aimed at weakening the president and his reforms. The angry antigovernment populism of the John Birch Society returned, this time in the form of the Tea Party movement. Both right-wing efforts were financed with Koch money. However, in the Obama era, the Koch family deployed a far more sophisticated strategy that included a nationwide network of conservative think tanks, students, scholars, media outlets, advertisements, lobbyists, and cutting-edge campaign technology.

The legacy of Fred cast a dark shadow over the Obama presidency. Fred showed that one man, and his wealth, could use conspiracies and effective propaganda to persuade thousands to protest their own self-interest. He purged the Republican Party of those insufficiently conservative moderates who dared to work with liberals in the name of pragmatism. His sons did the same thing, only on a grander scale. And unlike the previous attempts by the business class to undermine bold progressive presidents like Roosevelt or Kennedy, the Koch brothers were successful in blunting the impact of Obama and his short-lived congressional majority.

KOCH VS. OBAMA

The first clue about the Koch brothers' perception of Obama came shortly before the 2008 election. Charles gave a short interview to *Esquire*. Most of his comments were rather bland, like noting that his wife calls him "Chucky." Except for one response. Charles, who has long argued that American society should be run like a business, began riffing on the evils of having people in a "company" who are simply too "smart": "Every company wants smart people. Well, Hitler was smart. Stalin was smart. Mao was smart. If somebody's evil, the smarter they are, the more damage they're going to do."[13] The odd remark, made at the peak of the election season, sounded more like a shot at candidate Obama than a critique about the perfect employee. The erudite senator from Illinois could do a lot of "damage"—like Hitler or Stalin—Charles seemed to think.

As Obama prepared for his inauguration, the Koch family declared political war. In January after the presidential election, Charles proclaimed in a newsletter to his fifty thousand employees that America was quickly arriving at the "greatest loss of liberty and prosperity since the 1930s."[14] The somber warning noted what he saw as the parallels between Roosevelt's Keynesian response to the Great Depression and Obama's calls for fiscal stimulus in light of the financial crisis. He warned against "piling on even more regulations" and new "make-work" government programs modeled after the Roosevelt administration. Charles lectured, "it is markets, not government that can provide the strongest engine for growth, lifting us out of these troubling times." Many of the programs Roosevelt had started in reaction to the Great Depression persisted for generations, Charles warned. In challenging the new president, Charles appeared to be anointing himself the heir to Irénée Du Pont's crusade against Franklin Roosevelt, or his own father's fight against John Kennedy and moderate Republicans. Only this time, Charles hoped to succeed.

And inflaming Charles's worst fears, Obama gave a bold, progressive speech at his inauguration, making clear his intention to transition to a clean energy economy, to reform the nation's health care system, and to remake the country's sagging infrastructure. The financial crisis, Obama said, "reminded us that without a watchful eye, the market can spin out of control." "The nation cannot prosper long when it favors only the prosperous," he added. Billionaires like the Koch brothers took note.

As Obama announced his promise to change America, it seems doubtful that he could have known that among the many entrenched business interests gearing up to lobby against reform, a single ultrarich family was preparing to fight him across the board. He didn't even have to look far from where he stood to see their reach. Ironically, INVISTA, a Koch Industries subsidiary, had won the government contract to provide the imperial blue and red carpeting for the inauguration ceremony. The second Obama became president, he was standing atop a Koch product.

Within two days of Obama's swearing his oath of office, the Koch network sprung into action. A website called NoStimulus.com launched, along with a television advertising campaign, a petition, and a series of media events designed to defeat Obama's first signature accomplishment, the $800 billion Recovery and Reinvestment Act, better known as simply the stimulus. In what later blossomed into the Tea Party movement, Koch-funded organizers fanned across the country organizing "Porkulus" rallies decrying government spending and regulations. Koch-supported groups, for instance the Competitive Enterprise Institute and state-based think tanks like the Buckeye Institute for Public Policy, fired off a volley of antistimulus press releases, op-eds, and joint events with Republican lawmakers. Koch operatives staged media events with the most vitriolic opponents of the stimulus, like Governor Mark Sanford and Senator Jim DeMint, both from South Carolina.

By early February, as the vote neared, Americans for Prosperity, one of the main Koch-financed front groups, sent a letter to congressional Republicans instructing them to oppose the stimulus, regardless of any amendments or adjustments made to the bill. Indeed, in a bid for bipartisanship, Democrats offered a slimmed-down version of Obama's proposed stimulus. In order to gain the vote of three Senate Republicans, tax cuts comprised a third of the stimulus.

While the stimulus ultimately passed, the antistimulus hysteria helped conservatives shift the national debate from the causes of the financial crisis to issues like the national debt and government waste. More importantly, the right-wing echo chamber, comprised in no small part of dozens of Koch-funded nonprofits, provided cover for every Republican in the House and nearly every Republican in the Senate to vote against the bill.

Sporadic advertising from Koch groups attempted to spark populist outrage. One television spot, which began soon after Obama took office, featured a middle-aged man exclaiming loudly: "Congress should stop wasting our money and start focusing on real problems!" As the disheveled-looking man yelled about the government, text decrying global warming as a "hoax" flashed across the bottom of the screen. The ad didn't propose an alternative or any solution for that matter; rather it seemed to be crafted simply to stir general outrage. Another Koch ad, which began airing around the same time, showed an actor who said his name was "Carlton, the wealthy eco-hypocrite." The ad was not a large buy, but the script was a perfect specimen of Koch-funded fake populist outrage:

> Hey there, I'm Carlton, the wealthy eco-hypocrite. I inherited my money and attended fancy schools. I own three homes and five cars, but always talk with my rich friends about saving the planet. And I want Congress to spend billions on programs in the name of global warming and green energy. Even if it causes massive unemployment, higher energy bills, and digs people like you even deeper into the recession. Who knows, maybe I'll even make money off of it!

Of course, the Koch brothers inherited their money, attended elite private schools, and own an array of private jets and vacation homes. Their opposition to addressing global warming had nothing to do with energy prices. In fact, many of the serious plans from Democrats to tackle global warming would have lowered energy prices for the vast majority of Americans, according to the Congressional Budget Office. Denying the threat of global warming only permits the Koch brothers to make vast amounts of money from their pollution-based empire. But the Koch brothers weren't interested in an honest debate. They wanted to kill attempts to regulate their pollution, and were willing to say or do anything to provoke middle- and lower-income voters to turn against Obama.

By late February, after Rick Santelli's infamous rant on CNBC and a number of carefully orchestrated rallies, the Tea Party movement took off. The small Koch-funded Porkulus rallies morphed into Tea Party rallies. Koch's state-based network of think tanks and front groups quickly became the main drivers of the movement, offering everything from free advertisements to venues for protests (see chapter 1). Before long, Americans for Prosperity, the group David Koch serves as chairman, became the premier Tea Party organization, hosting the largest rallies, employing the greatest number of organizers, and generating lots of media buzz.

The ability of the Koch brothers to quickly build a national anti-Obama movement came as the result of thirty years of infrastructure building. Groups controlled directly by the Koch brothers include the Institute for Humane Studies, the Reason Foundation, the Bill of Rights Foundation, the Cato Institute, Americans for Prosperity, and the Institute for Justice. Moreover, Koch political officers sit on the board of many other right-wing groups, and Koch foundation grants are regularly dispersed to an even wider network of conservative nonprofits.

In the first two years of the Clinton administration, Koch front groups had played a similar, albeit smaller, role. The Koch group Citizens for a Sound Economy organized large rallies to kill the BTU tax, energy legislation that would have hit their refineries. In a strategy that was a precursor to the Tea Party movement, Koch operatives corralled conservative activists to ambush lawmakers on Capitol Hill with yelling matches about the BTU bill. The defeat of the BTU tax in 1993 was followed by an increased campaign from Koch-funded organizers to block any legislation proposed by Clinton. When Hillary Clinton decided to host events around the country to save her husband's health reform plan, Citizens for a Sound Economy followed her around, shouting her down at every opportunity. As PBS reported, Koch groups aggressively followed Clinton with a "broken-down bus wreathed in red tape symbolizing government bureaucracy and hitched to a tow truck labeled, 'This is Clinton Health Care.'"

The post-1994 Republican Congress, elected largely by the perception that Clinton's first two years had been a failure to accomplish anything, quickly reimbursed the Koch brothers for their assistance. A *BusinessWeek* investigation found that Senator Bob Dole attempted to suppress an investigation into allegations that the Koch brothers had stolen oil from Native American reservations. Speaker Newt Gingrich also attempted to attach language to his omnibus regulatory reform bill to help Koch avoid scrutiny for the Native American oil theft scandal, and in his budget, stripped power away from the EPA to investigate such crimes.

The Koch brothers had an interest in undermining Clinton, but the Obama administration's reforms posed a far greater threat to Koch Industries. Obama's promise to roll back the Bush tax cuts for the top earners came at a time when Koch Industries grew substantially; by 2010, the brothers' net worth had surged by $11 billion in a little over a year. Obama's proposed financial reforms included a new exchange system to provide oversight of the multitrillion-dollar derivatives market—a field in which Koch is a major, and secretive, player. The first derivative, based on the price of crude oil, was crafted by a Koch executive in 1986. In 1997, Koch Industries and Enron pioneered the first "weather derivatives," complex financial instruments to help power companies bet on future weather conditions. According to the Koch Trading and Supply website, the company expanded its financial practice over the years with a variety of financial products and opened trading offices in London and Singapore.[15] Bloomberg reported that Koch lobbyists were among the top players lobbying aggressively against provisions in Obama's financial reform bill to address the unregulated derivatives market. However, Obama's promise to address greenhouse gas pollution caused the most worry for Koch Industries.

Although Koch Industries is known largely as just an oil company, over the years it has expanded into some of the most carbon-intensive businesses. Much of Koch Industries' $110 billion-a-year revenues are derived from burning fossil fuels: oil refineries and pipelines, coal-fired power plants, fertilizer and manufacturing plants, and a sprawling business based around the shipping of coal and crude oil. In 2005, Koch Industries purchased Georgia Pacific, one of the largest timber companies. By cutting down large swaths of forests, Koch also contributes to global warming by decreasing the world's carbon sink capacity.

Koch even sets itself apart from other oil companies by specializing in particularly harmful high-carbon Canadian crude oil. One estimate made by climate journalist Brad Johnson found that Koch Industries is responsible for over 300 million tons of carbon dioxide a year—a greenhouse gas "externality" from which Koch wildly profits.

Obama promised to act on climate change, and this terrified Koch Industries. The primary threat came from legislation. In Congress, the Waxman-Markey energy bill was proposed to set up a "cap-and-trade" plan, a market-based scheme to regulate carbon emissions. A central authority would place a "cap" on overall carbon pollution, and a system of permits could be bought and sold to incentivize the most innovative way for either reducing emissions or creating alternative sources of energy. If Congress could not find a solution, the Supreme Court, in a landmark ruling in 2007, ruled that the EPA must enforce the Clean Air Act to regulate carbon pollution. Finally, Koch faced threats on the state level. A number of states, including California and the states of New England, had set up their own cap-and-trade systems. Koch set out to destroy all of these threats to their bottom line.

The threat of having to actually pay for their carbon emissions elicited a strong response from Koch Industries. Brad Razook, president of the Koch subsidiary which runs the Pine Bend refinery in Minnesota, said a low-carbon fuel standard—which many experts agree would be the most efficient mechanism to reduce our overall carbon footprint— "would be very bad news for our industry, our employees, and our customers." Koch lobbyists inundated the open rule-making process website for the EPA with letters demanding that the agency avoid forcing Koch facilities to monitor their greenhouse gas emissions. They also hired top K Street lobbying firms to press their case privately with lawmakers.

However, the real lobbying muscle from Koch came from the Koch brothers' financing of Astroturf front groups. At the very first Tea Parties' tax day on April 15, 2009, Koch's Americans for Prosperity group distributed talking points claiming, "the Obama budget proposes the largest excise tax in history, disguised as a cap-and-trade energy scheme." T-shirts, signs, and other free paraphernalia distributed by Americans for Prosperity emphasized the threat of cap and trade as the greatest threat that the Tea Party should fear. The multiprong strategy Koch had pioneered descended upon members of Congress contemplating support for clean energy legislation. In southwest Virginia, Democratic Rep. Rick Boucher was positioned as a key negotiator for the bill given his relationship with other conservative and rural Democrats. Koch fronts descended on his district, running attack ads and organizing Tea Parties. After Boucher ultimately voted for the bill, a Koch-backed candidate named Morgan Griffith ended Boucher's twenty-eight-year career. Griffith benefited from Koch campaign donations and received a boost to his campaign from three different Koch-funded bus tours in the district.

Although the clean energy bill passed the House, it died a slow death in the Senate. A group called Institute for Energy Research, funded by Koch, ExxonMobil, and coal interests, funded a series of rallies pressuring key senators to oppose the legislation. Koch-funded policy experts, from places like the Heartland Foundation, George Mason University, the Heritage Foundation, and elsewhere, provided a steady stream of anti–clean energy testimony before hearings. The combination of ads, Tea Party fury, constant attack ads, and insider pressure successfully pushed weak-kneed senators from even bringing the legislation to an up or down vote.

Koch groups also played offense while they slowed down climate legislation. A bunk study by a Spanish professor claimed, erroneously, that clean energy jobs "kill" jobs in the rest of the economy, as evidenced by the downturn in the Spanish economy since adopting similar clean energy standards. In fact, most of the downturn in the Spanish economy had more to do with a housing bubble similar to the one experienced in the United States. But reality made no difference: Koch-funded groups took the professor on a road show across the country, touting his findings in the media, at Tea Party rallies, and in the halls of Congress.

Similarly, after e-mails were hacked from a climate research center in England—the so-called ClimateGate scandal—Koch groups manipulated several of the e-mails to claim the science underpinning the concerns on climate change was a "hoax." Later investigations by the Commerce Department inspector general and British authorities cleared the scientists of accusations of manipulating any of the climate data underlying the worldwide scientific consensus on climate change. The facts did not matter. Americans for Prosperity sent its operatives to Copenhagen to disrupt the international climate accords of 2009. They demanded that global leaders negotiating an international solution to global warming acknowledge that the hacked e-mail "proved" that there was no crisis.

To stop the EPA from enforcing the Clean Air Act's duty to regulate carbon emissions, Koch started a new group called Regulation Reality Tour. The group paid staffers they called "Carbon Cops," who would go to Tea Parties and other events to claim the EPA would hire "Carbon

Cops" to regulate churches, refrigerators, and even "the air you breathe." The Regulation Reality Tour hosted its own Tea Party functions, particularly in states with crucial senators. In Arkansas, the group funded rallies with a moon bounce for children and free food for participants. The citizens, after being fed lies about the EPA, were told to call their legislators and demand legislation to gut the Clean Air Act. Arkansas's Sen. Blanche Lincoln, a Democrat, later cosponsored legislation to do just that. When Republicans took control of the House in 2011, one of the first items of the budget they decided to cut was the money for the EPA's Clean Air Act enforcement for carbon emissions. The freshman congressman who sponsored the effort, Rep. Mike Pompeo (R-KS), was a personal friend of Charles who previously worked for an oil company initially funded by Koch Industries.

On the state level, the Koch strategy was again on display. In California, Americans for Prosperity rallied around a proposition to repeal the state's landmark clean energy bill, AB 32. Flint Hills Resources, a Koch refining subsidiary, gave $1 million in direct funds to the forces working for the repeal. The Pacific Research Foundation, another Koch-funded group based in California, produced bunk studies claiming AB 32 would kill jobs. Although the repeal effort failed, a similar strategy later succeeded in weakening the cap-and-trade scheme in New England. After an aggressive lobbying effort facilitated by a Koch-funded group called the American Legislative Exchange Council, the Republican-controlled legislature in New Hampshire pulled out of the Regional Greenhouse Gas Initiative in February of 2011. Americans for Prosperity's New Hampshire chapter had helped elect many of the lawmakers responsible for the vote.

The Koch brothers poured resources into fighting Obama's other key legislative agenda items as well. Americans for Prosperity and the Americans for Prosperity Foundation (the same group essentially—the foundation was set up for a more favorable tax status) nearly doubled their budget from $15 million in 2008 to over $26 million in 2009. In 2010, the group financed over $45 million in direct campaign expenditures alone, largely television attack ads. According to a report by *Politico*, Koch secretly worked to funnel money to other leading groups responsible for running attack ads against Obama, including Independent Women's Forum and the 60 Plus Association, two pivotal groups running near-constant ads in 2009 against health reform.

Koch operatives were particularly powerful in GOP primaries. A Koch-funded group called the Hot Air Tour demanded that Republicans sign a pledge never to support efforts to address climate change. In 2008, pretty much the only issue both McCain and Obama agreed on was the need to deal with climate change. At the time, many in the Republican Party supported some type of cap-and-trade system, including Sen. Lindsey Graham and Rep. Bob Inglis. But by the dawn of the 2011 Republican Congress, over half of the entire caucus were on record doubting the belief in climate change at all. Inglis, Rep. Mike Castle, and other clean-energy-supporting lawmakers had been driven from the party in vicious primaries. Rep. Mark Kirk, a Republican who had voted for the Waxman-Markey clean energy legislation, had to disavow his support for the legislation to survive his primary.

While the Koch Industries political action committee was ranked as a "heavy hitter" by the Center for Responsive Politics for being one of the most active campaign contributors during the 2010 midterm elections, the most pernicious campaign strategy came in the form of its extensive field operation, done mostly through undisclosed nonprofits exploiting a loophole with the Federal Elections Commission (thus skirting any disclosure). They financed nonprofit bus tours with innocuous names like "Spending Revolt," "November Is Coming," and "Patients United." These efforts were deadly effective. Without the appearance of being a GOP front, the bus tours would sponsor rallies day after day for Republican candidates for local and federal office. Spending Revolt alone sponsored over 138 rallies, each one featuring Tea Party speakers and Republican candidates for office.[16] The November Is Coming group provided free food and Visa gift cards to its most active volunteers.

The massive gains for Republicans in the midterm elections were the direct result of a permanent campaign financed by Koch, from the Tea Party, to constant media distortions, to the elevation of hundreds of Republican candidates. It's impossible to truly quantify the amount of political money Koch infused in the first two years of the Obama administration. Koch's charitable foundations provide a clue, but the true extent may never be known. Direct corporate donations from Koch Industries through fronts like the Independent Women's Forum and Americans for Prosperity never have to be disclosed.

A month into the new Congress, Republicans slashed into the EPA's budget to oversee Koch's carbon pollution. Even by spending a few hundred million clobbering Obama, the Koch brothers reaped a windfall. The prospect of paying for their billions of tons of carbon pollution was completely swept off the table with the weakening of the EPA and destruction of state and federal clean energy laws. The Koch brothers also immediately benefited directly from the mid-term election. In December 2010, Obama backed away from his promise to roll back the Bush tax cuts for billionaires like Charles and David.

The Koch brothers' sizable role in shaping the first three years of the Obama administration—first by funding the Tea Parties and opposition to big progressive policies, then by financing the GOP takeover of Congress in 2010—was a preview of the strategy employed in Obama's reelection bid. Early reports signaled that the Koch political machine prepared to raise and spend more than $400 million in the 2012 election, routing the money through a wide array of conservative issue groups, including ones used in the past, like the seniors-oriented 60 Plus Association, as well as new groups, like the National Rifle Association. The same tactics employed in the past, from bus tours and paid grassroots campaigns, would be augmented by a new voter targeting system called Themis.[17]

The expanded Koch network resembled its own political party by the time of Obama's reelection. But the roots of this radical expansion are multifaceted. While self-interest is at the heart of the Koch political machine, not every Koch political decision is guided strictly by business. Rather, a large part of the Koch philanthropy operation seems to exist to validate the brothers' belief system and their own prestige. In a speech to the reclusive Council for National Policy in January of 1999, Charles summed up his funding of conservative groups as an almost messianic higher calling. "I'm dedicated to living by and advancing these principles and values. In that, I echo Martin Luther," he told the gathering of right-wing leaders and philanthropists in Naples, Florida.[18] In a letter I uncovered from Charles to dozens of the nation's wealthiest conservative donors, many of them billionaires, he portrayed himself as a revolutionary fighting an uphill battle against the tide of Obama's reforms. Asking a small set of billionaires to join his efforts against Obama, Charles wrote, "It is up to us to combat what is now the greatest assault on American freedom and prosperity in our lifetimes."

Indeed, Charles's commitment to antigovernment politics is deeply personal. He once confided to Stephen Moore, a *Wall Street Journal* writer also employed by a Koch-funded nonprofit, that he gives "dozens and dozens" of lectures on libertarian philosophy to Koch Industries employees. Perpetuating the lie that Koch Industries operates on the free market, without government contracts, is part of Charles's deeply ingrained identity. On occasion, he has even compared himself to great libertarian thinkers. An academic association (funded by a Koch charitable foundation) presented Charles an award in 2007 for his deep commitment to libertarian philosophy.

David, who ran for vice president on the Libertarian Party ticket in 1980, began re-creating presidential nominating ceremonies for himself every year since 2007. In what he calls the "Defending the Dream" summit, David hosts hundreds of activists from Koch-funded groups. Delegates carry vertical signs displaying which state they are from, similar to the signs carried by delegates to the major party conventions. Representatives from each state ritualistically stand and inform David of their progress in advancing the antigovernment cause. At his summit in 2009, several Americans for Prosperity staffers stood confidently in the audience reporting about their success in organizing the largest Tea Parties in their respective states. David laughed and clapped approvingly from the podium. Although Charles is known for spending most of his time tending to business or politics, David can be found in the pages of the *New York Social Diary*, attracting tabloid coverage for hosting the most fashionable dinners in the city. Although it has been said their approach to politics is indistinguishable, David and Charles both enjoy the limelight for very different reasons.

David was at hand for the new Republican Congress he helped elect. Before the official ceremony swearing in the members of the 112th Congress, David chatted with Rep. John Boehner in the Speaker's office. Meanwhile, Koch lobbyists met with the new chairman of the Energy and Commerce Committee to chart out a new course of action.

I caught up with David as he left the Capitol and strolled down Independence Avenue. "I'm curious to know, Mr. Koch, are you proud of the Tea Party movement and what they've achieved in the past years," I asked. "Yeah. There are some extremists there, but the rank and file are just normal people like us. And I admire them. It's probably the best grassroots uprising since 1776 in my opinion!" he said cheerfully. As soon as he finished the sentence, Tim Phillips, the Americans for Prosperity president who was escorting David around, pushed me back and started yelling into the video camera my colleague Scott Keyes was holding. David seemed amused by the attention, despite Phillips's demands that the "interview is over!" David boasted that his AFP group would do more going into the next few years, and along the way, "cut the hell out of spending, balance the budget, reduce regulations, and uh, support business."[19]

Our conversation eventually turned toward his secret fund-raising meetings. I asked if he had benefited from *Citizens United*, the Supreme Court decision allowing unlimited corporate spending in elections. He looked at me, and I caught a quick expression of guilt. He promptly ended the interview and walked away. It could have been because he genuinely felt bad about his oversized role in the democratic process. But then again, I was making him late for a party he was hosting for the dozens of Republican congressman he had helped elect to office.

4

REFORM HITS A WALL AT K STREET

"We ask you to use your important position to help protect seniors and other consumers in your district from higher electricity bills," wrote Helen Cast of the Dunmore Seniors Citizens' Center, in a letter requesting that Congressman Christopher Carney (D-PA) oppose Waxman Markey, the cap-and-trade legislation making its way through Congress in the summer of 2009. Helen Cast, however, didn't exist.[1] The senior center in Carney's district had no position on climate change and energy policy.

Similar letters, using almost identical language and formatting, were sent from local chapters of the NAACP, the Erie Center for Health and Aging, the American Association of University Women, and nearly half a dozen other organizations, to congressmen in competitive districts before the vote on the bill.[2] Staffers working for freshman Congressman Tom Perriello, a recipient of the anti-cap-and-trade faxes, decided to call some of the groups. They discovered that the letterhead was fake, the names made up, and the letters forged and sent without the consent of the groups. In fact, the letters were written by Bonner and Associates, a consulting firm based in Washington, D.C. that was working on behalf of the coal industry.

The lobbying coalition behind the forged letters, the American Coalition for Clean Coal Electricity, also funded a $28 million campaign of targeted advertising, rallies, and organizing around congressional town halls in 2009.[3] A loophole in lobbying law, however, ensured that none of this spending was recorded or disclosed at the time.

Perriello ultimately voted for Waxman Markey, but two other Democrats who received the fake letters voted no. The onslaught of lobbying slowed and watered down the legislation until it could be killed in the Senate months after it barely passed the House of Representatives.

The window of opportunity to deal with global warming closed largely as a result of the failures associated with Waxman Markey. Despite widespread belief in action on climate change among the American public, near consensus in the climate science community on the urgency of action, and the job-creating and utility rate–cutting benefits of clean energy policy, the bill still failed in a Democratic Congress with a Democrat in the White House. The coal and oil lobby proved to be too strong.

The secret to the failure to act on global warming lay in the dramatic expansion in what is known as "outside lobbying." This type of influence peddling seeks to manipulate the public into pressuring regulators and lawmakers. In many cases, like the coal industry's forged letters, corporate interests construct the perception of public support using deception and coercion. But this type of lobbying isn't registered, because registered federal lobbying only applies to firms that spend over 20 percent of their time speaking directly to lawmakers.

The work of integrating grassroots groups, orchestrating letter-writing campaigns, rallies in support of corporate lobbying goals, and phony studies published by think tanks is typically tasked to public relations companies that work in tandem with traditional K Street firms.

Managing public opinion has been a key component of lobbying since the early twentieth century. Edward Bernays, a nephew of Sigmund Freud living in America, developed some of the first major corporate campaigns to shift policy through public relations. For Mack Truck, for instance, Bernays set up conferences in the Waldorf Astoria and created front groups like the Better Living Through Increased Highway Transportation to influence the development of the interstate highway. His tactics remain the basis for an industry that is exploding in growth inside the Beltway.

Since President Obama took office, a glance at the most visible and highly engaged groups in the policy arena would seem to suggest conservatives mobilized at an unprecedented rate. Coalition to Protect Patients Rights, Conservatives for Patients' Rights, FACES of Coal, Regulation Reality, Regular Folks United, and other brand-new "grassroots" groups appeared out of nowhere in 2009 and 2010 alone.

But all of the aforementioned groups, and many more, were little more than smoke and mirrors, props created by public relations experts to advance a corporate, typically Republican, agenda. Regular Folks United, for example, was founded by Lori Roman, who said she started the group in response to President Obama's election and his "elitist comments" about rural Americans. In reality, Roman used the website, which catered to Tea Party and social conservatives, as a springboard for corporate advocacy. The Salt Institute, a trade association representing major salt producers including Cargill Salt and the China National Salt Company, paid Roman $251,321 the same year her Regular Folks United blasted e-mails to grassroots about salt regulations.[4] Roman's group attacked New York City's sodium-reduction campaign as an effort by "food nannies" to "control our lives." On the site, Roman called policies to curb salt intake an "arrogant quest for government control." Nowhere on Regular Folks United does Roman disclose that she was paid by the salt industry. But on a website for her consulting business, called Libertas Global Partners, Roman sells such services as "creative strategies for shifting public opinion" and "developing grassroots and grasstops support" to corporate clients.

Rather than appeal to the public directly, lobbying interests often set up what are known as "third-party authorities" to deliver a message. Again, corporations pursuing public policy through front groups is not considered lobbying by law. As such, front group–led campaigns not only confuse the public, but face very few disclosure requirements.

While front groups have existed for years, the use of such hoaxes has skyrocketed in response to Obama's election. Facing a tidal wave of progressive reforms promised by Obama on the campaign trail, corporations and the right wing leaned on a cadre of public relations operatives skilled in the art of manipulating policy debates and reshaping political discourse on a national level. These PR mavens sit at the hub of influence within the right-wing machine. They serve as the strategists who ultimately plan how to kill reform— from conducting the research, to inventing phony groups driving a certain message, to coordinating the attacks. With large-scale reforms promised in energy, health care, financial regulation, labor, and tax policy, front groups have multiplied and become more sophisticated than ever.

Some of the deceptive third-party groups used by political operatives of today are temporary, ad hoc "coalitions" created to sway a single issue area or piece of legislation. When Democrats pushed to pass student lending reform—which cut $60 billion in waste from private lenders who had been channeling the loans while skimming taxpayer money off the top—the private lending industry, including PNC, Sallie Mae, SunTrust, Nelnet, and others, contracted the PR firm Qorvis Communications to stop the legislation.[5] One of the many tactics used by Qorvis was the creation of a purportedly "grassroots" organization called Protect Student Choice. The website for the group did not disclose that it was bankrolled by profiteering student loan companies and banks. Qorvis staffer Karen Henretty[6] posed as a news reporter on the program "Focus Washington," along with officers of the College Republicans to criticize the legislation and falsely claim that it hurt students.[7] When the Senate passed lending reform, Qorvis's front lost a purpose and disappeared.

Other fronts are permanent rent-a-front groups—ostensible "think tanks" that serve as vessels for corporate lobbying campaigns. Many rental fronts pose as nonprofits dedicated to ideological goals, like removing regulation or cutting taxes. The specific issues triumphed by a rent-a-front are often linked to its donors. One of the loudest conservative groups defending BP after the Deepwater Horizon oil spill in the Gulf of Mexico, for example, was Dick Armey's FreedomWorks nonprofit. The group alleged that the Obama administration had no right to negotiate a $20 billion escrow account to compensate the victims of the spill.[8] A PowerPoint presentation showed that starting in 2007, the oil industry, including companies like BP, had concocted a multitiered campaign through seemingly grassroots groups like

Significant Grassroots Supporters

Trade Associations

API	IECA	Forest & Paper	NAM
NOIA	AGA	DPC	
IPAA	ACC	U.S. Oil & Gas Assn	

Companies

Shell	Anadarko	BP	Murphy
Devon	Marathon	ChevronTexaco	Exxon Mobil

Affiliated Groups

60 Plus	Freedom Works	American Conservative Union
BIPAC	Frontiers for Freedom	Partnership for America

Consumers/End-Users

Consumer Energy Alliance	Farm Bureaus (NC, CO, VA)
Ag-Energy Alliance	Affiliated Industries of Florida
U.S. Chamber of Commerce	Alaska Support Industry Alliance

Offshore drilling campaign supporters

FreedomWorks to promote offshore drilling in the Gulf of Mexico and off the coast of California.[9] FreedomWorks never disclosed this relationship, or the fact that FreedomWorks counts the American Petroleum Institute among its major donors. Armey's group positioned itself instead as simply a staunch defender of corporations against all government intrusion, even when that corporation spilled millions of barrels of oil into the Gulf.

Corporate efforts to steer the debate are often hidden behind nonprofits that are supposedly formed for a niche audience as well. An ExxonMobil-linked public relations firm called CDR Communications helped create a variety of fronts opposed to action on carbon pollution. One group, called the Cornwall Alliance, organized pastors and the evangelical community to oppose efforts to cap greenhouse gases.[10] Cornwall Alliance released a DVD, *Resisting the Green Dragon*, which compared the belief in global warming with paganism. Spokesmen for the group regularly appeared on conservative media, including the Glenn Beck program, to tout anticlean energy conspiracy theories under the guise of objective religious commentators.

The public relations industry is often paired with other influence-peddling strategies. While insider lobbyists work within the halls of Congress to pressure lawmakers, political operatives whip up public outrage and sow divisions among reform proponents. Most important, even though PR firms are akin to lobbying organizations, albeit through channels outside Congress, they do not have to disclose their clients or how much they are being paid. In many cases their true intent is never discovered. This chapter is a window into some of the new, innovative campaign strategies employed by public relation experts working against progressive reforms.

TIM PHILLIPS'S FRONT GROUP ROAD SHOW

In a rare public appearance speaking about his political beliefs in October 2009, David Koch could be seen escorted around the stage by a smiling figure. Tim Phillips, the Kochs' top political lieutenant, is not a registered lobbyist, but is perhaps the most influential operative working to advance the myriad corporate lobbying goals pursued by Koch's multibillion-dollar petrochemical and manufacturing empire. Phillips is a strategist and has served as David Koch's right-hand man at the helm of Americans for Prosperity, the massive conservative "grassroots" organization founded and financed by the Koch brothers.[11]

As one of the most prolific creators of front groups in the Obama era, Phillips stands out among other Republican operatives. From his work orchestrating the anti-Obama Tea

Parties to his sophisticated lobbying campaign to dismantle regional cap-and-trade programs in the United States, he has an outstanding track record of success.

Beginning his career as a Virginia-based political consultant, Phillips got his first big break managing the campaign of Congressman Bob Goodlatte (R-VA). After serving as Goodlatte's chief of staff for four years, Phillips joined former Christian Coalition director Ralph Reed in 1997 to create a lobbying and campaign consulting operation called Century Strategies.[12] The firm promised to mount "grassroots lobbying drives" and explained its strategy as "it matters less who has the best arguments and more who gets heard—and by whom."[13]

Through Century Strategies and other similar companies, much of Phillips's work has focused on exploiting traditional Christian values to advance one of two objectives. The first has been to shield his industry clients from laws against pollution, sexual exploitation, gambling, and corporate censorship. The second objective has been to deploy racial and ethnic slurs against a number of politicians, both Democrats and Republicans. Both efforts have met with considerable success, and neither has resulted in any serious repercussions for Tim Phillips or any of his companies.

Making its start with a recommendation from Karl Rove, Century Strategies signed one of its first major corporate clients—Enron.[14] Phillips and Reed were paid $380,000 to mobilize "religious leaders and pro-family groups" to push energy deregulation in Congress and on the state level, a policy shift that helped to lead to the energy crisis and recession of 2001.[15] The *Washington Post* reported that the pair informed Enron that they had leveraged their relationships with members of Congress and "placed" articles in prominent papers like the *New York Times*.[16]

In 1998, Phillips turned his attention to exploited women and children. The now-disgraced lobbyist Jack Abramoff hired Phillips's firm to pressure members of Congress to vote against legislation that would have made the U.S. Commonwealth of the Northern Mariana Islands subject to federal wage and worker safety laws.[17] A federal report found that "Chinese women [working in the Marianas] were subject to forced abortions and that women and children were subject to forced prostitution in the local sex-tourism industry." Part of Phillip's role at Century Strategies was to manage the firm's direct mail subsidiary, Millennium Marketing.[18] Accordingly, Phillips sent out mailers claiming Chinese workers "are exposed to the teachings of Jesus Christ" while on the islands, and many "are converted to the Christian faith and return to China with Bibles in hand."[19] The mailers then encouraged the recipients to contact lawmakers and ask them to oppose the Marianas labor reform legislation. Of course, none of the pamphlets revealed that Tan Holdings of Hong Kong, a sweatshop empire, sponsored the campaign.

The Marianas stealth lobbying effort was not the only time Phillips worked with Abramoff to manipulate Christian activists. Reed and Phillips conspired to generate conservative Christian outrage toward gambling in Indian casinos in a cynical plot to encourage those same tribes to hire Abramoff to lobby on their behalf.[20] In some cases, Phillips's antigambling crusade would simply be part of an effort to kill off competition to Abramoff's clients.[21] And while Phillips and Reed pretended to be motivated by antigambling Christian values, the pair received money from the gambling industry. One of Abramoff's gambling clients, an Internet company called eLottery, laundered its payments through a set of fronts. To conceal payments, eLottery would give donations to Grover Norquist's Americans for Tax Reform, another rent-a-front group, which would then be passed along to Phillips's Faith and Family Alliance, before eventually going to Century Strategies.

Whether he is attacking Net Neutrality (what Phillips calls a "government takeover of the Internet") or the Clean Air Act ("Churches would need an EPA permit"), Phillips furthers the corporate interest by combining right-wing resentment with folksy promises of "freedom." Almost every charge he flings is false: EPA carbon regulations would be aimed at coal plants, not churches, and Net Neutrality guarantees a free and open Internet without traffic controls. Although he refuses to divulge who, other than Koch, funds his organization, Phillips has long practiced the art of funneling corporate money and fooling the public with campaigns ostensibly based on religious or cultural motivations.

Though Phillips and Reed are best known in the campaign consulting world for engineering the dual victories of Senator Saxby Chambliss (R-GA)[22] and Republican Gov. Sonnie Perdue in Georgia (by associating images of Osama bin Laden with the incumbent Democratic senator),[23] the pair can also be credited with the most below-the-belt tactics ever seen in modern Republican primaries. The duo reportedly "spearheaded" the telemarketing and direct mail efforts for George Bush against John McCain in the 2000 primaries.[24] It is widely believed that Century Strategies executed the mass mailers and robo-calls that accused McCain of fathering an illegitimate child with a black woman, using the image of McCain's adopted daughter from Bangladesh.[25]

Phillips has managed to escape most of the controversy that eventually embroiled his partners Reed and Abramoff, and has gone on to represent a wide range of clients and causes. While remaining behind the scenes himself, he has orchestrated exuberant, gimmick-filled campaigns across the country. He contracted an actual hot air balloon to press his case that climate change is just "hot air," a hoax. Phillips's campaigns are national and multifaceted. He runs multiple "tours" crisscrossing the country and in crucial congressional districts where he is trying to place pressure on a particular member of Congress. His "Save My Ballot Tour" paid Samuel Joseph Wurzelbacher, the unlicensed plumber and would-be small business owner from the McCain campaign, to tour the country attacking the Employee Free Choice Act, a key labor reform. His "Regulation Reality Tour"—an outfit featuring inflatable moon bounces for children, as well as free food and drinks—went to states like Arkansas and Nebraska to convince people to call their senators to support an amendment to gut the Clean Air Act and remove its ability to regulate carbon pollution.

The bus tour method was expanded in 2010 as a undisclosed electioneering effort. Phillips developed multiple bus tours during the campaign to promote a general anti-spending message. His "Ending Spending," a thirty-city tour targeting vulnerable Democratic candidates, was clear election spending as each stop featured rallies against local Democrats with competitive challenges. The "Remember November" tour, another Phillips creation during the 2010 election, hosted phone banking parties to plug activists into Republican campaigns. As Kevin Gentry, a Koch public affairs officer, later noted during a private meeting with donors, the Tea Party bus tours during the midterms were "designed to help in the Congressional races."[26]

The effect in 2010 was so successful that Phillips expanded it in 2012, hiring over one hundred organizers for the election. Since taking over Americans for Prosperity's operations, Phillips has played a key role in helping to mastermind the rise of the Tea Parties (see chapter 1) and has also taken on some of the largest progressive agenda items and won. Phillips's organization is credited with pressuring Republicans firmly into the climate science denier camp following the 2008 election. One of his groups, No Climate Tax, issued a pledge, signed by nearly five hundred Republican candidates, to oppose efforts to tax and regulate carbon emissions. From climate change–related ads, Tea Parties organized around opposition to climate legislation, to aggressive media outreach, Phillips commanded an integrated public relations campaign that severely undercut reform efforts. In a meeting with conservative bloggers, Phillips explained that he worked to influence climate policy by increasing skepticism around climate science: "If we win the science argument, it's game, set, match."[27] Koch Industries, cited as a major polluter responsible for burning over 100 million tons of carbon a year by one estimate, clearly benefited from the failure of climate negotiations.[28]

THE SECRET CAMPAIGN AGAINST HEALTH CARE REFORM

The effort to pass sweeping health reform legislation under President Obama placed massive health care industries, particularly health insurance corporations, in a difficult position. For one thing, the industry genuinely opposed reform. Insurance companies viewed the "public option," a voluntary insurance program administered by the government to compete with private insurers to help bring down costs, as its greatest threat. Regulatory changes, such as a so-called

Medical Loss Ratio—a rule mandating that a certain percentage of every premium dollar go towards actual health care instead of insurance company profits and administrative costs—obviously threatened the bottom line of insurance corporations. Other regulatory proposals, such as ending the controversial practice of "rescissions," the canceling of coverage when patients get sick, and banning widespread discrimination based on broadly defined "preexisting conditions," also worried insurance giants. Making matters worse, the industry had become a regular punching bag for politicians. In the years prior to the 2009–10 battle over health reform legislation, Democratic candidates for president, starting with John Edwards, but also Hillary Clinton and Barack Obama, had demonized insurance companies for earning profits by denying care.

On the other hand, with Democrats proposing various methods to dramatically increase coverage for the uninsured, health insurance companies saw an opportunity to gain millions of new customers through the health reform bill. Wendell Potter, the former vice president for communications at Cigna, explained that this dynamic was clear to health insurance companies well before Obama even took office. Potter confided that his former boss at Cigna, CEO H. Edward Hanway, formed a group of other health insurance CEOs called the Strategic Communications Committee to develop an effective message and strategy for the industry. The committee, working with a bevy of public relations experts, lobbyists, and America's Health Insurance Plans (AHIP), the trade association for health insurers, decided early on that it would adopt a two-pronged strategy to deflate reforms that might hurt profits, while encouraging reforms that would increase the number of insurance industry customers. In public, according to Potter, the insurance industry would position itself as "changed" and supporting reform. However, the only reforms they would actually support were policies like the individual mandate to require people to purchase private insurance. Behind closed doors and through third parties seemingly unrelated to the industry, the insurers planned to orchestrate a massive campaign to smear reform and obstruct the legislative process.

The health insurers' duplicitous campaign was based partially on the industry's experience defeating President Clinton's health reform proposals, as well as with dealing with the documentary *SiCKO*, filmmaker Michael Moore's poignant takedown of the American profit-driven health care system. In 1993, the health insurance industry created a front called the Coalition for Health Insurance Choices to mobilize opposition to Clinton's proposals. The coalition hired focus groups to find the best arguments to encourage opposition to reform, then set about working with any group they could find as possible allies in the fight. Blair Childs, the lobbyist at the center of the insurers' campaign, explained that he found natural allies in right-wing attack groups, the tobacco industry (which Clinton planned to tax to pay for his plan), and employers who did not want to be required to provide insurance to their workers. To undercut initial support for Clinton's reform ideas, the industry worked secretly with right-wing journalists and celebrities such as Rush Limbaugh to drum up anger at reform. Sheldon Rampton and John Stauber detailed in their tome on deceptive PR tactics, *Toxic Sludge Is Good for You*, how Limbaugh's rants falsely accusing Clinton of trying to jail people for not complying with health reform and how reform would supposedly bankrupt the nation, figured directly into the health insurer's campaign:

First, Rush would whip up his "dittohead" fans with a calculated rant against the Clinton health plan. Then during a commercial break listeners would hear an anti-health care ad and an 800 number to call for more information. Calling the number would connect them to a telemarketer, who would talk to them briefly and then "patch them through" directly to their congressperson's office. The congressional staffers fielding the calls typically had no idea that the constituents had been primed, loaded, aimed and fired at them by radio ads on the Limbaugh show, paid by the insurance industry, with the goal of orchestrating the appearance of overwhelming grassroots opposition to health reform.[29]

Once much of the right's propaganda machine had soured the public discourse about reform, the insurance industry moved in directly with a national ad campaign to attack. The combination of Republican unity in opposition to any reform plan, along with the hard-hitting "Harry & Louise" commercials paid for by the health insurance industry, ultimately defeated Clinton's reforms.

When Michael Moore's award-winning documentary *SiCKO* came out in 2007, the insurance industry devised a detailed public relations plan to blunt Moore's argument that profit-based health insurance is both unnecessary and inefficient.[30] The industry understood that it suffered a negative public perception even before Moore's movie. So the industry, according to a PowerPoint presentation obtained by Bill Moyers of PBS, orchestrated an elaborate campaign to position Moore as simply an "entertainer" and "out of the mainstream."[31] The PowerPoint indicated that the industry worked with centrist Democrats and Republicans to cast Moore as too much of a "polarizing figure" for the Democratic Party, and to threaten Democrats aligned with him with the prospect of "returning to a minority party." According to their industry's own research, they believed that arguing that America should simply improve its own health system rather than move to government-run health care would be a "debate we can win." To shift the dialogue, one slide in the presentation recommended that the industry worked with various conservative think tanks, such as Heritage and the Pacific Legal Research Institute, as well as with conservative blogs and media, to produce a series of stories on the "horror stories of govt.-run systems" and positive steps industry could make to improve itself without the government involvement. Before the movie even premiered, the industry blasted the media with its own message. The PowerPoint, developed by the public relations firm APCO, demonstrated a preemptive plan to "reframe the debate" and "define the health insurance industry as the solution."

As the industry prepared to enter the debate under Obama, the insurance companies came to the conclusion that they were particularly unpopular and a vulnerable target for comprehensive reform. Out of all of the major industries involved in health care, the public hates and has long hated insurance companies, and there has always been wide consensus supporting some type of reform. Politically, President Obama, with his massive majorities in Congress, seemed more likely than any president in the past to enact sweeping changes. Adding urgency to the situation, when Obama was sworn into office, approximately 14,000 Americans were losing their health insurance every day because of the recession.[32]

Taking a page from the strategy they used against Moore, the industry tried to flank the Obama administration, com-

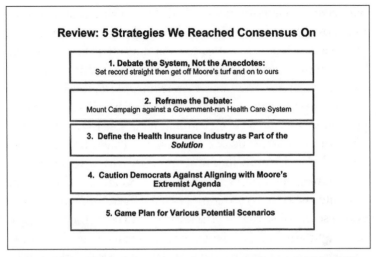

Screenshot from AHIP's Powerpoint presentation regarding anti–Michael Moore strategy

ing out quickly to announce that the industry would not fight reform as it had under the Clinton administration. The insurance industry's chief lobbyist, Karen Ignagni, made headlines when she told Obama, "You have our commitment to play, to contribute and to help pass health-care reform this year" at his health reform summit at the outset of the reform process. This, Wendell Potter explained, was part of the "charm" side of the duplicitous campaign. In public, the industry would commit to working proactively for reform. "They will talk about, in broad terms, how supportive they are of health care reform," said Potter, adding, "but they will be working behind the scenes to kill very, very crucial parts of reform legislation like the public option."[33] Just as soon as the charm campaign kicked into high gear, with pundits and editorials praising the insurance industry for changing its ways, the "dirty," underhanded campaign began.

In March, shortly before Obama's health reform summit announcing the beginning of health reform negotiations, a group called Conservatives for Patients' Rights (CPR) was launched to smear the effort. The group, managed day to day by Creative Response Concepts Public Relations, the Republican-friendly PR firm which had handled the "Swift Boat Veterans for Truth" campaign to smear John Kerry's war record in 2004, hosted a website, but had no grassroots support. Creative Response Concepts had worked in the past for health insurers, managing the Coalition for Patient Choice front group in the nineties. CPR immediately raised $20 million dollars for ads, in part funded by millionaire Rick Scott, who was forced to resign as the head of the Columbia/HCA hospital corporation amid Medicare fraud charges in the nineties, and in part from a group of mystery donors.[34] The ads disparaged reform with token catchphrases, accusing the public option of placing "a bureaucrat in between you and your doctor." Curiously, the Washington, D.C., address listed for CPR was a mailbox on the floor of an office building level owned by APCO public affairs, the same mega-PR firm that Potter said handled the strategy for the insurance industry's campaign against Moore. Representatives from CPR denied any relationship with APCO.[35] A document later obtained from the health insurance industry revealed that insurers had funneled over $3.8 million to APCO in 2009.[36]

Almost every day of the summer of 2009, the insurance industry pumped out two simultaneous messages. Starting in July of 2009, the insurance industry trade association began sponsoring millions of dollars' worth of feel-good ads promising to fix the health care system. "We're America's health insurance companies, supporting bipartisan reforms that Congress can build on," said the narrator in one ad called

"Illness." Starting around the same time, the U.S. Chamber of Commerce launched ads smearing reform, erroneously alleging that reform would kill jobs and would "make a tough economy worse." "Let's stop the new health care tax. Tell Congress to keep their hands to themselves and out of our pockets," said another chamber ad. The chamber spent more than $10 million on various attack ads against reform on television and on the radio. Well after health reform was signed into law, Bloomberg reported that the health insurance industry had channeled over $107 million to the chamber for the attack ads in 2009 and 2010.[37] Companies such as Aetna, Cigna, Humana, Kaiser Health Plans, UnitedHealth Group, and Wellpoint all participated in the donation.

Potter explained that despite the industry's promise to support reform, it still fed talking points and attack lines to right-wing radio and the larger propaganda chamber of the right, such as Fox News and the *Washington Times*. In February 2009, only weeks after Obama took office, the health insurance trade association AHIP conducted a secret poll to find the best language to defeat reform, particularly the public option. The best way to sour opinion over the public option, the poll found, was to brand it as the "government-run health insurance plan." AHIP lobbyists sent the polling memo to Republican staffers, and eventually, to right-wing media. In October, Fox News vice president Bill Sammon sent a stern warning e-mail to all Fox News reporters instructing them only to use the term "government-run health insurance" or "government option" when describing the public option In the weeks preceding critical votes in both the House and Senate, front groups like Americans for Prosperity, 60 Plus Association, Independent Women's Forum, the Susan B. Anthony List, and American Future

Fund ran millions of dollars' worth of ads attacking the legislation. Like CRC, none of the groups would reveal their backers. It is difficult to imagine that doctors' groups or hospitals were secretly funding these anti–health reform fronts.

The Obama administration successfully brokered deals to win support for health reform legislation from the hospital lobby, the drug industry, and professional associations representing doctors, nurses, and health-care unions. When President Harry Truman and Lyndon Johnson made broad attempts to reform the American health-care system, they faced rigorous opposition, particularly from the American Medical Association (AMA). The AMA also helped defeat President Bill Clinton's health reform plan in 1994. Although support within the AMA was divided, most of the organization, including its leadership, tossed support behind President Obama's health reform proposals—a first for the entire history of the AMA.

With the American Medical Association supporting reform legislation, the insurance industry turned toward PR operatives to manufacture its own doctor groups that would oppose reform. A new doctors' group formed in 2009, the Coalition to Protect Patients' Rights, began organizing press events and running ads of doctors saying they opposed any form of government-run health care, especially a public option. After meeting several of the group's staffers at the National Press Club, I was handed a business card with a newly registered telephone number and post office box. On the publicly available calendar for the Press Club, however, I noticed that a woman from the infamous DCI Group had registered the coalition's event. After calling the DCI Group and speaking with the staffer, I was able to confirm that the DCI Group had helped create the coalition and was managing its daily affairs.

The DCI Group, which came into prominence after working for the tobacco industry to create fake "smokers' rights" groups to lobby against tobacco regulation, had worked for the insurance industry in 2002 to build opposition to the Patients' Bill of Rights legislation. Similarly, an investigation I conducted into an outfit called the Center for Medicine in the Public Interest, which had been running online ads attacking the public option and calling to kill the bills in Congress, revealed that the group was secretly run by the PR firm Porter Novelli, which has long served the health care industry.

As corporate front groups and right-wing media fought to bring down the popularity of health reform throughout the summer, many still trusted the health insurance industry's charm campaign, despite clear evidence that they were lying. For instance, insurance industry lobbyists, including Karen Ignagni, spent the summer claiming that the industry was "the first to step up and offer real change," such as ending the practice of rescinding coverage after an applicant files a medical claim. But in a hearing under oath on June 16, 2009, executives from UnitedHealth, Assurant, and WellPoint specifically refused to "commit" to ending that practice, undercutting the public promises from their trade association.

As a pivotal vote in the Senate Finance Committee neared in October 2009, it became more difficult to believe the industry's charm campaign. Shortly before the Finance Committee vote, health insurance lobbyists distributed a report—funded by the insurance industry—falsely accusing the bill of raising premiums.[38] According to the Huffington Post, health insurance lobbyist Steve Champlin declared ten days later that bipartisan reform was dead, and he urged GOP lawmakers to refuse to help pass the bill.[39] "So when they vote for a health care reform bill, whatever it is, they are giving comfort to the enemy who is down," said Champlin at a closed-door meeting for insurance executives.

In the end, the insurance industry successfully removed the public option by spreading misinformation about it. Conservative Democrats, persuaded by an avalanche of ads and angry constituents, removed the public option before the Senate passed the bill on Christmas Day in 2009. Although the industry also succeeded in slowing the reform process down, the duplicitous campaign eventually unraveled. Rather than thanking the industry for changing its ways, as Obama and his officials were doing throughout the beginning of 2009, the administration changed its tone and declared that insurers were the problem by the end of that year. The final bill expanded private coverage to 31 million previously uninsured Americans, ended industry abuses like rescissions and preexisting condition discrimination, and removed lifetime caps on medical care.

After the bill passed, front groups, many of them funded by health insurance companies, began pummeling legislators with attack ads in a bid to replace them with lawmakers who would repeal or weaken the bill. But as they had during the legislative debate over the bill, the companies hid their identities while funding the ads. It wasn't until June 2012 that Aetna, in what appeared to be an accidental regulatory filing, revealed that it poured some $7 million into undisclosed nonprofits, like the American Action Network, to help elect Tea Party Republicans promising to repeal health reform.[40]

DIVIDE AND CONQUER
Instead of focusing solely on natural allies in the right-wing movement, corporate front groups have conducted strate-

gies aimed at dividing liberals or convincing them to oppose progressive reforms. During the debate over the Wall Street reform bill in Congress, a group unknown to the larger progressive community emerged called Stop Too Big to Fail. The group attacked the bill from the left, running $1.6 million worth of ads in Nevada, Virginia, and Missouri asking constituents to call Democratic senators and tell them to "vote against this phony 'financial reform.' Support real reform, stop 'too big to fail.'" While the bill did not explicitly limit the size of banks, it provided vast new powers for the government to identify risky banking institutions and close them before they can harm the broader financial system. Instead of calling for stricter amendments, the ads simply called for killing the bill. However, reporting on the failed amendment sponsored by Senator Sherrod Brown (D-OH) to limit the size of large banks and force some of the largest banks to sell off some divisions, progressive blogger David Dayen remarked grimly, "Wall Street won big."[41] Complaints that the bill did not do enough to deal with the problem of overly large banking institutions caused great concern for liberals who appeared to have been won over by the Stop Too Big to Fail campaign.

Stop Too Big to Fail also wrote posts on liberal blogs like DailyKos and FireDogLake. One guest posting by Stop Too Big to Fail on DailyKos erroneously claimed that the $50 billion resolution fund to liquidate failing banks, a mechanism actually proposed to prevent future bailouts, was a "bailout fund for large institutions funded by small investors." In fact, the purpose of the fee was to collect funds for liquidating failing firms from the very largest financial institutions, not small investors. DailyKos commenters were not fooled. One immediately disputed the "funded by small investors" claim, remarking, "It's funded BY THE BIG BANKS." Another commenter chimed in, calling the guest posting "as deceitful as I thought." [42]

The liberal bloggers were right to expose Too Big to Fail's trickery. Robert Johnson and Jim Conran, the two individuals running Stop Too Big to Fail, are longtime front group lobbyists. The pair founded Consumers for Competitive Choice, a nonprofit which lobbies for deregulation of ownership rules for the cable industry. Deregulation, of course, allows telecommunication giants to further monopolize the market and does not necessarily provide more choices. And despite the name of the group, it was not funded by consumers. Rather, Conran and Johnson collected large sums from the telecom industry, like Verizon, to fund the venture.

The investigative blog Talking Points Memo revealed that Stop Too Big to Fail had been directed in part by the DCI Group, the same lobbying firm that had set up fake groups for health care interests, tobacco firms, and other corporate interests. According to reporter Justin Elliot, Stop Too Big to Fail tried to fool Simon Johnson, the former chief economist for the International Monetary Fund, into joining their campaign against financial reform. Johnson told Elliot that he had been contacted to participate in a Stop Too Big to Fail conference call by DCI Group director Oliver Wolf. Although Wolf and the organizers of Stop Too Big to Fail refused to divulge their funders, the subterfuge they concocted served only the interests of Wall Street firms attempting to kill reform.

A more subtle, and successful, effort to divide the left and motivate progressives to oppose reform was deployed by lobbyists from the Blue Cross Blue Shield (BCBS) Association, a lobbying group representing thirty-nine independent BCBS companies. Like most of the health insurance industry, BCBS engaged in the duplicitous campaign of telling the public they fully support the concept of health reform, while continually demanding drastic changes to the legislation and funding stealth efforts to kill the bills.

One of the reforms BCBS actually wanted was a strong individual mandate, including stiff penalties for anyone refusing to purchase private health insurance. Most legislators balked at the type of individual mandate proposed by BCBS and other insurers, but still included a version of the individual mandate with a sliding scale of subsidies. Without healthy people in the health insurance market, premiums would skyrocket for others who need it. An individual mandate ensures that there isn't a "free rider" problem where people only sign up for insurance when they get sick. As health economist Jonathan Gruber has noted, reform without an individual mandate would result in a "death spiral" making it nearly impossible to cover sick people in a fair, affordable way.

However, without the public option, many progressives opposed the individual mandate, balking at the idea of being forced to buy private insurance. DailyKos founder Markos Moulitsas tweeted "kill [the bill] if it includes mandate. Strip out the mandate, then what's left is inoffensive." Howard Dean echoed this sentiment, spending several weeks calling for the death of the Senate version of health reform because it lacked a public option and contained the individual mandate. Indeed, the individual mandate is the least popular part of health reform, particularly to progressives. A *Wall Street Journal* poll in July of 2009 found 60 percent of Americans opposing it, even with subsidies for low- and-middle income Americans to help them afford insurance.

Understanding that reform cannot be implemented without an individual mandate, BCBS capitalized on progressive discontent. BCBS began working with the American Legislative Exchange Council (ALEC), a D.C.-based front group which helps state lawmakers craft corporate-friendly legislation. Early in the national health reform debate, ALEC began circulating template health care "states' rights" legislation to its member state legislators in an attempt to encourage every state to propose a ban on the individual mandate.[43]

According to the ALEC website, the draft legislation banning the individual mandate was developed by a three-member task force of industry representatives. One of the members was Joan Gardner, who simultaneously served as the lead lobbyist for state-based affairs at the BCBS Association policy office. In an interview, Christie Herrera, the director of ALEC's health task force, told me that Gardner played a pivotal role in crafting the anti–individual mandate states' rights initiative. According to Herrera, Gardner's position at the BCBS brought "great knowledge" to the issue, and Gardner lobbied to press forward with the campaign. Another ALEC staffer I spoke with at one of their conferences in the fall of 2009 said the individual mandate was the "perfect issue," because it cuts across party lines and provokes both liberals and conservatives to be against the health care bill.

Ironically, shortly before my interview with Herrera, the BCBS called for scrapping the Senate health reform bill because the individual mandate *that the BCBS had proposed* was too weak. However, at the same time BCBS fired off a report criticizing the Senate bill's individual mandate, the ALEC website, which was largely controlled by BCBS, accused the very notion of an individual mandate as "anti-freedom." Either way the Senate had acted—with a strong mandate, with weak, or with no mandate at all—BCBS could attack the bill and give a different, conflicting reason for killing it.

Similar efforts by right-wing operatives to sow doubt and uncertainty within liberal ranks have sprung up. Operatives working for white nationalist John Tanton and his anti-immigration Pioneer Fund started Progressives for Immigration Reform (PFIM) early in 2009. The group, which advertises in liberal publications, fakes concern for environmental issues like overconsumption and urban sprawl, to call for a halt to new immigration into America. Before starting PFIM, staffers for the group bought nearly half a million in advertising from climate change–denying organs like NewsMax. Like Stop Too Big to Fail and BCBS's anti-individual mandate initiatives, these overtures to progressives are thinly masked attempts to drive a political wedge.

* * *

The decline of newspapers, particularly layoffs of investigative reporters, has dramatically increased the vulnerability of the public to exploitative public relations campaigns. As public relations firms increase their arsenal with more sophisticated ways to fool the public about any given policy or politician, there are fewer and fewer institutions dedicated to rooting out dishonesty in the public sphere.

In a nationally televised speech to Congress in September of 2009, Obama tried to call out the lies leveled against his policies. "If you misrepresent what's in the [health reform] plan, we will call you out," he said. But a poll taken around the time of the speech showed that nearly half of the public believed in the ludicrous falsehood that there were "death panels" in the bill. What President Theodore Roosevelt called the president's power of the "bully pulpit" to command public opinion had faded. While Obama could grab headlines at times, he did not have the tools to move the public that his opponents in industry wielded. Although unions made meager efforts to help bring the public around to supporting policies like health reform, they were outgunned by industry opponents with a vast array of public relations strategies at their fingertips. Obama could not generate mass protests, divide and conquer his enemies, nor develop dozens of front groups to advance his policies—or any policies in the public interest. No matter how much of a mandate voters handed Obama on election day, or how personally popular he remained, control of public opinion rested far from his grasp, and remained far from a reflection of reality or a rational discussion of policy.

5

A SOCIAL MEDIA FACE LIFT
FOR CONSERVATISM

o borrow a Sarah Palin aphorism, after their election defeat in 2008, conservatives didn't retreat, they "reloaded." Instead of finding new solutions to public policy problems or seriously reevaluating Bush's failures, conservatives focused almost solely on new ways to communicate their old ideas. To do so, they looked to their natural allies in corporate marketing for inspiration; and they looked to the left for imitation. The result has been a recent and profound turnaround that has allowed the right the bury Obama's message and dominate the political debate.

HISTORICAL RIGHT-WING DOMINATION OF THE MEDIA

Traditionally, conservatives have almost always dominated direct mail solicitations, retained the best pollsters money could buy, and paid for the most celebrated advertising makers. Message discipline is the first lesson for any Republican politician. Talk radio? Unquestionably controlled by conservatives.

Cable news? Fox News couldn't be more right-wing and popular. The right had also dominated the Internet for most of the Internet's fledging history. Throughout the nineties and for much of President George W. Bush's first term, conservatives easily ruled online news. And much of that initial success stemmed from foundations and entrepreneurial pioneers, like Matt Drudge, creator of the wildly popular headline-aggregating site Drudge Report, and Jim Robinson of the news message board Free Republic. The pair formed a symbiotic relationship. Drudge, who played a role in breaking the Monica Lewinsky story, made waves in the media with scoops on the latest Clinton scandals, and Free Republic provided a platform for conservatives to share conspiratorial perspectives and to organize their own rallies and events. Many of the angry mobs hounding Clinton at public events were mobilized by Free Republic. The Free Republic–organized impeachment rally, "Treason Is the Reason," featured Republican lawmakers and writer Christopher Hitchens.[1]

Their efforts were enhanced by well-funded conservative investments in internet technology. The first major foray into purely ideological online news came from the Heritage Foundation, which worked with *National Review* magazine to create Town Hall in 1992. The Town Hall bulletin board forum on Compuserve required users to pay to dial into a central terminal to share information and read conservative publications. It later morphed into an Internet site with links to conservative opinion pieces, studies, and syndicated columns from newspapers. Town Hall helped organize the top conservative arguments, studies, and articles. The one-stop shop, similar in utility to Drudge Report, provided direction for various conservative websites, talk radio, and Republican politicians to get on the same message.

Conservatives maintained their dominance by constantly making investments in online news portals. In 2000 James Glassman, previously a fellow at the American Enterprise Institute, launched a website called TechCentralStation with the corporate lobbying firm DCI Group. The website, with funds from corporations such as Microsoft and ExxonMobil, published reports from right-wing think tanks as news pieces. Glassman, who later became the director of the George W. Bush Institute in Dallas, eventually closed TechCentralStation after a round of criticism that the site was essentially a smoke screen for corporate propaganda.[2] In 2004, Bush strategists hired a number of firms to develop online tools to help supporters place op-eds and letters to the editor, well before MoveOn adopted a similar tactic. As even Karl Rove conceded, conservatives held an advantage in online news through 2004—but the right lost its edge after Bush's victory over John Kerry.

CHANGE IN MEDIA ENVIRONMENT

Conservatives soon slipped to second place in the media war. Comfortable controlling the gears of government for so long, the right had largely ignored the rapidly shifting media landscape. John McCain, for instance, used an outdated e-mailing technology and had no functioning social network of his own. By Election Day, 2008, the Republican Party did not even have its own national list of supporters they could reach through text messages. While candidate Barack Obama talked about hope and change, an entire universe of liberal websites lobbed attacks and criticism every day at the McCain-Palin ticket. There were structural reasons for this decline. During the latter half of the Bush administration, triumphant Republican consultants who had won in 2004 largely with traditional spending on television ads, telemarketing, and direct mail had every incentive to encourage the party and the right-wing movement to continue spending on traditional outlets. Many television consultants receive up to a 15 percent cut of an entire advertising buy—which of course can be many of millions of dollars during an election season. Moving to online and nontraditional communications would result in a financial loss for some of these consultants, who doubled as advisors to the Republican National Committee and contractors to major conservative foundations.

Yet, while Republicans were expanding their traditional marketing strategies, some of the most cutting-edge corporate advertising campaigns of the twenty-first century intentionally abandoned using billboards, television commercials, and other traditional forms of branding. Ironically taking their cues from the socialist writer Naomi Klein—whose book *No Logo* detailed a world alienated by the overabundance of corporate brands on every T-shirt, building, and bus—brand managers skillfully slipped their products into the background of movies, seemingly amateur blog posts, and the most popular YouTube channels. The corporate public relations firm Edelman, one of many advertising and marketing behemoths that specialize in this form of stealth salesmanship, carefully chronicled how the public shifted toward trusting "peer-to-peer" endorsements of ideas and products. They found that one of the efficient ways to mediate peer-to-peer marketing is through impersonal social networking and online content platforms. The USC Annenberg School for Communications and Journalism found that 80 percent of Internet users considered the Internet to be an important source of information for them in 2008—up from 66 percent in 2006—and already higher than television, radio, and newspapers. By 2010, USC found that over 82 percent of Americans were regular Internet users.

Edelman published a study, "The Social Pulpit," revealing the various ways the 2008 Obama campaign wove campaign engagement into the social media habits of his supporters, from ethnic social networking websites like Black Planet to innovative campaign widgets for local bloggers. Ironically, the study was written in consultation with Mike Krempasky, an Edelman executive who also helped found the conservative blog Redstate (a blog that duplicated the diary system of the left-wing blog DailyKos). Krempasky would later assist various corporations and right-wing blogs in deploying Obama campaign tactics to boost the nascent Tea Party movement.[3]

However, out of power in 2006 and 2008, it was the left that had a greater incentive to experiment with alternative methods for organizing and delivering their ideas to the public, and it was the left that took the lead in the tactics proposed by Krempasky and others. Simon Rosenberg of the New Politics Institute and other left-leaning think tanks contributed resources to developing best practices for new communication tools as well as opportunities for incubating talent. Democratic campaigns sought outsiders adept at online strategy. Progressives developed online fund-raising schemes, like Act Blue, and experimented with new ways of connecting with voters, such as targeted SMS text messages. The Obama campaign's decision to announce the selection of Obama's running mate via text message netted an additional two million cell phone numbers to its database, which could then be used to plug voters into other election season notices. The unprecedented investments from the left coincided with rapid shifts in the media landscape. Perhaps most important, much of the institutional assistance simply buoyed left-wing initiatives that began organically, like DailyKos or MoveOn. As the progressive "blogosphere" swelled with traffic and influence during the 2008 Democratic presidential primaries, the momentum gave the impression that liberal bloggers would always be the prevailing force on the left.

"DON'T RETREAT, INSTEAD RELOAD!"

Much of the right-wing's resurgence is due to its intense investment in technology and communications. Republicans, as well as right-wing conservatives, realized that their image could be salvaged if repackaged properly. And the most discussed post-2008 election concern was the advantage held by the left in communication infrastructure. In a December 2008 reflection piece titled the "Roots of Defeat," Republican consultant Patrick Ruffini wrote in the *National Review* that progressive news sites, like the Huffington Post and Talking Points Memo, were the constant purveyors of "attack memes" against the conservative movement and its candidates.[4] Talking Points Memo had led the liberal blogosphere's mobilization against President Bush's attempt to privatize Social Security in 2005. In addition to its rapid news coverage, the website posted the phone numbers of Democratic politicians who had indicated support for Bush's proposal and encouraged readers to call. The groundswell of opposition from bloggers, then the general public, marked the first significant policy defeat for President Bush. As Ruffini noted, the defeat punctured Bush's "aura of invincibility and presage[d] the death spiral to come." ThinkProgress, where I began working in 2009, had helped expose much of disgraced lobbyist Jack Abramoff's relationship with the Bush administration, and Talking Points Memo broke the story of the Bush Justice Department's systematic political firings of U.S. Attorneys around the country. As the 2008 election unfolded, the McCain campaign's positions and statements were instantly fact checked and scrutinized by leading progressive websites. Ruffini observed that progressive blogs did actual research and reporting while most conservative bloggers were "generally commentators and not reporters." He also noted that the right lacked many of the technological innovations employed by Barack Obama's campaign, and, more important, lacked a powerful online megaphone for its ideological goals.

As conservative writer Ross Douthat noted in a postelection interview about the future of conservatism, the Internet also served as a vital organizing platform for progressives. DailyKos, Douthat said, was one of the main sources of "left wing populist anger against the excesses of the Bush Administration." The DailyKos system allows the public, after registering, to post blog entries, which are either selected by moderators or voted up to the "Recommended" list by other users. Other organizations, from MoveOn, to Democracy for America, to the message board Democratic Underground, had helped feed the surge in leftist populism through the Internet by providing opportunities for likeminded people to find each other instantly.

In more apocalyptic terms than usual, Media Research Center founder L. Brent Bozell III addressed the Council for National Policy in February of 2009 and warned of an entire media revolution the conservative infrastructure had "missed." He rattled off a series of negative stories about Barack Obama, and claimed that during the course of the 2008 campaign, only two stories had been written about the Tony Rezko scandal, and by the time the national networks ran "a single story on Reverend Wright, 42 States and the District of Columbia had voted." According to a search of transcripts supplied by Nexis, the major networks ABC, CBS, and NBC ran at least a combined 57 segments or mentions of Obama's controversial pastor Rev. Jeremiah Wright well before November. Countless news stories were written about Barack Obama's relationship with Chicago developer Tony Rezko: the Associated Press (41); *Washington Times* (13); *Los Angeles Times* (6); the *Chicago Sun-Times* (78).[5]

The gross exaggeration notwithstanding, Bozell went on to complain that these stories "weren't told" because the right had failed to continue to build its communications apparatus. "We have Fox News," Bozell said, "we have mastered talk radio," referring to the fact that nine out of ten talk radio programs are conservative. But on the Internet, Bozell said that Matt Drudge's Drudge Report—"our top guy"—barely had half the readership of Arianna Huffington's liberal-leaning Huffington Post. He then went on to run down a list of technologies, from podcasting, to text messaging, to YouTube and on to blogging, all areas where the left had gained a strategic advantage—and, more important, places where the American public increasingly was turning for news and information. With enough investments, Bozell said the right could compete. If "any of us have made the

Internet a top priority and made the information world a top priority," then the American public would see Obama as a "socialist," he concluded.

Bozell closed his remarks to the assembled group of conservative leaders and donors with a futuristic vision crafted perfectly for his audience of former Reaganites. "Do you realize that we have the technology actually to hologram ourselves? This is not Star Wars stuff," Bozell exclaimed to the group. "Did you know we can have a three-dimensional image of [Focus on the Family founder] Jim Dobson standing right next to me talking to you," beamed Bozell. He closed on an optimistic note. "The technology is wondrous that we have out there."[6]

Bozell was a true pioneer in media technology. Although he is best known for using his well-funded think tank to conjure the "liberal media" myth, Bozell also started some of the first conservative news websites in the nineties. In 1998, Media Research Center founded conservativenews .com, a unique site with its own staff of reporters and editors, funded with a three-year budget of $5.46 million. The site later rebranded as CNSNews.com, which became a popular newswire and reporting outlet for conservatives. In 2008, Bozell began touting a website his organization created called Eyeblast, which he hoped would be an "alternative" to YouTube. YouTube, according to Bozell, had a pernicious liberal bias. Bozell stipulated that Google, Facebook, and even Wikipedia were "run by liberals" and are "openly hostile to conservatives." To combat this, Bozell asked for money—lots of it.[7] (In 2009, Bozell's Media Research Center raised over $10.5 million from over eighty family and corporate foundations, as well as from donations from a number of individual contributors.)

Ruffini, like Bozell, had a financial stake in demanding that the right stock up its communications arsenal. His
EngageDC political consulting firm specializes in new media technology, and a shift in resources to the Internet would
be a boon to his business. But they were both correct to argue that the right had skimped on investments in technology
during the 2006 and 2008 election cycles, and in doing so,
were losing an opportunity to communicate with millions of
Americans.

Meanwhile many progressives were taking a laissez-faire
approach to developing online tactics. From the 2008 election through the 2010 midterms, there were few, if any,
serious innovations or new online breakthroughs for the
left. Some, like political science professor Russell Dalton,
argued that the decentralized nature of the Internet allowed
liberals to naturally outpace conservatives on the medium.
Dalton reasoned that because conservatives philosophi-
cally embrace ideological loyalty and are generally more
comfortable with authoritarian, top-down communication, they would never really harness the potential of new
media. Liberals on the other hand automatically flourish
in environments where users are granted freedom to communicate with infinite possibilities. According to this line
of thinking, liberals would inherently succeed online, and
investments weren't quite necessary. The right's ability to
effectively harness the Internet to achieve tremendous political goals after Obama election, however, demonstrates
the weakness of this theory.

As Patrick Ruffini recalled later, "in the wake of the 2008
election, after four years of aloofness from most of our party's leaders about the role of new media and technology in
electoral politics, we took a break from the day to day of

campaigns and thought seriously about how to help our party move forward." The series of targeted investments and strategic nurturing of new communication vehicles bore fruit quickly. From the rise of the Tea Parties to the upset victory of Senator Scott Brown in Massachusetts, Republican operatives outmaneuvered their counterparts on the left by imitating and improving on the online approach of Obama's 2008 campaign. Moreover, the right-wing noise machine became more sophisticated in its ability to smear Obama and his policies, again making use of the Internet and broadening its reach in the media. The right not only convinced their ideological funders and the Republican Party to invest in creating the next wave of communication tools, but corporate lobbyists desperate to manipulate public opinion against reform aided in the process.

ATTACK OF THE CLONES

One of the most defining differences between new media and traditional media is the role of the user. With new media, anyone with Internet access has virtually unlimited power to comment on, modify, or discuss content with which they come into contact. Traditional media—whether it is broadcast television, print, or newspaper—does not allow the same type of instant, unrestricted interactivity, although some television shows are increasingly finding ways to better incorporate their audience's feedback. Fundamentally, traditional media delegates power to the broadcaster, the editor, or the radio host. Conservatives seeking to take control of the media spent years under the traditional media paradigm creating their own media outlets while casting doubt or public skepticism on ones outside their grip. The "liberal media" myth was one of the most potent strategies to discredit outlets that reported critically on Republican politicians or did not generally skew toward the right. Many of the early Internet innovations from conservatives relied on simply creating new models of one-way content distribution. But the rise in Internet culture, in which users expect decentralized networks and user-created content and control, has forced the right to adopt more sophisticated strategies to reach the public.

A central dynamic created by the growth of new media is the proliferation of virtual communities. The Obama campaign in 2008 tried to harness this trend by creating MyBarackObama, an interface for campaign supporters to create online identities, connect with other supporters, and publicize their campaign activity. The technology was based on Howard Dean's successful use of the website MeetUp, used in 2004 to network and find fellow supporters. By showcasing their own contributions, in the form of pictures, videos, and "points" for volunteer service, MyBarackObama did more than simply foster engagement. They created a social premium for volunteers to share their contributions with others. Also, users of MyBarackObama, like the Obama campaign generally, saw themselves as insurgents fighting against entrenched powers, from the Democratic establishment during the primary with Hillary Clinton, to special interests and Washington insiders during the general election. The online community gave Obama campaign operatives a wealth of information about its supporters, and the seemingly walled structure (although it was open to anyone) of such a network provided a sense of togetherness for people inside that community.

Just as insurgency helped the large MyBarackObama

community create tight bonds as an ideologically coherent community, Obama's victory undid them. Shortly after Obama took office, Democratic planners moved the MyBarackObama listserv and online community into the apparatus of the Democratic National Committee, converting it into Organizing for America. The social capital of the community evaporated quickly as the DNC ordered the community to support conservative politicians, like Democrat Ben Nelson of Nebraska, or to simply fall in line with the agenda of the president, even when policies drifted from ideologically pure campaign promises that had brought people to the website initially.

While MyBarackObama died a quick death as a functional community, the right went to work building communities to oppose Obama and his agenda. Republican consultants flocked to Ning, an easy tool to create entire social networks for niche communities. Ning replicates common features of any social network: users may create online identities, send messages within the network, post links and news articles, and create events for offline activities.

Template Ning networks provided the right with the ability to quickly assemble Tea Party groups without the appearance of top-heavy Republican partisanship. Eric Odom, the former new media director of Sam Adams Alliance, used his consulting firms Strategic Activism and American Liberty Alliance to create dozens of ready-made Ning websites to cultivate the early stages of the Tea Party movement. Some Tea Party groups he created, like the Patriot Caucus, were geared toward a national constituency, while others catered to specific localities, such as Lehigh County in Pennsylvania. Although the websites appeared to be citizen generated, all of Odom's sites were actually centrally planned and operated. Every major Tea Party organization got in on the act: Smart Girl Politics, working with Odom's colleagues, created a Ning for Tea Party women; Ginni Thomas, the wife of Supreme Court Justice Clarence Thomas, used her Liberty Central group to help local Tea Parties in Florida build Ning websites; and the lobbying firm Libertas Global Partners created Regular Folks United using Ning to organize Tea Parties. Grassroots Action Inc., a company that thrived by building huge e-mail and petition lists using conservative outrage over immigrants or gay rights, operated as a business by selling its lists to corporate or politics interests. After Obama's election, Grassroots Action redesigned their network as a Ning, called ResistNet. Even Glenn Beck, with his so-called 9/12 movement, used Ning to develop local and national communities of supporters.

The power of Ning is the illusion of open, democratic communities. Republican operators and consultants in control of most of the Tea Party Nings set the agenda, administer the talking points available on the main page, and have the ability to censor information they disapprove of. Tea Party Patriots, one of the largest Ning communities of over 100,000 members, was regularly fed action items by lobbyist-run entities such as FreedomWorks.[8] So when members of Tea Party community websites received e-mails from website administrators to call Congress to oppose a student lending bill or hold a rally against a Democratic member of Congress, the orders appeared to come from community members of their respective Ning networks. To the casual user, the site appeared to be maintained by citizen activists, but in many cases the actual online organizers worked for right-wing corporate fronts or a Republican campaign. Functionally, the Ning social networks provided grassroots cover for the oil interests funding FreedomWorks or Republican campaigns paying Odom.

Republicans in Congress also seized upon a similar Internet technology to create an illusion of popular support for their corporate-friendly agenda. The best example would be a program touted by House GOP leadership called America Speaking Out. America Speaking Out offered the public the ability to submit policy ideas, and then vote them up or down. Republicans promised to campaign and eventually legislate on the most popular policies using the website's results.

The campaign document Republicans produced shortly before the 2010 midterms, supposedly based on the America Speaking Out–voted ideas, actually ignored the will of the people. First, any idea to raise taxes was censored from the site. But even the most popular ideas did not make the cut. In one section, four out of the five ideas with the most votes concerned marijuana decriminalization and legalization. In the economy section, the top idea was the legislation, proposed by Democrats, to end tax loopholes for companies that ship jobs overseas. In another section, ending earmarks ranked as one of the most popular ideas. However, the final Republican "Pledge to America" contained boilerplate Republican campaign pledges, like repealing Obama's reforms and reducing the deficit. It omitted many of the most popular ideas from their website, even earmark reform. Regardless, the House Republican leadership hailed their pledge as revolutionary because of the America Speaking Out voting system. Shortly before unveiling the pledge, Representative Mike Pence (R-IN) declared, the "Democrat [sic] majority isn't listening, but House Republicans will."

This trick deflected the fact that Republicans in 2010 failed to produce any ideas to address climate change, energy independence, job creation, rising inequality and poverty, or America's health-care crisis. America Speaking Out was more of a public relations gimmick than an actual way to incorporate public opinion into policy making. Similarly, Congressman Eric Cantor (R-VA) created a website called YouCut for the public to vote on federal programs to eliminate. Many of the programs were simplified or distorted with wasteful-sounding names. One such program targeted by YouCut, the Temporary Assistance for Needy Families Emergency Contingency Fund, created 240,000 jobs in a matter of months, but YouCut falsely characterized it as a job-killing welfare program. Another item on YouCut, the Exchanges with Historic Whaling and Trading Partners Program, had already been eliminated by Obama's budget, yet the Republican website claimed killing the project would be a YouCut idea. The first few months of YouCut targeted only 0.017 percent of the federal budget for elimination, but the online vote platform gave the impression that Republicans were serious about incorporating the public's ideas for eliminating "waste."

In many cases, conservatives sought support in areas where there wasn't enough interest to build voting platforms or community sites. But with enough money and other incentives, Internet gimmicks could be used to boost the cause. Porter Novelli, a PR firm for health-care companies, used its front group Center for Medicine in the Public Interest to design online video games to build its anti–health reform listserv. To encourage the public to fill out surveys and sign online petitions to oppose health reform, the U.S. Chamber of Commerce offered gift certificates to Hooters through Internet ads.[9] The oil-and-industry-friendly Heritage Foundation tapped a Republican consulting firm called the David All Group to create a social media game to give away "points" for people to send public messages opposing clean energy reform. The game was replicated for the College Republicans to mock health reform and was even sold to the British Conservative Party. The Tories employed David All to set up an almost identical game to encourage the public to use social media to draw attention to corruption scandals in Gordon Brown's Labour government.[10]

Some online strategies the Obama campaign developed to fight against right-wing smears were picked up and used by the right to spread myths. In a presentation I obtained from Fleishman-Hillard, a public relations company working for a number of corporate clients, executives revealed that they designed their corporate lobbying campaigns on the Obama model. For instance, Obama's Fight the Smears website was a rapid-response database to debunk the many smears about Obama, from his citizenship to his family history. Explicitly referencing this strategy, Fleishman-Hillard executives built similar websites for the U.S. Chamber of Commerce and other trade associations. However, instead of correcting the record, the chamber's websites would spread falsehoods. For example, after I wrote a story detailing the chamber's solicitations of foreign money for its main 501(c)(6) campaign account, the chamber used its Fight the Smears–based website to attack me and falsely claim that it received no direct foreign money (even after chamber press officials had admitted they had received direct foreign funds). The chamber paid Google so that when anyone searched my story or any words associated with it, a link would appear directing the user to their erroneous chamber website "debunking" my story.[11]

The special election in January of 2010 to replace Ted Kennedy provided Republican consultants with an opportunity to test a range of new techniques. Every campaign brings a new search for better voter data. In 2004, Karl Rove boasted that he had the most sophisticated information, obtained by purchasing lifestyle and consumer data from guns and sporting magazines. In 2008, Democrats claimed they had significantly improved their data files and digitized the information to better prioritize which neighborhoods to canvass and where new voters could be found.

However, in the special election for Kennedy's seat, Republican nominee Scott Brown innovated the use of voter data in two new ways. First, Brown's campaign established a large network of field offices throughout the Bay State and inundated Republican-leaning households within a 20-mile radius of the field offices with highly targeted online ads and canvassing contacts. Second, his campaign utilized a new mobile technology to give every canvasser a walk list system for knocking on doors and updating the voter file in real time through their iPhone or BlackBerry. The mobile application also synced voter information with the smart phone's GPS, so that finding each household was easier.[12] This system was far more efficient than previous walk lists, done largely on paper or at best by calling back to headquarters, and provided superior data used to turn out voters. Republican campaigns all over the country adopted this mobile technology for the midterm elections. American Crossroads, one of Karl Rove's front groups, even spent $1 million equipping volunteers in key states with state-of-the-art iPads to better use the technology for canvassing. (However, Dino Rossi and Ken Buck, two Republican Senate candidates aided by Rove's iPad investment, lost.)

While the Brown campaign adopted important innovations, including Ning and its new walk lists applications, Brown was also aided by a stealth online smear campaign. The secretive Republican front group American Future Fund helped elect Brown by spamming Twitter with attacks against his Democratic opponent Martha Coakley. A study by two Wellesley College researchers found that American Future Fund set up nine Twitter accounts to pump out 929 tweets with attacks against Coakley in a short period of time. The "Twitter-bomb" reached 60,000 people before Twitter administrators recognized the messages as spam and shut the accounts down. Informal discussions on Twitter can often be a barometer of popular news stories. But in this case, smears—including messages like "AG Coakley thinks Catholics shouldn't be in the ER, take action now!"—were meant to fabricate actual online dialogue.[13]

The manipulation of "open" platforms should be expected and is difficult to prevent. But right-wing operatives streamlined the process. The well-funded front group American Majority hosted 395 training sessions in 2009 and 2010 to teach Tea Party and Republican volunteers how to abuse open platforms like Twitter to spread the conservative cause—usually by spam attacks on Democrats. Austin James, a trainer with American Majority, taught a session on "guerrilla warfare" against liberals at a retreat in Pittsburgh. One technique he recommended was to go on Amazon and for "every Obama book" he told attendees to rate it down with one star (the lowest rating). "I mean, 80 percent of the books that I view and put stars on online, I never read, people. That's just how it works," he said.

Beginning in 2009, my colleagues and I noted that Think-Progress stories no longer appeared on popular websites like

Digg and Reddit, sites where users submit and comment on the best content on the web. ThinkProgress, where I blogged, had been wildly popular on both sites for years. In August of 2010, AlterNet revealed a massive conspiracy by a small cabal of Digg users to systematically "bury" news content from liberal sources like Talking Points Memo, the *Atlantic Monthly*, the Huffington Post, and my own site, ThinkProgress. A secret list of Digg users called "DiggPatriots" had worked for over a year to coordinate their efforts. It was never clear if the group was acting on its own or working with an established GOP consulting firm or other entity. In 2006, liberals had attempted a similar strategy. The website OpenLeft and others encouraged readers to "Google-bomb" Republican candidates by constantly blogging or searching negative stories about them. The strategy was to ensure that when anyone googled the candidate's name, the negative stories targeted by the bloggers would come up first. Google later modified its search algorithm to prohibit such abuses. Still, the Digg conspiracy revelation confirmed that on either side, a small band of committed partisans can shape online news in subtle ways.

Internet culture has given rise to a public obsession with voyeurism and a certain form of authenticity. Twitter is a great example. Conversations on Twitter are almost all public, so anyone can read what a celebrity, politician, or normal college student tweets at any given time. The limitations of Twitter, 140 characters for each tweet, force users to be pithy and creative, and the most popular tweets are usually the most personal expressions. However, the American Future Fund demonstrated that Twitter "conversations" can be completely fraudulent; a single political operative can flood the system with phony tweets. Although tweets are typically so personal in nature, they are not always real reflections of a person's thoughts.

The Internet-driven voyeurism fetish, evidenced by the popularity of reality television shows, has affected how people view the world around them. In political campaigns, grainy YouTube videos revealing gaffes, confrontations, or other unscripted events have gained a certain place in the public mind. In an environment where every campaign activity is overly produced and candidates recite talking points verbatim, missteps recorded on amateur video have the potential of gaining far more public interest than traditional news packages or campaign videos. Perhaps this phenomenon relates to the same fatigue of consumer brands and overcommercialization seen elsewhere in American society. In any case, a video shot by a Democratic "tracker" of Senator George Allen (R-VA) calling the Indian American holding the camera a "macaca" erupted as the biggest campaign upset of all 2006. The video seemed to capture a side of Allen that was vicious and hateful, and it quickly went viral. Allen had a long history of outright racism, but the racist charge had never defined him until the macaca video. Allen, viewed by many as a rising GOP star, lost to a lesser-known Democratic rival.

Similarly, a shaky shot of John McCain suggesting that America should occupy Iraq for one hundred years became one of the most notorious viral videos of the 2008 campaign. These videos were of low quality, but that fact seemed to make them more credible and authentic for millions of online viewers. By appearing amateur and off-the-cuff, they seemed to portray Republican politicians revealing a side of themselves they would rather have kept secret. Most of all, these videos became Internet lore, attracting thousands of bloggers, discussions, remixed videos, and other spontaneous forms of online commentary.

Recognizing the explosive potential of viral videos capturing politicians in ugly or embarrassing episodes, Republicans set out to create their own for the 2010 midterms. Of course, the most successful viral videos of this genre appear amateur and unplanned—but clever tactics could fake this as well. A training session I attended at the Conservative Political Action Conference of 2010 taught attendees to use a video camera to harass Democratic officials until their inevitable outbursts were caught on tape. As I heard from attendees of Americans for Prosperity, FreedomWorks, and American Majority training sessions, the tactic was recommended all year.

As I reported in August of 2009, a memo on how to harass Democratic officials and videotape their frustration at town hall meetings was widely distributed among Tea Party groups before the infamous health reform town hall protests of 2009. Several of the videos, showing ordinary-looking men and women screaming their lungs out at sputtering Democratic lawmakers convinced several incumbents to retire. A video of a military veteran dressing down representative Brian Baird (D-WA)—for allegedly disrespecting the Constitution with his support of health reform—gained over a million views within a matter of weeks. After the viral confrontation, Baird announced that he was not going to run for another term, citing a new level of vitriol in politics as the reason.

Many of the Democratic casualties of the 2010 midterms fell victim of embarrassing viral videos. Before a fundraiser, a group of young men approached congressman Bob Etheridge (D-NC) yelling, "Do you fully support the Obama agenda?" Etheridge asked, "Who are you?" to which the young men replied that they were "just students" working on a "project." Etheridge grabbed one of the individuals taping him, shaking him and demanding to know their identity. The video, which went viral, was also incorporated into an attack ad from the Republican front Americans for Job Security. Although Republicans denied any involvement in the incident, it was revealed after the election that the students harassing Etheridge were actually staffers working for Republican strategists.

Shoving a camera in his face, Tea Party activists berated congressman Phil Hare (D-IL), asking him what part of the Constitution authorized health reform. An exasperated Hare eventually blurted, "I don't worry about the Constitution." Hare's opponent, Republican Bobby Schilling, distributed the video far and wide among conservative bloggers, and it became a popular clip for Fox News and talk radio. Schilling also retained Craft Media, a firm run by in part by Jon Henke, the Republican consultant for George Allen in charge of responding to the macaca video back in 2006.

Congressman Lincoln Davis (D-TN) faced a little-known Republican opponent, Scott DesJarlais, whose reputation suffered from the revelation that he had threatened his ex-wife with a gun and had physically attacked her on multiple occasions.[14] Favored to win up until the last month of the election, Davis was targeted by Republican operatives. One night during the campaign, young men claiming to be "Young Democrats" from "Lee College" approached Davis and began secretly taping him. Once he realized he was being filmed, Davis quickly walked away. The two young men then started screaming, "Did you know about

Wanda or Norma Jean, about your family values, sir?" The insinuation that Davis had cheated on his wife was completely unfounded. According to the *Knoxville News Sentinel*, Republican staffers set up Davis. Within moments of the video going online, National Republican Campaign Committee staffers promoted the video, and it bounced around the conservative blogosphere and to constituents in Davis's district.[15]

In similar fashion, Representative Tom Perriello (D-VA) faced a number of dirty tricks. Offline, the coal industry targeted Perriello and forged a number of letters from the local NAACP and several women's groups to ask him to oppose clean energy reform. But the most devastating attacks were through online viral videos. I witnessed the process by which Republican operatives went fishing for such online hits. At a town hall in Ruckersville, Virginia, I saw several angry constituents step to the microphone and scream at Perriello, calling him a traitor to the country for supporting Democratic policies, like health reform and a price on carbon pollution. There were three Republican staffers videotaping the event. One constituent barked, "I'm angry that you ignore the law of the Constitution that requires Obama to prove that he is a natural born citizen." I approached this particular attendee after the event. He was busy handing out paraphernalia for Americans for Prosperity in the lobby of the building. He told me that Ben Marchi, the state director of Americans for Prosperity, had encouraged him to follow Perriello around at town halls with such "questions." Before being hired by Americans for Prosperity, Marchi had served as a campaign staffer for the National Republican Campaign Committee and had served as an aide for former Republican Majority Leader Tom

DeLay. Although none of the videos that evening became viral hits, other ambush videos, such as one of Perriello appearing to say, during an argument with Tea Party activists, that Congress "steals" from the taxpayer, gained hundreds of thousands of views.

Perriello, Davis, Hare, and Etheridge all lost to their Republican opponents. Other Democrats targeted with similar viral video harassment tactics, including Alexi Giannoulis, Rep. Ciro Rodriguez (D-TX), Rep. Steve Kagen (D-WI), also lost on Election Day. Of course the viral videos weren't the only reason these candidates lost, but the videos chipped away at their popularity, provided fodder for Republican online fund-raising drives, and gave hours of grist for conservative talkers looking to gin up smears against these Democrats.

Moreover, conservatives vastly expanded their online network for distributing such videos and other smear pieces against liberals. Launched early in 2010 by Tucker Carlson with funds from wealthy mutual fund founder Foster Friess, the Daily Caller was designed to mirror the success of the Huffington Post. It blended investigative research with up-to-the-minute breaking news, entertainment, political gossip, and opinion columns. And it heavily recruited conservative journalism talent and opposition research veterans, including David Martosko, a skilled dirt digger who had spent much of his career working for the lobbyist Rick Berman. In a similar format, Glenn Beck launched the Blaze—written by former Republican staffers and producers at his radio program.

One of the more ambitious efforts for conservatives to branch out into multimedia has been Pajamas Media, a new media company that was founded in 2005 by a group of right-wing bloggers. The outlet, known largely for its PJTV video component, was funded by two investors, Aubrey Chernick and Jim Koshland, who provided approximately $7 million for the venture. PJTV provides daily programming with conservative comedians Alfonzo Rachel and Stephen Kruiser creating satirical skits mocking liberals, as well as online news analysis with Glenn Reynolds, of the popular right-wing blog Instapundit, Tea Party coverage with radio host Dana Loesch, and about a dozen other online conservative personalities appearing in various video shorts. Other than promotional coverage of Republican events and Tea Party rallies, much of PJTV broadcasting consists of segments based on an anti-Islam, neoconservative viewpoint. PJTV and Pajamas Media gave rise to Pam Geller, of the anti-Muslim Atlas Shrugs blog. Her blog posts frequently accused Obama of being a secret Muslim bent on the destruction of America, and she regularly used the PJTV website to encourage sending B-52 bombers to the Arab side of Jerusalem. Geller's hate speech had been confined to the media fringes for years, but PJTV gave her a far greater platform. In 2010, her aggressive blogging about a planned Muslim community center and mosque in downtown Manhattan, several blocks from the Ground Zero site, created a mass hysteria in the media. Geller—who described the community center as "the second wave of 9/11"—led demonstrations, garnered interviews on mainstream news outlets, and provided many of the talking points for Newt Gingrich, Congressman Peter King (R-NY), and others who latched onto her manufactured controversy.

Like much of the conservative blogosphere, PJTV is known more for outrageous commentary than actual reporting. PJTV made a splash when it briefly hired the McCain campaign's "Joe the Plumber" to go to Israel and cover the

Gaza conflict as a "war correspondent." PJTV's Michael Leeden, a dedicated prowar blogger, got caught in what fellow conservative blogger Michelle Malkin described as a "major embarrassment" when he falsely reported that Ayatollah Ali Khamenei, Iran's supreme leader, had died.[16]

It's possible that PJTV's near-daily hyperbolic segments about the threat of radical Islam are a direct result of the anti-Muslim views of some of its funders. Investor Aubrey Chernick, one of two main people underwriting PJTV, has also given to several hawkish pro-Israel, anti-Muslim groups, including the American Freedom Alliance, a group sponsoring various campaigns warning against the threat of "Islamic penetration" into "Western civilization."[17] The Foundation for the Defense of Democracies, one of the main neoconservative think tanks promoting a war against Iran, provides in-kind backing to PJTV by granting it a studio space.

PJTV never made a serious shift in the new media paradigm, but has established itself as part of the larger online political news establishment. PJTV, like the Daily Caller and the Blaze, is important to the right-wing movement because it provides video coverage of issues before a larger outlet, like Fox News, take an interest. For instance, as oil industry lobbyists and Americans for Prosperity kicked off their campaign to promote a piece of legislation that would remove the EPA's power to enforce the Clean Air Act to regulate carbon emissions, the first few events on Capitol Hill were only covered by PJTV. The PJTV correspondents interviewed Americans for Prosperity's speakers and created a series of news packages repeating the distortion that the EPA would destroy the economy.

During the Obama era, conservatives added new walls to their echo chamber. Before Obama's presidency, conservatives could invent a story on a blog or an ideological outlet like the *Weekly Standard*, then blast it from the Drudge Report to Fox News, then to talk radio and finally the pages of the *Washington Times* and the *Examiner*. It would inevitably end up in a Republican speech, or perhaps on an e-mail forwarding chain or a conservative mailer. With enough buzz, it would also end up in the rest of the mainstream media. After two years of the Obama administration, the right could continue this strategy, but then amplify its reach through Ning networks across the country, fake Twitter feeds, and an online documentary on PJTV telling the same story in video format. Follow-up stories written by the Daily Caller and the Blaze would keep the story in motion, while a viral video would be made of a Democratic lawmaker being asked about the story, and finally any attempt by liberals to fact-check it could be buried from the public by "guerrilla" Digg users. The new spin cycle looks familiar, but it's enough to still confuse the public.

THE NEXT FRONTIER:
ENTERTAINMENT

Creating a self-sustainable business model for conservative movies, comedies, and pop culture has been a goal for decades, but so far, the right has not enjoyed any serious breakthroughs in entertainment mass media. Many attempts have been made, however, with the goal of creating a popular following for a forum with an explicit political message, even if profits are not immediately forthcoming.

In September of 2010, an ambitious new cable channel called RightNetwork premiered. It featured a lineup including a conservative stand-up comedy show called *Right to*

Laugh; *Running*, a reality series promoting Republican candidates running for Congress; *Politics and Poker*, a half hour of random conservatives arguing over a game of poker; and a promise to dedicate coverage to all things Tea Party. Woven throughout the different shows are hardcore conservative topics. *Jackpot Justice* is part of a running series attacking class-action lawsuits and highlighting cases to make the argument for across-the-board tort reform. *Stakelbeck on Terror Show*, a criminal justice–style show, picks up on far-right neoconservative themes and dedicates most of its time to spreading hatred about Muslims in America. For instance, the third episode opened with the following monologue:

> Well, New York City Mayor Michael Bloomberg has been a huge supporter of the proposed "Ground Zero Mosque." And he said recently that one reason U.S. troops are fighting Islamic jihadists overseas is that Muslims here have the freedom to build mosques wherever they please in America, including at Ground Zero. Really? That may come as a surprise to our troops, Mr. Mayor. You know, your predecessor Rudy Giuliani may have been known as America's Mayor, but you'll always be known as Arabia's Mayor.

Shortly after it launched, RightNetwork went to work providing free campaign advertising to the Republican Party. *Running* helped showcase little-known Republican candidates for Congress in 2010 with essentially hour-long promotions. Rich Lott, a Republican candidate in Ohio, had faced mounting criticism after it was revealed that he belonged to a group that dressed up as Nazi soldiers for World

War II reenactment games in the woods. RightNetwork helped Lott push back against the embarrassing pictures of him in an SS uniform by producing an episode of *Running* dedicated largely to his candidacy, portraying him as a loving family man. Although Lott didn't win, many candidates given sympathetic *Running* puff pieces, like Kelly Ayotte in New Hampshire, did.

To fill gaps in programming, RightNetwork features documentaries produced by right-leaning think tanks, as well as a set of short videos, including *Five 4 Friday*, lighthearted interviews conducted by the Christian Broadcasting Network's Davidy Brody with various conservative talkers and politicians. "You got a top pet peeve?" asked Brody in one segment to Michael Savage, the popular hate radio host from San Francisco. "Noise! Noise pollution," replied Savage, "flying on an airplane with loud people talking and you have no way to get out of there."[18]

The project is funded by Ed Snider, a top Republican donor who helped bankroll Freedom's Watch, a Bush administration–aligned front group that ran ads attacking Democrats who did not support the Iraq war. A CEO of the Comcast subsidiary that operates various theaters, stadiums, and convention centers, Snider used his ownership of the Philadelphia Flyers hockey team to allow Sarah Palin to drop the puck at ceremonial opening games during the 2008 election.

Snider's network tries to straddle the line between open partisanship and mainstream appeal. Its brand symbol is a "Gazelephant," an orange Republican Party elephant appearing to sprint. RightNetwork says it "combined the power of the largest land mammal on earth with the agile, fast as all get-out, Gazelle." Pitching the channel to the press, Snider played coy. "We're creating a welcome place for millions and millions of Americans who've been looking for an entertainment network and media channel that reflects their point-of-view," he explained to the *New York Daily News.* To gain credibility with the right, Snider hired Jim Hoft of the Republican blog Gateway Pundit to be the network's voice in the conservative blogosphere. But in promotional advertisements and on television, actor Kelsey Grammer is the face for RightNetwork. "Things that just aren't right," Grammer says in a spot of him in front of a white background, "Trillion dollar deficits, baby carrots, left-handed scissors, thousand dollar toilet seats!"

Although liberals viciously mocked the RightNetwork preview materials, particularly one featuring a Tea Party rap video, Snider's foray into the world of entertainment builds on a daring campaign by the conservative movement to radically transform the American entertainment industry. Even if RightNetwork is a flop, it may contribute to the success of another right-wing effort, or inspire other conservative donors to fund a similar project. In fact, Fox News took a similar route in its path to power.

Fox News dominated cable television during most of the Bush years, and with Obama's election, its ratings soared. In 2010, Fox News attracted 1.8 million prime-time viewers on average—more than CNN, MSNBC, and HLN combined.[19] Fox News also set the agenda, using its hosts to encourage people to attend Tea Parties, to disrupt Democratic town hall meetings, and to protest the Obama administration. Glenn Beck's vitriol gained a vastly expanded platform when he launched his afternoon television program on Fox in January of 2009. Fox News was instrumental in generating countless smears about progressive reforms: attacking Obama as a "socialist," fundamentally lying about almost every aspect of health reform, and falsely accusing the stimulus of creating "no jobs." Trying to gin up racial and ethnic hate during the lead-up to the 2010 midterm elections, Fox News aired over ninety-five segments about a meaningless "New Black Panthers" scandal, while spending several weeks in August accusing a proposed Muslim community center and mosque in lower Manhattan of being a "terrorist command center."[20]

The power of Fox News cannot be underestimated, but its position as the right wing's premier propaganda outlet took many years to accomplish. Fox News chief Roger Ailes, a former Republican campaign consultant who got his start advising Richard Nixon on his television appearances, tried to bring his own brand of partisan Republican politics to television for years. Quitting traditional campaign work shortly after helping Lee Atwater engineer President George H.W. Bush's victory in 1988, Ailes linked up with Rush Limbaugh—"two look-alike, sound-alike ideologues," according to *New York* magazine—to try to bring Limbaugh's zeal for liberal bashing to a video format in 1992. As the executive producer to his newly created television show, Ailes helped Limbaugh try to deliver his largely uninterrupted monologues railing about "apocalyptic environmentalism," the evils of government, and the "fundamental differences between men and women." Ailes was confidant Limbaugh's style would revolutionize television. "I want them to unthink all they thought they knew about TV," said Ailes, brimming with enthusiasm about the potential of his show. His enthusiasm did not last, and Ailes eventually left the program in frustration before Limbaugh quit as well. Although the franchise collapsed due to low ratings, Ailes kept trying to reach his larger goal.[21]

Conservative icon Paul Weyrich also dabbled in his own attempt to create a bastion for right-wing conservatism on television. In 1993, Weyrich—with funds from tobacco giant Philip Morris, Newt Gingrich's Progress and Freedom Foundation, and his own Free Congress Foundation—launched the National Empowerment Television network, a station filled with right-wing promotional videos and Republican advertisements portrayed as unbiased information. The channel featured a show by Newt Gingrich called *The Progress Report*, an antiregulation and antitax program called *The Cato Forum*, which was produced by the Cato Institute, as well as programming directly from the National Rifle Association, the Family Research Council, and the Competitive Enterprise Institute. The shows all suffered from low ratings, and the network consistently lost massive amounts of money. Although Weyrich's National Empowerment Television mirrored the type of content seen on a regular basis on the modern Fox News, it lacked quality production and its partisanship was too thinly veiled.

While working at CNBC in 1994, Ailes founded America's Talking, a network with a less overtly political message, but with plenty of conservative content woven in. Ailes crafted his own programming, including a show called *Pork*, a call-in show about government waste and fraud. After bitterly clashing with NBC executives, Ailes was forced out of the company when it signed a deal with Microsoft to transform America's Talking into MSNBC in 1996. Ailes then gained News Corporation CEO Rupert Murdoch's trust. Both men reportedly shared vindictive personalities and a distaste for the ruling media establishment in New York, and Murdoch allowed Ailes to try to fulfill his dream of creating a purely right-wing twenty-four-hour cable program with Fox News.

While Fox News was slow to gain much of an audience in the midnineties, part of the reason was that Ailes placed partisanship over profits. As David Brock noted, Clinton scandals held a prominent place in the news lineup: for instance, Fox "was the only network to carry GOP senator Fred Thompson's" committee investigation of the so-called Chinagate scandal "live, gavel to gavel, even though the channel took a hit in the ratings." Providing Republicans with an unfiltered forum, instead of attracting a larger audience, was paramount. The channel ran up over $100 million a year in operating losses, but Murdoch personally saw value in a right-wing alternative to the mainstream news and continued subsidizing Ailes's red-ink venture. Fox News steadily gained a wider audience and exploded into prominence as the Bush administration gave it a preferred status with media scoops and exclusive interviews.

It was not a typical rags-to-riches story, of course; Murdoch had powerful political and corporate allies helping him along the way. But Ailes's story of perseverance and vision mirrors the wider effort in the conservative movement to establish greater control over entertainment industry.

Conservatives have labored for decades to break into the Hollywood movie industry and establish a norm of right-wing films. Certainly, many widely distributed movies already regularly extol wealth and privilege, glamorize guns and violence while obscuring pain and suffering, and often censor even the slightest scene suggesting gay romance. But conservatives have sought to create an entertainment culture in which movies with far more conservative messages, for example Social Security privatization, are able to gain mainstream audiences.

Several organizations have been set up to create such a dramatic cultural shift. The Motion Picture Institute (MPI) is one of the main groups dedicated to changing the nature of the movie industry by cultivating conservative filmmakers and supporting "their work through grants, fiscal sponsorship, promotion, marketing, internships, training workshops, networking opportunities, distribution consulting, and production assistance." In 2005, staffers from the Foundation for Individual Rights in Education—a conservative think tank that pressures colleges to welcome free-market and antigovernment causes—founded MPI with the belief that, as board member Rob Pfaltzgraff explained, a "single well-timed film can change the way this country understands itself; a number of them can change the country as a whole."

Pfaltzgraff admitted that many Hollywood films already carry "capitalist ideas" of individual responsibility, citing Will Smith's *Pursuit of Happyness* and some of Clint Eastwood's movies. However, Pfaltzgraff has said that there is still a great void in the conservative movement for harnessing the "transformative power" of film.[22] Many of the MPI-supported films represent a mix of conservative ideology. MPI helped finance a short film series called Free Market Cure, which largely attacked single-payer health systems. In 2010, MPI made an aggressive push to promote a movie it helped finance called *The Cartel*, a documentary about corruption in public schools that MPI says makes a "compelling case" for "far-reaching" public school privatization. Some films supported by MPI have a more artistic feel, like *2081*, an adaptation of Kurt Vonnegut's short story "Harrison Bergeron" about a dystopian future where everyone is "equal"—beautiful people wear masks, athletes are strapped with weights, and intelligent people are forced to wear devices that disrupt their thoughts.[23]

MPI has had some considerable successes. Its *Indoctrinate U*, a movie condemning the culture of liberal college campuses, was aired several times on cable television, and *The Cartel* took a more traditional route of appearing in several film festivals before being released in theaters in ten cities. *Waiting for Superman*, a scathing critique and critically acclaimed documentary attacking the public school system released in 2010, borrowed many of the themes from *The Cartel*.

It's not clear where MPI receives its funding, but MPI has collaborated closely with the Pacific Research Institute, the Competitive Enterprise Institute, and the Koch family foundations. Elizabeth Koch, the daughter of Koch Industries' owner Charles Koch, sat on MPI's board for several years.[24]

MPI also benefits from cooperation with other conservative efforts in Hollywood. David Horowitz, the former sixties communist radical turned far right ideologue, has spent over two decades funding insurgent programs to foster conservatism through culture, particularly in film. Aided by funds from the Scaife family foundations and the Bradley Foundation, Horowitz sponsors a program called The Film Institute (TFI) in partnership with the right-wing evangelical organization Youth with a Mission (YWAM). TFI's mission statement declares that it is "dedicated to a Godly transformation and revolution TO and THROUGH the Film and Television industry," and its publications claim that it places YWAM interns in film industry jobs "so that they can begin to impact and transform Hollywood from the inside out." TFI gained wide notoriety for its first major project, *Path to 9/11*, a two-part miniseries that pinned the blame for the 9/11 attacks on President Clinton.[25] Despite criticism about the absurd distortion of history portrayed in the film (one scene, invented out of whole cloth, depicts Clinton officials aborting a mission to capture Osama bin Laden), ABC still aired the "docudrama."[26] Since the resulting controversy, TFI has stuck to more low-key projects, like *Hakani*, a film about infanticide in indigenous cultures of Brazil. Critics have pointed out that *Hakani* lacks evidence for many of its claims, and the film appears intended to further the goals of YWAM's missionaries in the Amazon.

Horowitz, through his Freedom Center think tank, also sponsors a special club to bring people from the entertainment industry into contact with right-wing Republicans and conservative speakers. Steve McEveety, who produced Mel Gibson's *Braveheart* and *The Patriot*, helps Horowitz with outreach to the Hollywood elite.

Horowitz's work of changing Hollywood from the inside compliments the long-running effort of Ted Baehr, publisher of *Movieguide*, who has dedicated his life to furthering Christian right movies. In addition to providing many Christian right organizations with a list of movies deemed offensive to his values, Baehr hosts the Movieguide Awards, also known as the "Christian Oscars." There, through the Templeton Foundation, Baehr presents a series of awards and cash prizes (ranging from $50,000 to $100,000) to filmmakers who have created pieces that best further a "traditional view of the Bible and Christianity." At a conference I attended hosted by Phyllis Schafley in St. Louis in February 2010, Baehr exclaimed that not only had his efforts brought Christian movies to a mainstream audience, but that he had also successfully converted several "Jewish producers." A woman next to me prominent in the Missouri homeschooling movement stood up to applaud him.

Right-wing filmmakers have made recent gains since Obama's election, and several dedicated right-wing producers stand out as the movement's future leaders. Conservative filmmaker Ray Griggs dedicated himself to anti-Obama videos shortly after the election, creating a series attacking health reform, then a "documentary" called *I Want Your Money*.[27] *I Want Your Money*, which premiered in October of 2010, features Claymation and 3-D animation to portray Barack Obama and Ronald Reagan in a boxing match, while right-wing commentators are interviewed explaining how dangerous Obama's policies are in contrast to Reagan's. The usual cast of conservative think tanks, including the Heritage Foundation, the Hudson Institute, Pacific Research Institute, among others, supplied most of the research used for the film.

Starting in 2005, Govindini Murty and Jason Apuzzo, two spirited right-wing activists, created a popular conservative entertainment blog as well as the Liberty Film Festival to air "politically incorrect" conservative movies. The pair, aided at one point by Horowitz's think tank, created an independent film called *Kalifornistan* in 2009 about a terrorist in Los Angeles. They energetically promote the work of their conservative peers in the film industry. Along with blogging insider gossip and commentary about right-leaning screenwriters and their projects, Apuzzo and Murty help generate buzz for right-wing films. Throughout 2010, they heavily promoted a project by MGM Studios to remake the Cold War cult hit *Red Dawn*. Instead of high school students fighting as insurgents against invading Russians, the remake features a veteran of the war in Afghanistan leading a resistance against occupying Chinese soldiers. After hearing some early rumors about the film, Apuzzo excitedly blogged that the movie could be a "patriotic smack-down of Obama-era socialism" because themes in the movie equate "certain tendencies in contemporary American liberalism with Chinese-style communism."[28] Apuzzo's rumormongering helped bring similarly giddy buzz about the film from much of the right-wing blogosphere, from Michelle Malkin to the *National Review*.

Apuzzo helped cultivate the careers of Joel Surnow and Manny Coto, creators of the popular television series *24*, a show starring a federal agent named Jack Bauer who would, time and time again, save the nation by torturing terrorists into confessions. Surnow and Coto crafted a conservative alternative to Jon Stewart's *Daily Show* called *The Half Hour News Hour*, unveiling it at Murty and Apuzzo's Libertas Film Festival. After an introduction to Roger Ailes by way of mutual friend Rush Limbaugh, *The Half Hour News Hour* enjoyed a brief run on Fox News in 2007. More recently, Surnow created *The Kennedys*, a 2010 miniseries produced for the History Channel which portrays President Kennedy as sex crazed (with a dozen sex scenes) while largely ignoring major points during the presidency, like the Cuban missile crisis. In one scene, Kennedy brushes off a Secret Service agent with an urgent national security message because he is busy having sex in a swimming pool. In another fictional scene, Kennedy says, "If I don't have some strange ass every couple of days, I get migraines."

Behind the scenes of the right-wing beachhead into Hollywood stands a single committed financier, Stephen Bannon. A former Goldman Sachs banker and CEO of a specialty media investment banking firm called Bannon & Company, Bannon has done everything from help pay for the Libertas Film Festival to provide free office space to Breitbart when he first got off the ground. Bannon has worked with oil billionaire Phil Anschutz to finance the *Chronicles of Narnia*, based on C.S. Lewis's books, and fused together a network of Hollywood conservatives. The *New Yorker* noted that he has brought together a diverse collection of right-leaning A listers:

> They include strongly identified Catholics like Mel Gibson and the manager-producer Doug Urbanski (*The Contender*), and evangelicals like Ralph Winter, who produced *X-Men* and *Fantastic Four*. One of their leading voices has long been Lionel Chetwynd, a Jewish neo-conservative whose credits include the 1987 pro–Vietnam War feature *The Hanoi Hilton*. A collection of what might loosely be styled conservative libertarians includes the actors Clint Eastwood, Drew Carey and Gary Oldman, along with the producers Jerry Bruckheimer and Gavin Polone.[29]

Bannon himself is an active filmmaker. In 2010, he directed *Fire from the Heartland*, a movie about conservative women featuring Representative Michele Bachmann, Ann Coulter, and Tea Party blogger Dana Loesch. A frequent speaker at Washington events, Bannon has openly described his efforts as "the right's propaganda war with the left."

Outside Hollywood and tightly connected with political insiders in Washington, a well-established media firm called Citizens United has reemerged as a major player. Run by longtime Republican operative David Bossie, the firm is best known for its role in crafting the "Willie Horton" ad used against Democratic presidential nominee Michael Dukakis in 1988. Citizens United also gained wide notoriety as the plaintiff in the *Citizens United v. Federal Election Commission* Supreme Court case. Citizens United's *Hillary: The Movie*, a feature-length film attacking Hillary Clinton, was created with the expectation that she would be the Democratic nominee in 2008. Citizens United and its donors wanted to play the Hillary movie on cable television, but the FEC intervened, calling the film a violation of long-standing rules banning corporate money from politics. The resulting legal battle ended with Citizens United winning a 5-to-4 decision overturning nearly a century of campaign finance law and opening the floodgates of unlimited corporate money in elections. The Roberts court ruled that corporate spending and corporate communications on behalf of candidates is protected under the First Amendment as "free speech." While the movie wasn't designed to spark the greatest upheaval in campaign finance law in over a century, the unintended affect was a welcome development for those on the right.

Aside from the Supreme Court decision, Citizens United has rebranded itself as a major right-wing production house. Citizens United rushed a highly produced attack film against Barack Obama, *Hype: The Obama Effect*, shortly before the 2008 elections, but the movie did not appear to be widely distributed. Acting almost as a personal studio for the former Newt Gingrich, Citizens United has produced almost nothing recently but films starring the former Republican Speaker. Citizens United's *Ronald Reagan: Rendezvous with Destiny* hosts Gingrich talking about the legacy of Reagan, *Nine Days That Changed The World* has Gingrich and his wife providing a biographical sketch of Pope John Paul II, *Rediscovering God in America* is a remake of Gingrich's book arguing that the Founding Fathers envisioned religion in government, and *We Have the Power* is a sixty-one-minute video about Gingrich's positions on energy policy. On September 11, 2010, Citizens United distributed a new film, *America at Risk*, essentially arguing that the Obama administration's refusal to participate in demagoguery against Muslim Americans placed America at risk of another terrorist attack.

RightNetwork, the nascent right-wing cable channel, began distribution through its own website, on-demand through Verizon cable, and the online streaming television hub Hulu. It's not clear if cable providers will rush to offer the channel on basic or digital subscription services throughout the country. News Corporation's Rupert Murdoch heavily subsidized Fox News' success by paying as much as $11 per subscriber for local cable providers to offer Fox News. Typically, new networks work the other way around—providers pay for the content. Many analysts expected RightNetwork content to eventually be carried by major cable providers.

Few could have predicted the explosive growth and level of influence that Fox News has had in television news. But it didn't happen in a vacuum or through the competitive free market. News Corporation, along with years of investments from ideological corporate interests and right-wing partisans, made it possible by forgoing profits for the goal of having a decidedly right-wing news network. With the increase in the number of conservative foundations and organized interests concentrating resources into converting Hollywood and much of the entertainment industry into a far-right bastion, success might not be around the corner, but a beachhead seems an eventual certainty.

Shortly before the 2012 election, Barron released *The Hope and the Change*, a movie featuring disaffected former Obama voters. Barron's former billionaire collaborator, Phil Anshutz, owner of the Regal Entertainment Group, helped bring another election-season anti-Obama film, *2016: Obama's America*, to box office success with screenings across the country. The investments, at some level, have paid off.

RightNetwork ultimately failed—a lack of viewership and corporate interest doomed the project. But it was one among over a dozen seedlings planted to grow an alternate media universe.

Backstage at a Tea Party Patriots' convention in February of 2011, I spoke to Foster Friess, the wealthy proprietor of the Daily Caller. It hadn't turned a profit, but he said he wasn't worried about that: "They're breaking great stories and changing the discussion."

6

TAKING IT TO THE STATES

The 2008 federal elections were a disaster for Republicans. Having already been the minority party in both the House and the Senate, they shrank to being even a smaller minority, while the Republican-controlled White House passed to Obama. Recognizing that they had at least temporarily lost power on the national level, Republicans and their corporate benefactors turned to the states. At the outset of 2009, Republicans held key governorships around the country. Many state legislatures were also either held by the GOP or a majority coalition of conservative Democrats and Republican lawmakers. Even in states controlled by Democrats, conservatives had dug in with a powerful array of front groups and media outlets to effectively broadcast their message. Far from Washington, where President Obama's agenda items were being debated, conservatives pushed back in every way possible.

Decades before Obama's ascent, right-wing operatives began building a labyrinth of trenches for political outreach in state and local governments. Although this framework wasn't new, Obama's election sweep accelerated the growth of such local right-wing fronts as conservatives strategized over ways to counter progressive reforms on the national level. Local think tanks were expanded; new staff was hired; and efforts were reorganized to make local think tanks more effective. The constellation of state-based conservative think tanks and front groups now rivals the number of organizations in Washington, D.C.

National conservative groups leaned heavily on this network to generate local opposition to health reform, the stimulus, and other major issues. While many regional or state conservative think tanks appear to specialize in local policy, their existence relates largely to a media and political influence strategy coordinated at a national level. Few of these so-called policy nonprofits develop new ideas or solutions to problems. Rather, these local think tanks translate right-wing lobbying efforts into a format that appears credible since they are supposedly close to home.

The state-based conservative infrastructure also provided the muscle for conservatives to go on the offensive. With immigration efforts stalled at the national level, Republicans on the state level, with help from local think tanks and front groups, pushed draconian reforms like Arizona's SB1070, a law providing police with a broad new mandate to racially profile and to arrest anyone in the country illegally. And in states across the country, the size and scope of the conservative infrastructure helped Republicans turn back the clock on labor rights—a two-pronged attack designed both to help businesses and to weaken Democrats in future elections.

Moreover, after Republicans gained nineteen legislative bodies and elected six new governors (in addition to winning Virginia and New Jersey in the 2009 off-year elections) in the 2010 midterm elections, the state machine moved to solidify their gains. State-level conservative front groups are now some of the most important cogs in the larger Republican machine. This is the story of their beginnings—and of how Obama's election spurred their continued growth and heightened relevance.

A MESSAGE MACHINE
FOR EVERY STATE

Founded at about the time President Clinton was elected in 1992, the State Policy Network (SPN) is an organization dedicated to building a conservative infrastructure on the state level that mirrors the right-wing machine that now dominates government on the national level. Key conservative leaders began planning the SPN model of state-based conservative organizations through the now-defunct Madison Group.[1] Among the founding members of SPN was Thomas Roe, a successful South Carolina businessman who played an active role in the Heritage Foundation in the eighties. Impressed by the success of Heritage in influencing national policy through the Reagan administration, Roe gathered a group of businessmen to found a state-based clone of Heritage in his home state, the South Carolina Policy Council.[2] Staffers for the South Carolina Policy Council took policy recommendations, such as public school privatization and the elimination of environmental regulations, from Heritage and modified them to recommend to legislators in the state capital.

SPN flourished by serving as a nexus between existing local conservative groups and the national conservative policy centers. Initially, SPN think tanks worked closely with a parallel network of right-wing religious Family Policy Councils, which lobbied on mostly evangelical and Christian right issues such as abortion. These councils operated on the state level and were organized through James Dobson's Focus on the Family. As SPN began to grow, seeding each state policy think tank with staff members and money, it worked with Dobson's groups to connect with local conservative activists largely through joint conferences and Dobson's Community Impact Seminars, which trained activists and indoctrinated them with religious right talking points.[3]

By the midnineties, SPN had thirty-seven think tanks in thirty different states. Each SPN think tank maintained an operation on the state level that was similar to that of the Heritage Foundation, which had guided the direction of the Reagan administration through its "Mandate for Leadership" set of policy prescriptions and by supplying an experienced cadre of conservative staff members. For example, after his election in 1994, Massachusetts Republican Governor William Weld "hired almost everybody out of the Pioneer Institute," the SPN satellite in the Bay State, said Laurence Cohen of Connecticut's Yankee Institute, another SPN affiliate.[4] The Pioneer Institute then produced the "Agenda for Leadership" in 1998, filled with deregulation plans formulated into academic-appearing reports, for incoming Republican Governor Paul Cellucci. Hal Eberle, the late director of the South Carolina Policy Council, explained that state-based advocacy was often effective because most local legislators and officials are usually "part-timers, mostly business people and professionals. They're used to rubber-stamping what the bureaucracy wants or the ways things have always been done. But if you just show them how something has been done better somewhere else, you can really change their minds." Eberle, who died in 2009, served as SPN founder Tom Roe's political deputy and helped plot the growth of the SPN's mini-Heritage think tanks.

Like most right-wing think tanks, SPN's Heritage clones are rigidly Republican but maintain a veneer of independence by posturing as simply ideological. SPN think tanks are so sensitive about their image that they explicitly advise their local affiliates to be wary of local media portraying them as "pseudo think-tanks" created "by public relation firms and industry to promote single issues." Jeff Judson and Larry Reed, two Republican operatives active in the SPN world, advise each SPN affiliate to adopt the following language in their charter:

> [Name of organization] is a 501(c)(3) nonprofit research and educational entity, supported by charitable gifts from individuals, foundations and businesses. As such, we have met the Internal Revenue Service "public support" test, which evidences a broad and diverse funding base.
>
> [Name of organization] does not accept contributions intended to "purchase" a predetermined research outcome or in any way compromise the intellectual integrity of our work.
>
> [Name of organization] seeks to advance the principles of liberty, limited government, free enterprise and civil society and to foster public policy that solves real problems within the context of those principles.[5]

Even the language from SPN groups promising "intellectual integrity" is a carbon copy of a document handed down from political operatives in D.C. The legitimacy of SPN affiliates hinges on the ability of each local think tank to appear independent. But in reality, SPN is just another cog in a corporate-backed right-wing messaging machine. In fact, the DCI Group, a corporate lobbying firm, routinely "invests" in SPN network think tanks to advance their clients' interests. DCI executives Kent Lassman and Stacey Chamberlin attend SPN events to help connect SPN think tanks with corporate donors, including DCI Group clients. DCI Group clients run the gamut of Fortune 500 companies, and have included big tobacco, ExxonMobil, Verizon, AT&T, McDonald's, and the mortgage insurance industry.

The Louisiana Pelican Institute, one of SPN's newest additions, was founded in 2008 with a $240,000 grant from SPN. One of Pelican's first initiatives was a report critiquing the Democratic mayor of Shreveport for spending $4,475 to attend events for the U.S. Conference of Mayors and the presidential inauguration.[6] Although Pelican promised nonpartisan coverage of public officials, the report ignored the fact that Republican Governor Bobby Jindal spent over $45,000 of taxpayer money for campaign-related helicopter trips.[7] During the health reform debate, the Pelican Institute recycled a study by economist Art Laffur calling for Medicaid privatization and hosted a series of events with Senator David Vitter (R-LA). The Pelican Institute also conducted a series of investigations into ACORN and invited dirty trickster James O'Keefe to give a speech around the time of his attempt to tamper with Senator Mary Landrieu's (D-LA) phone system.

The SPN website now boasts fifty-eight affiliate think tanks, with at least one in every state. But the network is actually even larger than that. In California, for example, SPN has only one official member, the Pacific Research Institute.[8] But SPN also helps provide training and support to SPN "associate member" organizations like the Claremont Institute, David Horowitz's Freedom Center, the Oakland-based Independent Institute, the National Tax Limitation Committee, Reason Foundation, and the Prometheus Institute. SPN no longer relies heavily on religious right organizations like Focus on the Family, although ties still exist. Instead, there is expanded cooperation with corporate fronts such as FreedomWorks, the Sam Adams Alliance, and Americans for Prosperity. While SPN continues to serve as a bridge between state governments and a variety of national right-wing groups, Heritage continues to provide monitoring and guidance as the dominant organization overseeing SPN's activities. Heritage officials sit on the SPN board, and Heritage helps manage the flow of ideas and experts to each SPN affiliate through its "Resource Bank" and "Insider Online" initiatives.

Since Obama came into office, Republicans state office-holders have served as the vanguard to launch repeated attacks on national policy, and they have done so with the eager cooperation of SPN. When the stimulus was first signed into law, a handful of Republican governors grandstanded against the money, threatening either to reject all of it outright, or reject portions such as the expansion of unemployment insurance. "We can take care of ourselves. And we do not need any more strings from Washington attached to programs," said Texas Governor Rick Perry, who was joined in his opposition by fellow Republican governors Bobby Jindal (LA), Haley Barbour (MS), Mark Sanford (SC), and former half-term governor Sarah Palin (AK).

SPN think tanks went into action, firing off weekly reports and op-eds criticizing the stimulus. The Texas Public Policy Foundation, an SPN member, claimed the mandated expansion of unemployment insurance would "de-stimulate" the Texas economy.[9] In Maryland, the Free State Foundation branded the stimulus as a "bailout," and lampooned Democratic governor Martin O'Malley for promoting the program. Staffers from the Evergreen Freedom Foundation, the SPN affiliate in Washington State, helped administer a weekly update, recommending SPN-generated opposition to the stimulus in every state.

In the end, every governor wound up accepting the money, including Perry, who briefly made threats that Texas should secede from the United States, and Sanford, who likened President Obama to Zimbabwe dictator Robert Mugabe for offering the stimulus.[10] The SPN studies maligning the stimulus helped the governors disguise their grandstanding as motivated by economic interests rather than just partisan politics.

After the stimulus diminished as a national issue, SPN continued to celebrate victories both large and small. One of SPN's most profound accomplishments has been on health reform. From the beginning of the health reform process, SPN think tanks acted as echo chambers, reissuing national rightwing studies attacking the bill. Studies from the Heritage Foundation, anti–health reform business trade associations such as the National Association of Manufacturers, and others were promoted aggressively by SPN think tanks.

Each think tank was encouraged to orchestrate opposition to health reform. The Independence Institute, the SPN affiliate in Colorado, commissioned a short video depicting the public option as a plane jettisoned the elderly and sick once it was in the air.[11] The Show Me Institute of Missouri organized a full-court response: guest columns, Tea Party rallies, studies claiming health reform would kill jobs, and finally an effort to pass a referendum declaring that the individual mandate was unconstitutional. The ballot issue passed by an overwhelming majority in August of 2010. After the bill passed, the attacks continued, with the Goldwater Institute of Arizona mobilizing a coalition of SPN groups to file a lawsuit claiming that health reform is unconstitutional.

But smaller battles are waged with just as much intensity. After providing expert testimony, SPN's Idaho Freedom Foundation helped delay a proposed smoking ban in the town of Eagle, Idaho.[12] In Kentucky, the Bluegrass Institute "led the charge" in pressuring a local board of education to drop a labor agreement for the construction of an elementary school.[13] Other efforts include working with corporate partners to develop short documentaries "exposing" the left, free-market scorecards for state legislators, and a constantly evolving series of tactics through which every SPN think tank works to promote conservative ideals.

The State Policy Network consciously aims to be just as media savvy as its parent Heritage Foundation. In most cases, the network devotes a majority of its resources to communications. Some of the first SPN think tanks not only conducted aggressive outreach to local media outlets, but created their own ways of getting a message directly to the public. In the nineties, the Colorado Independence Institute conducted its own news show on cable television, and the director of the Vermont Ethan Allen Institute had a regular commentary position with Vermont Public Radio. By the twenty-first century, every SPN think tank had a permanent presence in local media, through opinion columns in the newspaper, a close relationship with local conservative radio hosts, a stream of press releases, and more recently, blog posts and podcasts.

Despite its willingness to experiment with new media and outreach, the message has never really changed. SPN serves the same supply-side, "transfer the wealth to the rich and to business" philosophy as any other right-wing corporate front group. What makes SPN unique is its size, its ability to adapt its communication techniques, and its track record in fooling local reporters into believing they are quoting a reputable source.

TRICKLE-DOWN ECHO CHAMBER

The next horizon for the SPN is an attempt to undermine government through a large-scale opposition research program posing as objective journalism. Starting in January 2009, the secretive Sam Adams Alliance started the Franklin Center for Government and Public Integrity. The Franklin Center partnered immediately with the SPN to help each of its think tanks create state-based news websites and to hire investigative journalists. Jason Stverak, the president of the Franklin Center, a former executive director for the North Dakota Republican Party, was a longtime operative in various stealth lobbying campaigns conducted by the Sam Adams Alliance.[14] The Sam Adams Alliance was funded by political operatives such as Eric O'Keefe, who has a history of working for Koch Industries–funded front groups and for the reclusive real estate mogul Howie Rich.

Within its first year of operation, the Franklin Center helped hire or train at least one investigative reporter for most of the states in which the SPN operates. Longtime right-wing journalism foundations have supported some of the Franklin Center's operatives. Bill McMorris, a staff researcher and writer with the Franklin Center, was awarded a Robert Novak fellowship, which ranges from $50,000 to $75,000, from the Phillips Foundation to support his work.[15]

However, the effort to recruit veteran reporters has required competitive salaries. The Associated Press reported that the Alaska Policy Forum, an SPN affiliate advised by the Franklin Center, offered a $75,000 starting salary to cover state politics in Juneau.[16] The same AP story noted that Wayne Hoffman, the executive director of the SPN's Idaho Freedom Foundation, operates IdahoReporter.com, a website run with Franklin Center support, while also coordinating Tea Parties and lobbying drives on behalf of his organization. Despite his conflicting roles, Hoffman challenged the AP reporter to find any bias in his group's reporting.

Questions have been raised about the role of Franklin Center "reporters" in local newsrooms around the country. According to PBS's MediaShift blog, the Franklin Center's Illinois Statehouse News was denied "a spot in the Illinois capitol press bureau and is regarded with suspicion by the press."[17] Illinois reporters were well aware of the Chicago-based Sam Adams Alliance's long history of creating fake grassroots groups and were right to be wary of the Franklin Center. Similarly, because Stverak and his fellow Franklin staffers have refused to reveal any of their financial backers, other Franklin Center reporters have failed to obtain press credentials in states like Missouri as well. Phil Brooks, director of the University of Missouri's State Government Reporting Program, told the Associated Press that such reluctance to reveal their financial backers is a "red flag."[18]

The Franklin Center's first major scoop was a story about "phantom stimulus districts." Jim Scarantino, the investigative reporter for the SPN- and Franklin-supported New Mexico's Rio Grande Foundation, found a large number of stimulus projects that were listed in 440 nonexistent congressional districts on the Recovery.gov website. The story jumped from the Franklin Center newswire to right-wing blogs, to Drudge Report and Politico, and finally to much of the mainstream press, including ABC News.[19] While administration officials apologized for the error, they noted that the "phantom districts" did not actually show misappropriated funds. The mistake was due to early mis-reporting of zip codes, and in fact all of the stimulus dollars appearing in "phantom districts" had gone to actual projects in real congressional districts. Regardless, the story played out for weeks of Fox News denunciations and provided grist for congressional Republicans eager to knock the stimulus as a failure. "I'm appalled by the recklessness and disregard this Administration has demonstrated for Americans' hard-earned taxpayer dollars," said Republican Congresswoman Mary Fallin of Oklahoma, commenting on the story.[20]

Franklin Center reporters also helped senators John McCain and Tom Coburn produce a report on so-called wasteful projects within the stimulus.[21] Like the "phantom districts" story, the report gained wide coverage in both the ideological and mainstream press. But as White House official Jared Bernstein noted, many of the projects slammed by the McCain-Coburn report weren't actually stimulus funded, while others were blatantly mischaracterized: "Take for example an award that McCain and Coburn describe as funding a WNBA Practice Facility, when in fact the award is building a tribal government center that will create education and health facilities while also creating hundreds of jobs. Moreover, the tribe has agreed to disallow any commercial use of the facility."[22]

By wooing experienced reporters from the traditional media, the Franklin Center helped gain credibility. The SPN think tank in Michigan, the Mackinac Center for Public Policy, founded the Michigan Transparency Center with the Franklin Center's help, then hired broadcast journalist Kathy Hoekstra from local NBC affiliate WEYI-TV. Hoekstra has produced a variety of reports, including one attacking Michigan legislators for passing a film tax credit.[23] The Mackinac Center had long criticized the tax credit as wasteful, but Hoekstra's news item helped push the issue into a statewide controversy, particularly after her piece highlighted how the credit benefited left-wing filmmaker Michael Moore. Steven Greenhut, a longtime columnist to the *Orange County Register*, was tapped by the SPN-supported Pacific Research Institute to lead its news outlet, CalWatchDog. Clint Brewer, a well-respected journalist and the former national president of the Society of Professional Journalists, was hired for a 14-month stint to advise the Franklin Center's project with the Tennessee Center for Policy Research.[24] Brewer has said the Franklin Center helped him after his previous newspaper job laid him off.[25]

While some of the reports done by the Franklin Center are legitimate journalism, most of its work is typical Republican opposition research and press releases dressed as news. Earl Glynn, a Franklin Center staff reporter in Missouri, wrote an article promoting the far-right Association of American Physicians and Surgeons and their work organizing Tea Parties for Republican candidates.[26] In his reporting, Glynn glossed over the association's radical positions. For instance, the group declares that the FDA and the Centers for Medicare and Medicaid are unconstitutional, and has argued that President Obama may have used "covert hypnosis" to bring supporters to campaign events.[27] Andrew Griffin, a staff reporter for the Franklin Center's Oklahoma Watchdog site, wrote a story citing conspiracy theorist Alex Jones that President Obama is a secret CIA spy who was born in either Kenya or Indonesia. "We will post more here as we come across new information related to the mysterious Barack Obama (aka Barry Soetoro)," notes Griffin at the end of his story.[28] Many other articles from Franklin Center sites essentially repost right-wing think tank studies as their own stories or repackage content created by corporate front groups as "breaking news."

Despite the often-transparent partisan bias of many of the Franklin Center reporters, the group is well positioned to make a sizable impact for years to come. The websites, to any casual observer, appear independent and professional. Local news stations around the country, desperate for content, have used its network of WatchDog.org and StateHouseNewsOnline.org websites as a neutral source. In Wisconsin alone, eighteen newspapers syndicated the Franklin Center affiliate, WisconsinReporter.com.[29]

In Alaska, the Franklin Center reporter gained a weekly show promoting the Franklin Center's local news blog content. The SPN website advertises that the Alaskan reporter, in turn, will be promoting "education choice" policies from the local SPN affiliate, Alaska Policy Forum, in her broadcast segments.

The Franklin Center has indicated that it intends to continue its expansion after its first two years. In August 2010, the Franklin Center announced a formal partnership with *National Review* to report on key battleground congressional and gubernatorial races for the fall elections.[30] The Franklin Center also announced additional training programs for other right-wing think tanks considering opening journalism centers or news websites.

The Franklin Center's foray into state-based journalism is part of a larger scheme to enhance the power of state-based corporate front groups, including the State Policy Network. While the goal of providing additional oversight is ostensibly positive, the Franklin Center appears to have a singular focus on delegitimizing government institutions, promoting myths about left-leaning groups, and weakening programs that regulate their corporate sponsors. Just as the SPN attacks progressive policies by creating a local messaging entity in each state, the addition of localized dirt digging presents new opportunities for the right to flood the news media with smears.

FOR-PROFIT FEDERALISM

In the early seventies, lobbyists from nearly a hundred major corporations and trade associations, ranging from the Aluminum Company of America to the U.S. Brewers Association, founded the State Government Affairs Council (SGAC) to "enhance [state] policy-makers' knowledge of various business perspectives." The 2010 SGAC board of directors included representatives from Kraft Foods, Wal-Mart, International Paper, the Coca-Cola Company, Hewlett-Packard, and Tyco International, and had affiliations with many other corporate entities. SGAC helps underwrite a professional, nonpartisan organization called the Council of State Government (CSG), which in turn provides policy and practical training resources to the state legislators, governors, and their staff.[31] Although CSG, because of its reliance on SGAC funding, leans conservative and pro–big business, it avoids hot-button, controversial issues. To fight tooth and nail against progressive reforms, corporate America turns to a more rabidly right-wing state-based group called the American Legislative Exchange Council (ALEC), which also receives funds from SGAC.

Paul Weyrich, an architect of much of the modern right, founded ALEC to help corporate interests establish relationships with state legislators. Unlike the SPN think tanks, which serve as a clearinghouse for Republican staffers as well as a hub for distributing conservative ideas to local government and media, ALEC directly writes pieces of legislation for state lawmakers and coordinates multistate lobbying campaigns. ALEC has grown precipitously over the years and includes over 2,000 members, almost all of whom are Republican. Corporate members pay at least $50,000 a year to play a role in the group.

Through issue-based task forces, ALEC pairs right-wing state lawmakers with corporate lobbyists to draft business-friendly legislation. The Economic Development Task Force, which includes Ed Conklin, a lobbyist for Mc-Donald's Corporation, and Jamie Clark of the American Banking Association, produced the Minimum Wage Repeal Act, a law that preempts local governments from enacting their own wage laws. ALEC estimates that every year, one thousand bills around the country are introduced based on its model legislation, and of these, an average of 20 percent become law.[32]

Although ALEC is limited to state lawmakers, corporations use the group to send strong messages to federal policy makers. When President Bush fought to privatize Social Security, ALEC, through its Economic Development Task Force, distributed resolutions supporting privatization. In 2010, ALEC pressed forward with an aggressive campaign to encourage lawmakers to pass resolutions opposing Net

Neutrality, a regulation that bars telecommunication companies from blocking traffic or charging different rates depending on the website and user. Jim Epperson, an executive for AT&T, served as national chairman of ALEC during the anti–Net Neutrality campaign. With funding from polluters like Koch Industries, BP, ExxonMobil, and much of the coal industry, ALEC is also leading a fight to compel states that have signed carbon emission standards to repeal their efforts to address climate change.

A glance at the ALEC website does not convey how powerful the organization really is. Although ALEC sometimes celebrates its success, such as when it vigorously publicized its own role in coordinating an effort to declare health reform unconstitutional in many states, it typically maintains a low profile. Most of its promotional materials follow the pattern of other corporate fronts by presenting itself as simply a group of "Jeffersonian" lawmakers who share a "common belief in limited government, free markets, federalism, and individual liberty."[33] But ALEC is actually an extremely productive vehicle for corporate and right-wing interests to dominate state legislatures.

Arizona's radical immigration law—a 2010 measure called SB1070 that grants a broad new mandate for local police to target and arrest undocumented immigrants—is a quintessential example of ALEC's quiet, yet formidable, power. In December of 2009, Arizona state senator Russell Pearce, a top Republican in the legislature, attended a private meeting at an ALEC conference in Washington, D.C. The private meeting, a "task force" on public safety and immigration, featured several lobbyists, including Laurie Shanblum, an executive at the large private prison company Corrections Corporation of America. At the meeting, Shanblum, Pearce, and others came together to write a new legislative item that would become the baseline for Arizona's SB1070 law. Within two months of the meeting, ALEC distributed a template version of the law, titled Support Our Law Enforcement and Safe Neighborhoods Act of 2010, as model legislation for its members in every state.

The legislation called for requiring police to determine the immigration status of anyone they encounter as part of a "lawful contact," and for police to arrest any undocumented immigrants they might find. Critics rightfully pointed out that the law compels police officers to discriminate based on race. What does an illegal immigrant look like? One SB1070 advocate claimed police could figure it out based on a person's "shoes." The law also contained a provision allowing citizens to sue any police force believed to be not enforcing immigration law, as well as outlawing the transportation of any undocumented person for any reason.

In Arizona, where Corrections Corporation of America already operated three private prisons, executives believed the state's large immigrant population, coupled with a rising tide of anti-immigrant sentiment, could be harnessed for profit. According to NPR's Laura Sullivan, around the same time prison lobbyists were crafting anti-immigrant legislation through the auspices of ALEC, executives at Corrections Corporation were shopping the idea of new private prisons in Arizona to detain immigrants. Glenn Nichols, the Benson, Arizona, city manager, told Sullivan that a Corrections Corporation executive came by his office to pitch the idea of an immigrant detention center for the city. Nichols referred to the man as a "car salesman."

Reporting on this story, I also found a financial outlook presentation prepared by Pershing Square Capital, a hedge fund with a large stake in Corrections Corporation, suggesting that immigrant detention prisons would be an important part of the company's growth strategy. Indeed, Corrections Corporation, along with the Geo Group and other private prison companies, is notorious for leveraging its political relationships to increase profits. Lobbyists working for the industry have played a key role in passing three-strike laws and other efforts to increase the prison population. Prison privatization is also a top priority for the industry.

To ensure passage of the ALEC-crafted immigration law, the company forged close relationships with public officials. Arizona Governor Jan Brewer hired Corrections Corporation's top lobbyist as her campaign chairman, and another lobbyist with close company ties secured a position as her deputy chief of staff. As NPR's investigation found, two-thirds of the state legislators cosponsoring the SB1070 bill proposed by Pearce were either card-carrying ALEC members or were present at the ALEC conference where the law was devised. As the bill was debated, thirty of those same lawmakers received campaign donations from Corrections Corporation, as well as from other private prison companies like Management and Training Corporation and the Geo Group.

Although Arizona was the first state to pass ALEC's template Support Our Law Enforcement and Safe Neighborhoods Act of 2010 in the form of SB1070, many other states attempted to follow suit. In Pennsylvania, Republican state representative Daryl Metcalfe filed a bill identical to ALEC's template legislation shortly after attending the same ALEC convention with Arizona's Russell Pearce. Similar measures were also introduced in Oklahoma, Tennessee, Colorado, and Florida.

For reactionary right-wing groups hostile to Hispanic immigrants, the law was the perfect way to enlist local police officers in their fight to arrest and deport the millions of undocumented people in America. Many Tea Party groups, like Americans for Prosperity, ResistNet, and Tea Party Patriots, rallied around the Arizona law, which the governor signed in April of 2010. However, behind closed doors, the conservative movement had again played a convenient political role in helping a large corporation, in this case the private prison industry, take advantage of a policy crisis. With a federal stalemate on immigration policy, groups like ALEC were able to manipulate the process and achieve sweeping results for corporate interests on the state level.

Many conservatives clamor loudly for more state power. Congressman Tom Price, the former Republican Study Committee chairman and a former ALEC member before going to Congress, declared, "Our Founding Fathers understood the danger of amassing broad powers in the federal government at the expense of individual liberty."[34] But given the influence of groups like ALEC and SPN, decentralization can be a backdoor attempt to make broad, industrywide regulations more difficult to enforce. An example would be the Republican alternative idea for health reform: allowing insurance plans to be purchased across state lines. This health policy would replicate the failures of credit card deregulation, which allows companies to flee to states with the fewest consumer regulations. Employer-based health insurance policies could shift at any moment to plans in states where policyholders have limited coverage options or could be dropped for any reason.

Despite the bluster about individual and states' rights, these policies are always about corporate profits first. Indeed,

ALEC proposals—like the ALEC-drafted Independent External Review for Health Benefits Plans Act—have sought to strip the right of patients even to file a lawsuit against an insurance company.[35]

As the right continues to build its state-based infrastructure, corporate fronts like the State Government Affairs Council and the American Legislative Exchange Council will gain more influence. Lobbyists have always existed in state capitals around the country. But only until recently have right-wing activists exported sophisticated lobbying campaigns using front groups and think tanks to the state level. And at a time when state-based media is diminishing, groups like ALEC allow corporate lobbyists to wield unprecedented power without detection from the public.

PLAYING OFFENSE

Control of state governments has allowed conservatives to advance far right policies, even with President Obama in the White House. Most of this chapter has been devoted to how the state-based conservative infrastructure fought proxy battles against reforms at the national level, and how the network of state groups has grown significantly since Obama's election. But the chance for state-level fronts to really show their worth came only two years after Obama's election. When Republicans swept the 2010 midterm elections, they won unprecedented gains. By 2011, with GOP leadership in state capitals across the country, conservatives were ready to declare war. In ten states where Republicans made gains in 2010, restrictive voting laws were passed the following year.[36]

While the right has sought to chip away at worker protections as part of a broader antilabor agenda, their primary motivation has been to defund and weaken Democrats for future elections. Ed Gillespie, the Republican strategist co-ordinating a $40 million fund to help elect more Republican state legislators in 2010, saw state government as the path forward. First, he reasoned that because of the 2010 census, control of state legislatures would be critical in terms of the redistricting process that happens every ten years. "This will be the last election before redistricting, and there are 18 state chambers that could go either way and affect between 25 and 32 U.S. House seats," Gillespie told the *National Review* before the election.[37] Haley Barbour, the chairman of the Republican Governors Association, was just as candid, displaying the goal of redistricting prominently on the website for his group. With control of enough state chambers, Republicans hoped to gerrymander their way into power for at least ten years.[38]

Gloating shortly after the midterm election, Karl Rove spoke to an audience of Marcellus Shale gas-drillers (commonly known as the "fracking" industry) in Pittsburgh. In classic Rove fashion, he emphasized the partisan ramifications of the election as just a new policy landscape. Republicans had swept state legislative offices across the country, meaning the GOP could now gerrymander themselves into a power for the next decade. "He who controls the pen draws the line," Rove said, "and he who draws the line decides the outcome of most contests."

The second reason national GOP strategists focused on gaining state-level control was to defund labor unions, thus weakening the Democratic Party. Controlling state government would provide an opportunity for Republicans to de-certify and break public employee unions—one of the largest contributors to Democrats in elections. The American

Federation of State, County, and Municipal Employees spent $12.4 million in federal elections in 2010, making it one of the top pro-Democratic spenders in the country outside the party committees. Taking out AFSCME and unions like the Service Employees International Union would deprive Democrats of some of their greatest allies during elections.

To test the waters, Resurgent Republic, a polling nonprofit Gillespie had founded with Rove in 2009 to provide constant messaging advice for the conservative movement, began producing surveys about attitudes related to public employees. The polling found that direct attacks on public employees, like teachers, as overpaid, could be effective with voters. The analysis found that the public viewed teachers' unions with "disdain." Resurgent Republic circulated a memo claiming that an assault on public employees could "galvanize citizens" against "the new federal bureaucrat elite—paid for by struggling private sector families." Portraying public employees as leeches fed by taxpayer dollars could be a "tipping point" in the war on the labor movement, Gillespie and Rove argued.

The strategy also made sense given budgetary realities. By the end of 2010, resources allocated by President Obama's economic stimulus plan, a third of which was composed of direct funding to the states, would be drying up. Most state governments, unlike the federal government, require balanced budgets. A confrontation was brewing, and groups like the U.S. Chamber of Commerce preferred that public servants—not businesses—feel the pain. If conservatives could convince the public to blame both state and federal budget woes on public employee salaries or pensions, then the problem could be solved by axing workers and their benefits instead of raising taxes on businesses or the rich.

The trickle-down infrastructure of conservative front groups, which had grown in leaps and bounds during this period, carefully planned for the upcoming battle. In 2009 and 2010, the State Policy Network teamed up with strategists from the Sam Adams Alliance and American Majority to hire web developers to modify the websites of each state-based think tank. One fairly simple innovation they stressed was a searchable, public database for salary information for public servants—everyone from janitors to university professors, police officers, teachers, and nurses. In some cases, this data was already public but difficult to find. In other cases, the State Policy Network or staffers from the Sam Adams Alliance would inundate state governments with record requests for the information.

State Policy Network affiliates set up new websites to track public servants, along with reports to document how they are supposedly "overpaid." The Caesar Rodney Institute, the SPN affiliate in Delaware, set up the website DelawareSpends .com in July of 2009 to track state and county employee salaries.[39] In September of 2009, at the same time that it produced studies opposing an increase in the state corporate income tax, the Nevada Policy Research Institute produced a website called TransparentNevada.com to showcase salary data for teachers and college professors. Other SPN affiliates followed suit: the Yankee Institute for Public Policy set up a similar database in February of 2010, as did the Cascade Policy Institute in Oregon that same month.

Speaking with Politico reporter Ken Vogel, Matt Mayer, an official with the State Policy Network front in Ohio, the Buckeye Institute, boasted that his group had set up a state employee salary website as part of a plan to call for cuts to public employee unions later on.[40] When Governor John

Kasich, a conservative Republican, and the newly elected Republican legislature made ending collective bargaining— in effect, killing off the state employee unions in the state— their top priority at the outset of 2011, Mayer claimed partial responsibility. By setting up an online salary database and producing anti–public employee studies, Mayer said his group had been "hugely influential in the decision" to ulti- mately eviscerate public employee unions. Both Kasich and the collective bargaining bill sponsor had cited the work of the Buckeye Institute.

Serving its typical role as the engine for actual state legisla- tion, the American Legislative Exchange Council distributed a series of template legislation and guides for ending collec- tive bargaining and stripping public employee labor rights. Throughout 2010, the group held multiple conferences with workshops about its "Budget Reform Toolkit" to slash pub- lic employee benefits. Unsurprisingly, ALEC legislators in Maine, New Hampshire, Wisconsin, Ohio, and other states proposed draconian cuts to public employee unions based upon ALEC legislative ideas.

In Wisconsin, the newly elected Republican governor Scott Walker came into office and immediately pushed legislation to end collective bargaining for public employee unions, along with a series of budget and pay cuts for state workers. The move was quickly met with large protests, which gained headlines for weeks in the first few months of 2011.

Behind the headlines, the Republicans making the head- lines, and the strategy to go after the unions, the trickle- down lobbying infrastructure was hard at work. Americans for Prosperity, the national right-wing front group financed by the Koch brothers and other corporate interests, had created a local chapter called Fight Back Wisconsin. By organizing Tea Party rallies, boosting GOP candidates, and assisting with get-out-the-vote efforts, the Americans for Prosperity group—which was staffed by a number of long-time Republican operatives—set the stage for the Republican takeover of the state. Koch Industries, a company with a large stake in lumber mills, pipelines, and coal interests in Wisconsin, also funneled over $40,000 in donations in Walker, making the firm one of his greatest contributors. After Walker won his election, Americans for Prosperity president Tim Phillips traveled to Madison to persuade him to make targeting collective bargaining rights a priority.

State-level think tanks and front groups in Wisconsin also paved the way for Walker to go after public employee collective bargaining rights. The Wisconsin Policy Research Institute, a State Policy Network–affiliated group, produced polling claiming that the public supported Walker's power grab. Officials from the institute authored studies pinning blame for Wisconsin's deficit on public employee benefits and then promoted their work by writing opinion pieces, including one in the *New York Times*, to support that position. Another State Policy Network front in the state, the John K. MacIver Institute, provided similar work by producing studies that claimed public employee union officials were also overpaid.

The critics of public-employee pay, particularly that of public teachers, exaggerated their claims. Several Republicans and right-wing commentators claimed teachers in the state made "double" the average of private sector employees, or that the average teacher is paid over $100,000. In reality, the average teacher salary in Wisconsin is about $51,264, according to PolitiFact, the nonpartisan fact-checking website.

The sustained focus on teacher and other public servant salaries obscured the true drivers of Wisconsin's budget deficit. The budget gap could have been filled by simply closing an Internet sales tax loophole, getting rid of a special interest property tax exemption, and forcing Wisconsin corporations to pay their share of state corporate income taxes (many Wisconsin corporations, like many American companies, set up offshore accounts to avoid paying taxes). Rather than taking a pragmatic approach to ending the deficit, Walker's budget included tens of millions in additional tax cuts. Moreover, ending collective bargaining rights alone does nothing to affect the budget. Wisconsin public employee unions voluntarily offered full concessions on pay and benefits. The Walker administration demand to end collective bargaining was only an effort to weaken progressive institutions, not fix the budget.

Senator Scott Fitzgerald, the Republican majority leader in the state senate and a key ally to Walker, even admitted during an on-air interview that the bill to remove collective bargaining was political in nature. Speaking with Fox News' Megyn Kelly, Fitzgerald said, "If we win this battle, and the money is not there under the auspices of the unions, certainly what you're going to find is President Obama is going to have a much difficult, much more difficult time getting elected and winning the state of Wisconsin." The manufactured outrage about public employee pay was simply a distraction to further a right-wing political goal.

Beyond producing studies and being quoted in the media, which is typical for any think tank, the MacIver Institute had created a communications war room to bolster Walker's antiunion efforts. In October of 2010, shortly before Walker's election victory, the shadowy Franklin Center reached out to the MacIver Institute to establish a state-based news site. To run this media operation, MacIver hired Bill Osmulski, a reporter from WKOW 27 news, and Brian Fraley, a Republican campaign staffer.[41] The newly minted MacIver News Service quickly went to work creating video reports and articles complaining about the pay for teachers and other public servants.

In addition to MacIver, American Majority also launched a project called Media Trackers to "dig up dirt on the left," as one Politico story described it. After a meeting with wealthy GOP donors in the summer of 2010, American Majority president Drew Ryun came up with the idea of developing an army of opposition researchers and videographers to catch liberals making mistakes. As *Mother Jones* described the project, Ryun sought to develop a network of "nimble attack blogs that could quickly capitalize on the latest missteps by big-government politicians" using "hard-hitting, opposition-research-style shops that prize scoops, speed, and scandal."[42]

But like many of these thinly disguised partisan projects, Media Trackers simply turned out poorly researched attacks. The very first story published by the group, by one of its Wisconsin-based affiliates, claimed to show evidence that a labor union–backed group provided free BBQ to Milwaukee residents in exchange for a promise to vote for Democrats. The story predictably gained bounced through the echo chambers of the right-wing media. But a subsequent investigation by a local district attorney found absolutely no wrongdoing.[43]

CONCLUSION

> Like the Bourbon kings of France, the lords of
> unrestrained, amoral capitalism never forgot anything.
> They learned from their defeat how to organize new
> strategies and messages, furnish the money to back
> them, and recapture control of the nation's life.
>
> —*Bill Moyers and Bernard Weisberger*

Elections affect the occupancy of certain seats in government, but they do not alter the fundamental power dynamics in Washington, D.C. Barack Obama, awarded a second term by the American people, will have to contend with the right's political machine, which emerged from the election fresh with cash, new tools, and a renewed commitment to dig deeper ideological trenches.

On paper, Democrats won decisive victories in 2012. But even though Democratic House candidates earned more votes than their Republican opponents in this election, gerrymandering—engineered by the wave of Tea Party–

backed politicians two years prior—ensured that Democrats could only secure less than ten seats, far from the twenty-five necessary to win any substantive power.

The net result is a second term that consists of fighting to retain the few achievements from the first, endless political squabbling over minor issues, and, ultimately, stalemate on the big issues that grip society, from climate change to America's disappearing middle class. Republicans failed to deliver Mitt Romney to the presidency, but the conservative machine has largely triumphed in preventing the wave of progressive reform that seemed quite possible at the end of the Bush presidency or any permanent realignment toward liberalism.

One must marvel at the right, at least with the same respect given to an early venture capitalist whose savvy investment reaped an incredible return. Wealthy patrons and big business plowed money into stopping what seemed like an inevitable wave of progressive reforms, and were ultimately successful in many ways. Of course, it wasn't just financial advantage. Smart decisions were made to duplicate and build upon the few tactical advantages built by Democrats over the years and to block progressive legislative items writ large. The resources of ideological billionaires teamed with the near-limitless corporate treasuries of Fortune 500 companies (and their K Street lobbyists) swallowed and defeated much of President Obama's hopeful plans for America.

They also had the privilege of building upon success.

The model, of course, had been there all along. Lewis Powell, the corporate lawyer who eventually made his way to the Supreme Court, penned his influential memo in 1971 calling for corporations to stem the tide of activism in the country by funding a vast array of organizations for the defense of the "American business executive" and all he stands for.

Charles Koch's model of fabricating dozens of front groups ensured that by the time Barack Obama had ascended to the Illinois State Senate, there were already dozens of think tanks prepared to oppose his agenda years later when he occupied the White House. The Heritage Foundation, founded in the seventies in the wake of Powell's memo and funded over the years with help from Koch grants, expanded over the course of Obama's administration. Many other fronts, such as the American Action Network, were created after the 2008 election to overwhelm Democrats and extinguish the promise of wide-ranging economic reform.

The conservatives and the Republican Party were not building a new machine; they were simply retrofitting one that had lasted for some thirty years. If anything, the shock of Obama's first election served simply as a reminder that this machine had to be improved for the twenty-first century.

The conventional wisdom regarding the 2012 elections concluded that big money went largely to waste and that Super PACs played little role in shifting the electoral battle in favor of conservatives. A closer reading of how the right used its political bulwark shows that the hundreds of millions spent by deep-pocketed donors prevented a greater Democratic sweep.

The brand-new fronts devised early to combat the Obama administration were deployed to account for the Republican's key disadvantages. Several of the groups formed to manufacture Tea Party outrage in 2009, including American Majority, set up over dozens of "Get Out the Vote" offices in swing states to provide Republican candidates with support. Romney's biggest phone-banking center was far from the headquarters in Boston—it was actually an office complex in Idaho, set up by Americans for Prosperity, with resources lent to the group from a telemarketing mogul.

The billions spent on political advertising had a diminishing impact over the course of high-profile races, like the presidential contest, where many voters became oversaturated with partisan content. Down ballot, however, unlimited political money helped conservatives grow majorities in many state legislatures and insulated many right-wing congressional incumbents from being hit by a popular Democratic wave.

Despite what voters communicated on Election Day, entrenched interests were quick to continue their permanent campaign. Within hours of the results, the Heritage Action released a video scorched with apocalyptic scenes of American decline, promising, "To win this war, we must remain committed to fighting President Obama's agenda." Within a week of Election Day, an oil industry group with deep Republican ties began airing the first ads of the following cycle, hammering incumbent Senator Kay Hagan of North Carolina, one of twenty Democrats up for reelection in 2014.

Republican strategists have launched new think tanks and front groups to better communicate to gay Americans and Latinos; but there is little talk of reorganizing the machine to enact more inclusive policies or to better address the problems faced by society. The powerful forces that fought back against reform for Obama's first term have little incentive, and face no democratic mechanism, to change course.

The end result may seem, at first, political. Labor unions will continue to decline as a part of political life while Democrats will struggle one day to achieve the same window of partisan advantage enjoyed for those vital two years after Obama's victory. Corporations and the wealthy will continue to invest in an ever-expanding communications infrastructure designed to shape public opinion and policy, as well to win elections for favored candidates.

But the success of the conservative machine is more conse-
quential than politics. Overall economic growth is no longer
coupled with broad prosperity. While corporations achieved
records profits in 2012, the nation's top CEOs made over
3,486 times the salary of the average American worker, according to one survey. During the economic recession, the
typical American family's wealth plunged 40 percent, a sta-
tistic that only underscored the long-term unemployment
that has become normalized in many parts of the country.

The human toll of the political imbalance is striking. The
latest research shows that suicides and domestic violence are
closely linked with unemployment, meaning the conservative pressure to enact austerity over stimulus has a human
cost. The foreclosure crisis, unaddressed because of intense
lobbying by the banks, has left families in turmoil and entire
communities in ruin.

Can anything be done to change this trajectory? The
problem can be distilled into a set of choices.

On one hand, there is a call from the left to construct a political arsenal of think tanks and communications tools and
somehow outraise Republicans every election cycle using its
own set of corporate alliances and benevolent plutocrats. The
recent history would suggest that this approach, while possible in the short term, cannot match the combined resources
of the right. First, the underprivileged, the unemployed, the
debt-ridden, and the impoverished will never be able to mus-
ter the resources to finance a real left-wing political machine.
And why would corporate America dig its own grave, so to
speak, by supporting causes that would enact more consumer-
friendly laws and close tax loopholes? A case could be made
that such an alliance would be a breach of corporate fiduciary
duties to shareholders to make the highest quarterly profit

possible. These corporate partnerships, as Obama's first few years made clear, serve largely for entrenched interest groups to co-opt progressives so their lobbyists can delay and deter reform.

The second approach is that of populist action, the same tradition of civil disobedience that brought forth the first labor laws; the Civil Rights Act; the environmental movement; and, most recently, the Arab Spring. The experience of the Occupy Wall Street protests, however, suggest a modern limitation to this approach, at least in America. The protesters were quickly maligned by a twenty-four-hour news cycle media campaign and brutalized by the full power of the police and surveillance state. Public opinion might have been with the Occupiers for the first few weeks, just as the public supported virtually all of Obama's progressive reforms at the outset of his administration. But a persistent propaganda campaign and relentless smears from corporate-friendly political types proves that public approval, like legislation, can be bought. In the end, Occupy came to be perceived as an ugly, uncivilized embodiment of the left—not the wellspring for justice the organizers had envisioned.

Thomas Jefferson feared for this era. As he spent time in France, admiring a country filled with rich traditions and seemingly forward-looking cultural attitudes, he noted that a powerful elite could harness all political power in even the most tranquil of nations. In a letter to George Washington, Jefferson wrote: "Though the day may be at some distance, beyond the reach of our lives perhaps, yet it will certainly come, when a single fiber left of this institution will produce an hereditary aristocracy, which will change the form of our governments from the best to the worst in the world."

America's aristocracy is not hereditary, and government still functions with democratic designs. But Jefferson's dark vision of an America governed not by and for the people but ruled instead by a small, selfish oligarchy is coming true because of the conservative machine.

NOTES

1. THE TRUE HISTORY
OF THE TEA PARTY

1. "Democrats' 2008 Advantage in Party ID Largest Since '83." *Gallup*, Jan. 23, 2009.

2. Charles Adams, "The Rocky Road of American Taxation," *Mises Daily*, April 15, 2006.

3. Thomas Hartmann, *Unequal Protection* (Berrett-Koehler Publishers, 2010), 77.

4. Stephanie Mencimer, "Is the Tea Party Movement Like a Pyramid Scheme?" *Mother Jones*, Oct. 19, 2010.

5. Brian Beutler, "Industry-Backed Anti-Health Care Reform Group: Yeah, We're Packing and Disrupting the Health Care Town Halls," Talking Points Memo, Aug. 4, 2009.

6. Benjamin Carp, "The Tea Party's Appeal Across the Political Spectrum," *History News Network*, July 19, 2009.

7. Burson-Marsteller letter, Legacy Tobacco Documents Library, Apr. 6, 1992, http://legacy.library.ucsf.edu/document Store/v/b/i/vbi08b00/Svbi08b00.pdf.

8. "Tobacco Strategy," Legacy Tobacco Documents Library, June 5, 1998, http://legacy.library.ucsf.edu/tid/dtv34e00.

9. Jack Guthrie and Associates, "Recommended Public Relations Plan for Philip Morris U.S.A.," last modified October 5,

1995, http://legacy.library.ucsf.edu/action/document/page?tid
=hof57d00.

10. Michael Miles, letter to shareholders, last modified
March 7, 1994, http://legacy.library.ucsf.edu/tid/stc11d00.

11. Christ Wright, "The People's Party," *Boston Phoenix*,
May 30, 2002, http://www.bostonphoenix.com/boston/news
_features/top/features/documents/02289605.htm.

12. Jane Mayer, "Covert Operations," *New Yorker*, Aug. 30, 2010.

13. Walter Jenny, "Look More Closely at TABOR Petition to
Find Slimy Politics." *Edmond Sun*, Sept. 17, 2006.

14. Scott Mooneyham, "Tar Heel Tea Party," *Raleigh News and
Observer*, Apr. 9, 2002.

15. Internet archives of www.cse.org.

16. Edmund Andrews, "Clamor Grows In Privatization
Debate," *New York Times*, Dec. 17, 2004.

17. "Six Local Liberty Activists Recognized with Sammies
Award," *Washington Examiner*, Dec.17, 2007.

18. Internet archives of http://hoosiersforfairtaxation.blogspot
.com.

19. Associated Press, "Ron Paul Collects More Than $6
Million in a Single Day," Dec. 12, 2007.

20. Archived websites within samadamsalliance.org and terra
eclipse.com.

21. Alex Brant-Zawadzki, "A Time for Tea: A Tea Party Time
Line," Huffington Post, Apr. 15, 2010.

22. Lee Fang, "Tea Party Profiteers: How Republican
Operatives Are Exploiting Economic Anxiety for Power, Cash,"
ThinkProgress, Feb. 2, 2010.

23. "Behind the Tea Party Effort," *Verum Serum*, Apr. 17, 2009.

24. Alexander Brant-Zawadzki. "Tempest in a Tea Bag,"
Huffington Post, November 11, 2009, http://www.huffingtonpost
.com/dawn-teo/tempest-in-a-teabag-tea-p_b_354649.html.

25. Jane Hamsher, "A Teabagger Timeline: Koch, Coors,
Newt, Dick Armey There From The Start." *Alternet*, Apr. 16,
2009.

26. Amber Ellis, "Thousands Gather for 'Tea Party,'"
Cincinnati Enquirer, Mar. 15, 2009.

27. Search of media archives using LexisNexis.

28. Search of media archives using LexisNexis.

29. American Petroleum Institute 990 tax returns filed for year 2009.

2. COORDINATING THE MESSAGE

1. Byron York, "Same Old Party: Tranquility in the Ranks," *World Affairs Journal*, http://www.worldaffairsjournal.org /articles/2009-Winter/full-York.html.

2. Philip Klein, "The Future of the Right," *American Spectator* (2008). http://spectator.org/archives/2008/11/06/the-future-of -the-right/#.

3. "Election Roils Republican Leadership in House," *Washington Times*, Nov. 7, 2008.

4. Dan Gilgoff, "Newt Gingrich Steps Up Efforts to Mobilize Religious Conservatives," *U.S. News & World Report*, March 20, 2009.

5. Lee Fang, "GOP National Council Stumped When Asked to Offer Health Care Solutions," ThinkProgress, May 4, 2009.

6. Andy Barr, "Huck: Hard Not 'Laughing' at Cantor's Group," Politico, May 12, 2009, http://www.politico.com/news /stories/0509/22414.html.

7. Andy Barr, "GOP Base Rips Cantor's New Group," Politico, May 7, 2009, http://dyn.politico.com/printstory .cfm?uuid=1D05757B-18FE-70B2-A86FE47DB8EFA490.

8. Laura Blumenfeld, "Sowing the Seeds of GOP Domination, Conservative Norquist Cultivates Grass Roots Beyond the Beltway," *Washington Post*, Jan. 12, 2004, p. A01.

9. Robert Dreyfuss, "Grover Norquist: 'Field Marshal' of the Bush Plan," *Nation*, April 26, 2001, http://www.thenation.com /print/article/grover-norquist-field-marshal-bush-plan.

10. David Weigel, "Grover Norquist Joins GOProud," *Washington Post*, June 15, 2010, http://voices.washingtonpost.com /right-now/2010/06/grover_norquist_joins_goproud.html.

11. "FreedomWorks Grows Grassroots for BP Drilling Initiatives," Crooks and Liars, May 7, 2010, http://crooksandliars.com/karoli/freedomworks-grows-grassroots-bp-drilling-i.

12. Michael Scherer, "Grover Norquist: The Soul of the New Machine," *Mother Jones*, January 2004, http://motherjones.com/politics/2004/01/grover-norquist-soul-new-machine.

13. Michelle Malkin, "The GOP's Grover Norquist Problem and the RNC Debate," http://michellemalkin.com/2009/01/05/the-gops-grover-norquist-problem/.

14. Lee Fang, "Right-Wing Panel Agrees Obama Is the 'First Muslim American President,'" ThinkProgress, Sept. 29, 2009.

15. David Weigel, "Grover Norquist Joins GOProud," *Washington Post*, June 15, 2010, http://voices.washingtonpost.com/right-now/2010/06/grover_norquist_joins_goproud.html.

16. Lee Fang, "Tobacco Lobby Underwriting Part of the Conservative Anti-Tax Rally Tomorrow in Georgia," ThinkProgress, March 8, 2010.

17. Lee Fang, "Telecoms' Secret Plan to Attack Net Neutrality: Target Video Gamers and Stoke Fear of Chinese Censorship," ThinkProgress, May 11, 2010.

18. Jerry Markson, "New Media Help Conservatives Get Their Anti-Obama Message Out." *Washington Post*, Feb. 1, 2010, p. A01.

19. Faiz Shakir, "Once a 'States' Rights' Proponent, Thune Now Pushes Gun Law That Would 'Shoot Holes in State Sovereignty,'" ThinkProgress, July 22, 2009.

20. Barrett Kate, "Senators Reject Gun Proposal," ABC News/Politics, July 22, 2009.

21. Michael Scherer, "Grover Norquist: The Soul of the New Machine," *Mother Jones*, Jan. 2004.

22. John Micklethwait and Adrian Wooldridge, "The Right Rules: Conservatism Goes to the Heart of What It Means to Be an American," *National Review*, June 16, 2004, http://old.nationalreview.com/comment/micklethwait_wooldridge200406160902.asp.

23. Colin Hanna, the co-chairman of the Weyrich Lunch, confirmed to me that since 2008, groups associated with his coalition have received more of the share of conservative do-

nor money to run television advertisements. Jim Martin, of the 60 Plus Association, said that although Norquist is "trustworthy" and "tough," donors had indeed gravitated to the Weyrich Lunch groups after Bush.

24. Interview with Colin Hanna on November 17, 2011, at the Americans for Prosperity Defending the Dream conference.

25. Alex Isenstadt, and Josh Kraushaar, "GOP Pick Sparks Revolt on Right," Politico, Oct. 8, 2009, http://dyn.politico.com /printstory.cfm?uuid=31D2EEAE-18FE-70B2-A8921DB 076A7E7DF.

26. Joy Yearout, "Susan B. Anthony List Statement on Dede Scozzafava Suspending Campaign for NY-23," Christian News Wire, Oct. 31, 2009, http://www.christiannewswire.com/news /16711996.html.

27. Jerry Markson, "New Media Help Conservatives Get Their Anti-Obama Message Out," *Washington Post*, Feb. 1, 2010, p. A01.

28. John Tomasic, "Undeclared U.S. Senate Candidate Norton Receives National Nod, Frustrating Right Bloggers," *Colorado Independent*, Aug. 28, 2009.

29. Maggie Gallagher, "Marco Rubio Republicans," Real Clear Politics, March 10, 2010.

30. Maggie Gallagher, "The Fall of Dede Scozzafava," *National Review*, Oct. 16, 2009.

31. Interview with the author, Sept. 16, 2010.

32. "AIM: DC Conversations—Sen. James Inhofe on Cap and Trade," http://www.youtube.com/watch?v=LsFQJs34-es &feature=channel.

33. Alex Seitz-Wald, "Anti-Mosque Coalition's Website Owned by Neo-Conservative Islamophobe Frank Gaffney," ThinkProgress, Aug. 24, 2010.

34. Michael Scherer, "Grover Norquist Says Mosque Controversy Is Bad for Republicans," *Time*, Aug. 18, 2010, http:// swampland.time.com/2010/08/18/grover-norquist-says-mosque -controversy-is-bad-for-republicans/.

35. Interview with the author Sept. 17, 2010.

36. Bill Berkowitz, "The Heritage Foundation at 35,"

Transparency Media, http://old.mediatransparency.org/story.php ?storyID=229.

37. Heritage Foundation, "Issues 2010: The Candidate's Briefing Book," http://www.issues2010.com/.

38. Heritage Foundation, "Seek Social Justice: Transforming Lives in Need," http://www.seeksocialjustice.com/.

39. Heritage Foundation, "Breaking Health Care Research: 'Accountable Care' Unlikely," http://fixhealthcarepolicy.com/.

40. Lee Fang, "FLASHBACK: Heritage Touted RomneyCare, Key Elements of Health Reform Heritage Now Opposes," ThinkProgress, April 10, 2010.

41. "Becky Norton Dunlop discusses Time Capsule 2033," http://www.youtube.com/watch?v=RwYOSqtsNiI.

42. Heritage Foundation, "Becky Norton Dunlop, Vice President, External Relations," http://www.heritage.org/About /Staff/D/Becky-Dunlop.

43. "Inside the Council for National Policy," ABC News /Politics, May 2, n.d.

44. Bob Barr, *The Meaning of Is: The Squandered Impeachment and Wasted Legacy of William Jefferson Clinton* (Stroud & Hall, 2004).

45. Council for National Policy, "March 2008 Policy Council Speeches," http://www.cfnp.org/Page.aspx?pid=224.

46. Max Blumenthal, "The Council for National Policy Meets in Minn, Vets Palin," Talk to Action, http://www.talk2action.org /story/2008/9/1/24846/28141.

47. Media Matters, "In Fact, Hamilton's Decision Did Not Favor Islam over Christianity—It Simply Banned "Sectarian" Prayer," http://mediamatters.org/research/200911030023.

48. Meredith Shiner, "Senate Confirms Controversial Judge," Politico, Nov. 19, 2009.

49. Emmett Tyrrell, *After the Hangover: The Conservatives' Road to Recovery*, (Thomas Nelson, 2002).

50. Americans for Limited Government, "ALG Urges Senate Judiciary Committee to Reject Goodwin Liu for Ninth Circuit Court of Appeals," http://www.getliberty.org/content .asp?pl=10&sl=5&contentid=399.

51. "Senate Should Reject Radical Goodwin Liu for Seat on 9th Circuit," *Human Events*, March 29, 2010.

52. Charlie Savage, "Appeals Court Nominee Ignites a Partisan Battle," *New York Times*, April 12, 2010.

53. Jackie Calmes, "G.O.P. Group to Promote Conservative Ideas," *New York Times*, Feb. 10, 2010.

54. Peter Stone, "Rove Hosts GOP Fundraiser Conclave," *National Journal*, April 22, 2010.

55. Jeanne Cummings, "Republican Groups Coordinated Financial Firepower," Politico, Nov. 3, 2010.

56. Matea Gold, "$55 Million for Conservative Campaigns—But Where Did It Come From?" *Los Angeles Times*, May 28, 2012.

57. Keyes Scott, "Kissing Cousins: How the U.S. Chamber of Commerce and American Crossroads Hook Up To Elect Republicans," ThinkProgress, Oct. 31, 2010, http://think progress.org/politics/2010/10/07/122863/chamber-commerce -crossroads/.

58. "Chamber of Commerce 'Takes Both Sides' on Economic Stimulus," Associated Press, Oct. 4, 2010.

59. The chamber's donors largely came from multinational corporations, including Dow Chemical, Prudential Financial, and Microsoft. One of the largest checks to the chamber during the 2010 midterm elections came from America's Health Insurance Plans, a trade group representing all of the major health insurance companies.

60. Peter Stone, "Inside The Shadow GOP," *National Journal*, Oct. 4, 2010.

61. Angie Drobnic Holan, "Ed Perlmutter Voted for 'Viagra For Rapists' Paid for with Tax Dollars," PolitiFact, Oct. 26, 2010.

62. Matea Gold, *Los Angeles Times*.

63. Mike Allen, "GOP Groups Plan Record $1 Billion Blitz," Politico, May 30, 2012.

3. THE KOCH-FUELED
WAR ON OBAMA

1. Kim Phillips-Fein, *Invisible Hands* (New York: Norton & Company, 2009).

2. "The Plan." *Philanthropy Roundtable Magazine*, Spring 1997.

3. Brad Johnson, "Tim Phillips on Climate Policy: 'If We Win the Science Argument, It's Game, Set, and Match,'" ThinkProgress, Nov. 27, 2010.

4. Claire Kittle, "Why Don't You Get a Job?" America's Future Foundation, Washington, D.C., May 14, 2008.

5. Brad Friedman, "Exclusive Audio: Inside the Koch Brothers' Secret Seminar," *Mother Jones*, Sept. 6, 2011.

6. John Borowski, "Is the Trend of Trashing Textbooks in Texas Going National?" *Common Dreams*, Aug. 17, 2002.

7. Koch had a heavy hand in the Bush administration. Koch funneled large amounts of donations into electing George Bush in 2000 (even sending Koch-linked lobbyists to help disrupt the Florida recount). At the time, Koch Industries faced a ninety-seven-count federal indictment charging it with concealing illegal releases of 91 metric tons of benzene, known to cause leukemia, from its refinery in Corpus Christi, Texas. When Bush took office, his Justice Department dropped 88 of the charges and settled the case for a small amount of money. Bush officials also handed out no-bid contracts to Koch, including one massive contract to increase the supply of the Strategic Petroleum Reserve.

8. Another charter member of the John Birch Society, Harry Bradley of the Allen-Bradley Company, a major manufacturer of machine tools and electronics, eventually established the Lynde and Harry Bradley Foundation to support causes with goals similar to those of the John Birch Society. The Bradley Foundation, like the foundations run by Fred's sons today, is a permanent honeypot for the modern right-wing infrastructure. According to its website, the Bradley Foundation has granted over $530 million since 1985, mostly to conservative and neoconservative nonprofits. The Bradley Foundation also funds Koch's Americans for Prosperity front.

9. Rick Perlstein, *Before the Storm* (New York: Nation Books, 2009).

10. Rob Robinson, *Funding Fathers* (Washington, D.C.: Regnery, 2008).

11. Drew Pearson, "Kennedy's Death Is Used as Gimmick to Recruit New John Birch Members," *Gadsen Times*, Dec. 23, 1963.

12. Archives of Discoveries newsletter from Koch Industries.

13. Carl Fussman, "Charles Koch: What I've Learned," *Esquire*, Dec. 17, 2008.

14. Charles Koch, Loss of Liberties in the New Economy, Koch Industries, Jan. 1, 2008.

15. Lee Fang, "How Koch Became an Oil Speculation Powerhouse," ThinkProgress, June 6, 2011.

16. Review of records from EndingSpending.com and other websites.

17. Ken Vogel, "Inside the Koch World Convention," Politico, June 5, 2012.

18. Charles Koch, "Richard De Vos Award," Council for National Policy, Naples, Fl., Jan. 1999.

19. Interview with the author, Jan. 5, 2011.

4. REFORM HITS A WALL
AT K STREET

1. Brian McNeil, "Forged letters to Perriello's Office Came from Coal Group's Lobbying Firm," *Charlottesville Daily*, Aug. 5, 2009.

2. Kevin Grandia, "Five More Forged Letters Uncovered from Bonner & Associates' Work for ACCCE," DeSmog Blog, Aug. 6, 2009, http://www.desmogblog.com/five-more-forged-letters-uncovered-bonner-associates%E2%80%99-work-accce.

3. American Coalition for Clean Coal Electricity 990 tax disclosure (2009).

4. Salt Institute 990 tax disclosure (2010).

5. Daniel de Vise, "House Approves Huge Changes to Student Loan Program," *Washington Post*, March 22, 2010, http://www

.washingtonpost.com/wp-dyn/content/article/2010/03/21/AR
2010032103548.html.

6. Karen Hanretty, "Staff," Qorvis Company, http://www
.qorvis.com/staff/karen-hanretty.

7. ProtectStudentChoice, "Student's Speak Out About Student
Choice in Loan Legislation," http://www.youtube.com/watch
?v=yV3lMyGgPW8.

8. Amy Gardner, "Armey Questions Obama's Authority to
Seek BP Payment for Oil Spill," *Washington Post*, June 16, 2010.

9. Lee Fang, "BP Worked with FreedomWorks and the
Chamber to Build 'Grassroots' Support for More Drilling,"
ThinkProgress, http://thinkprogress.org/economy/2010/05/06
/95426/bp-freedomworks-ocs/.

10. Lee Fang, "Glenn Beck Brings ExxonMobil-Linked
Religious Front Group to Tell Christians Not To Believe In
Climate Change," ThinkProgress, Oct. 15, 2010. http://think
progress.org/media/2010/10/15/124583/glennbeck-oil-evangelicals/.

11. Adapted from Lee Fang, "Tim Phillips, The Man Behind
the 'Americans for Prosperity' Corporate Front Group Factory,"
ThinkProgress, May 29, 2009.

12. Center for Media and Democracy, "Century Strategies,"
http://www.sourcewatch.org/index.php?title=Century_Strategies.

13. Mark Shields, "In Politics, Money More Valuable Than
Speech," *Seattle Post-Intelligencer*, http://www.commondreams
.org/views02/0304-06.htm.

14. Joe Stephans, "$380,000 Pitch to Enron: Bush Campaign
Aide Devised Lobby Plan," *Washington Post*, Feb. 17, 2002.

15. Public Citizen, "Blind Faith: How Deregulation and
Enron's Influence over Government Looted Billions from
Americans," http://www.citizen.org/cmep/article_redirect.cfm
?ID=7104.

16. "Bush Adviser Ralph Reed Offered to Lobby for Enron,"
Associated Press, Feb. 17, 2002.

17. Susan Schmidt and James V. Grimaldi, "Abramoff Pleads
Guilty to 3 Counts," *Washington Post*, Jan. 4, 2006, http://www
.washingtonpost.com/wp-dyn/content/article/2006/01/03/
AR2006010300474.html.

18. Century Strategies, "Services: Millenium Marketing," accessed May 10, 2006, http://politicalvine.com/complaints /EXHIBIT%20A.pdf.

19. Thomas B. Edsall, "Another Stumble for Ralph Reed's Beleaguered Campaign," *Washington Post*, May 29, 2006.

20. "Ralph Reed," TPM Muckracker.com, n.d., http://tpm muckraker.talkingpointsmemo.com/reed.php.

21. Susan Schmidt, "Insiders Worked Both Sides of Gaming Issue," *Washington Post*, Sept. 26, 2004, p. A01.

22. Jeffrey Gettleman, "Senator Cleland Loses in an Upset To Republican Emphasizing Defense," *New York Times*, Nov. 6, 2002.

23. SoThisIsWashington, "Chambliss Ad (Cleland)," http:// www.youtube.com/watch?v=tKFYpd0q9nE.

24. Century Strategies, "Our Team: Timothy R. Phillips," http://web.archive.org/web/20041214162123/www.censtrat.com /index.cfm?FuseAction=Team.View&Biography_id=2.

25. Susan Schmidt, "Ralph Reed's New Role," *Washington Post*, Jan. 10, 2008.

26. Brad Friedman, *Mother Jones*, Sept. 6, 2011, http://mother jones.com/politics/2011/09/exclusive-audio-koch-brothers -seminar-tapes.

27. Brad Johnson, "Tim Phillips on Climate Policy: 'If We Win the Science Argument, It's Game, Set, and Match,'" ThinkProgress, Nov. 17, 2010, http://thinkprogress.org/green /2010/11/27/174846/afp-pollution-plan/.

28. Brad Johnson, "Koch Industries: The 100-Million Ton Carbon Gorilla," ThinkProgress, Jan. 30, 2011, http://think progress.org/green/2011/01/30/174900/koch-carbon-footprint/.

29. John C. Stauber, *Toxic Sludge Is Good for You* (Common Courage Press, 1995).

30. Michael Moore, *SiCKO*, directed by Michael Moore.

31. "Wendell Potter on Profits Before Patients," *Bill Moyers Journal*, July 10, 2009, http://www.pbs.org/moyers/journal /07102009/profile.html.

32. "Healthcare in Crisis," Center for American Progress, Feb. 19, 2009, http://www.americanprogressaction.org/issues/2009/02 /health_in_crisis.html.

33. Interview with the author, Sept. 13, 2009.

34. Igor Volsky, "Conservative Patient Rights Group Launches Attacks on Obama's Health Plan," ThinkProgress.

35. Interview with Wendell Potter in September of 2005.

36. An HIP 990 tax form filed with the IRS.

37. Chris Frates, "Exclusive: AHIP Gave More Than $100 Million to Chamber's Efforts to Derail Health Care Reform," *National Journal*, June 13, 2012.

38. Igor Volsky, "Insurance Industry Issues Misleading Report, Promises to Increase Premiums By 111%," ThinkProgress, Oct. 12, 2009. http://thinkprogress.org/health/2009/10/12 /170993/ahip-report/.

39. Lee Fang, "AHIP's Two-Faced Campaign Unravels: No 'Comfort To The Enemy' vs. 'Committed to Bipartisan Health Reform,'" ThinkProgress, Oct. 22, 2009, http://thinkprogress .org/economy/2009/10/22/65754/ahip-enemy-reform/.

40. Charles Riley, "Oops! Aetna Discloses Political Donations," CNN Money, June 15, 2009.

41. David Dayen, "Safe Banking Amendment Fails in Snap Vote, 33-61," FireDogLake, May 7, 2010, http://news.firedoglake .com/2010/05/07/safe-banking-amendment-fails-in-snap-vote -33-61/.

42. "New Stop Too Big to Fail $1.6 Million TV Ad Campaign Warns Small Investors of New Bailout Fund," DailyKos, April 19, 2010, http://www.dailykos.com/story/2010/04/19/858742/-New -Stop-Too-Big-To-Fail-1-6-Million-TV-Ad-Campaign-Warns -Small-Investors-of-New-Bailout-Fund.

43. Monica Davey, "Health Care Overhaul and Mandatory Coverage Stir States' Rights Claims," *New York Times*, Sept. 28, 2009.

5. A SOCIAL MEDIA FACE LIFT
FOR CONSERVATISM

1. Jeff Stein, "Free-for-all at Free Republic," Salon, July 13, 1999.

2. Nicholas Confessore. "Meet the Press," *Washington Monthly*, Dec. 2003.

3. Mike Krempasky, "Online Training for Tea Party Activists," RedState, July 7, 2010, http://www.redstate.com /krempasky/2010/07/07/online-training-for-tea-party-activists/.

4. Patrick Ruffini, "Roots of Defeat," Nation Review, Dec. 1, 2008.

5. LexisNexis news search.

6. Transcript provided by the Council for National Policy, Feb. 2009 conference.

7. Media Research Center 2010 Annual Report.

8. Author interviews with Tea Party Patriots members throughout 2011.

9. Zachary Roth, "Chamber of Commerce Campaign: Fight Health-Care Reform—and Win a Trip to Hooters!" Talking Points Memo, Dec. 16, 2009.

10. Steve Hanlon, "Conservative Party 'Cash Gordon' Campaign Was Designed by US Anti-Healthcare Lobbyists," Political Scrapbook, March 22, 2010, http://politicalscrapbook .net/2010/03/conservative-party-cash-gordon-campaign-was -designed-by-us-anti-healthcare-lobbyists/.

11. Lee Fang, "How the 'U.S.' Chamber Uses Its Money to Pay Pundits, Manipulate Google, and Create Fake News Outlets," ThinkProgress, October 28, 2010.

12. Chris Good, "Walking Edge: Canvassing with GPS," *The Atlantic*, Jan. 19, 2010.

13. Matt Viser, "Conservative Group Used Tweet Strategy Against Coakley," *Boston Globe*, May 4, 2010.

14. Jeff Woods, "Papers from DesJarlais' Bitter Divorce Pop Up in Media," *Nashville Scene*, Sept. 16, 2010.

15. Tom Humphrey, "NRCC, DesJarlais Promote Video of Questions Shouted at Lincoln Davis, Aide Blocking Camera," *Knoxville News Sentinel*, Oct. 18, 2010.

16. Glenn Greenwald, "Pajamas Media—'A New Method of Fact-Checking,'" Crooks and Liars, Jan. 2005, http://crooks andliars.com/2007/01/06/pajamas-media-a-new-method-of-fact -checking.

17. Archived from www.americanfreedomalliance.org.

18. Archived from www.rightnetwork.com.

19. Hal Boedeker, "News Ratings: Fox News Channel, NBC's Brian Williams Are Winners," *Orlando Sentinel*, July 27, 2010.

20. "Fox News has hyped phony New Black Panthers Scandal at Least 95 Times," Media Matters for America, July 16, 2010.

21. David Brock, "Roger Ailes: Mad as Hell," *New York*, Nov. 17, 2007.

22. Appenzel D. Bell, "Rob Pfaltzgraff on Free-Market Movies and the Future of Independent Films," Gold Speculator, March 14, 2010.

23. Archived information from the website www.thempi.org.

24. Newsletters from "The MPI Script," published by the Motion Picture Institute, 2006–2007.

25. Max Blumenthal, "Discover the Secret Right-Wing Network Behind ABC's 9/11 Deception," Huffington Post, Sept. 8, 2006.

26. "ABC Retained Fabricated Scene Showing Clinton Officials Aborting Mission to Capture Bin Laden," Media Matters for America, Sept. 11, 2006.

27. Christina Bellatoni, "Cartoon Obama Punches Out Reagan in New Conservative Anti-Spending Flick," Talking Points Memo, Aug. 6, 2010.

28. Jason Apuzzo, "The Red Dawn Remake: The Return of the Red Scare?" *Libertas Film Magazine*, June 8, 2010.

29. Rebecca Mead, "Rage Machine," *New Yorker*, May 24, 2010.

6. TAKING IT TO THE STATES

1. Frederick Clarkson, "Takin' It to the States: The Rise of Conservative State-Level Think Tanks," The Public Eye, http://www.publiceye.org/magazine/v13n2-3/PE_V13_N2-3.pdf.

2. State Policy Network, "SPN Leadership Team," http://www.spn.org/about/spn-leadership-team.

3. Clarkson. "Takin' It to the States."

4. Ibid.

5. State Policy Network, "SPN: BulletPoint December 2010—Guiding Principles for State Think Tanks," http://www

.spn.org/publications/spn-bulletpoint-december-2010-guiding
-principles-for-state-think-tanks.

6. Lamar White, Jr., "The Pelican Institute: Louisiana's First 'Astroturf' Think Tank," CenLamar.com. http://cenlamar.com /2009/08/01/the-pelican-institute-louisianas-first-astroturf-think -tank/.

7. Michelle Millhollon, "Governor's Sunday Helicopter Travels Have Come at Taxpayers' Expense," *Advocate Capitol News Bureau*, Aug. 30, 2009, p. 1A, http://www.2theadvocate.com/news /56139902.html?showAll=y&c=y.

8. State Policy Network, "Pacific Research Institute," http:// www.spn.org/directory/pacific-research-institute.

9. Texas Public Policy Foundation, "Foundation Study: Federal Stimulus Will Cost Texas Additional Jobs," http://www .texaspolicy.com/press_releases_single.php?report_id=2548.

10. Faiz Shakir, Amanda Terkel, Satyam Khanna, Matt Corley, and Benjamin Armbruster, "The Progress Report: Gubernatorial Grandstanding," ThinkProgress, March 26, 2009, http://www .americanprogress.org/pr/2009/03/pr20090326.

11. obamahealthcare. "Health Care Reform," http://www .youtube.com/watch?v=fKXuDPFz_9g.

12. Wayne Hoffman, "Eagle Considers Smoking Ban," Idaho Freedom Foundation, http://idahofreedom.net/blog/eagle -considers-smoking-ban.

13. State Policy Network, "SPN News November/December 2010 Newsletter Updates," http://www.spn.org/publications/spn -news-novemberdecember-2010-newsletter-updates.

14. Jerome Tuccille, "Online Outfit Trains, Empowers Journalists to Scrutinize Government," *Examiner.com*, Sept. 17, 2009, http://www.examiner.com/civil-liberties-in-national/online -outfit-trains-empowers-journalists-to-scrutinize-government.

15. Franklin Center for Government and Public Integrity, "Franklin Center Reporter Awarded Robert Novak Journalism Fellowship," http://www.franklincenterhq.org/1664/franklin -center-reporter-awarded-robert-novak-journalism-fellowship/.

16. John Miller, "News Sites Funded by Think Tanks Take Root," Sign on San Diego, April 13, 2010, http://www.signon

sandiego.com/news/2010/apr/13/news-sites-funded-by-think
-tanks-take-root/.

17. Stephen Ward, "How to Avoid Ethical Snags in Non-Profit
Journalism," PBS, http://www.pbs.org/mediashift/2010/01/how
-to-avoid-ethical-snags-in-non-profit-journalism004.html.

18. John Miller, "News Sites Funded by Think Tanks Take
Root."

19. "Did 'Phantom' Districts Get Stimulus Cash?" CBS News,
Nov. 18, 2009. http://www.cbsnews.com/stories/2009/11/18
/politics/main5701130.shtml.

20. Andrew Griffin, "Oklahoma's Phantom Districts," http://
www.house.gov/list/hearing/ok03_lucas/20091118_News_Red
DirtReportOKsPhantomDistricts.shtml.

21. Franklin Center for Government and Public Integrity,
"Local Watchdogs Included in Coburn/McCain Stimulus
Report," http://www.franklincenterhq.org/1858/local-watchdogs
-included-in-coburnmccain-stimulus-report/.

22. Matthew Yglesias, "The Bogus McCain/Coburn Campaign
Against Waste in the Recovery Act," ThinkProgress, Aug. 3,
2010, http://yglesias.thinkprogress.org/2010/08/the-bogus
-mccaincoburn-campaign-against-waste-in-the-recovery-act/.

23. Mackinac Center for Public Policy, "Kathy Hoekstra,"
http://www.michigancapitolconfidential.com/bio.aspx?ID=563.

24. Chas Sisk, "Clint Brewer Named Tennessean Political
Editor," *The Tennessean*, June 15, 2010, http://blogs.tennessean
.com/politics/2010/clint-brewer-named-tennesseean-political
-editor/.

25. The Heritage Foundation, "Resource Bank," http://www
.heritage.org/About/Resource-Bank/Resource-Bank.

26. Earl Glynn, "Doctors Hold Tea Party in Kansas City,"
Missouri WatchDog.org, Aug. 8, 2010, http://missouri.watchdog
.org/1770/doctors-hold-tea-party-in-kansas-city/.

27. Eric Kleefeld, "Rand Paul a Member of Right-Wing
Doctors Group That Pushes Conspiracy Theories," Talking
Points Memo, Aug. 6, 2010, http://tpmdc.talkingpointsmemo.com
/2010/08/rand-paul-a-member-of-right-wing-doctors-group-that
-pushes-conspiracy-theories.php.

28. Andrew Griffin, "Thoughts on new investigation—'Bombshell: Barack Obama conclusively outed as CIA creation,'" Oklahoma WatchDog.org, Aug. 19, 2010, http://oklahoma .watchdog.org/1144/thoughts-on-new-investigation-bombshell -barack-obama-conclusively-outed-as-cia-creation/.

29. Patti Wenzel, "State Democrats Toss Reporter Out of Recall Walker Training Meeting," Patch.com, Oct. 20, 2011.

30. Franklin Center for Government and Public Integrity, "The Franklin Center and National Review Partner For Election Coverage," http://www.franklincenterhq.org/1872/?utm _source=Government+and+Pols&utm_campaign=7a0dae7e47 -Franklin_Comm_Maine&utm_medium=email.

31. David Broder, "States Grown into a New Job," *Boca Raton News*, Aug. 4, 1982, http://news.google.com/newspapers?id=my0 QAAAAIBAJ&sjid=wY0DAAAAIBAJ&pg=3537,7612293&dq=st ate-government-affairs-council&hl=en.

32. American Legislative Exchange Council Watch.org, "ALEC's Corporate Special Interest Legislation," http://alec watch.org/harmfullegislation.html.

33. American Legislative Exchange Council, "History," http:// www.alec.org/AM/Template.cfm?Section=History&Template =/CM/HTMLDisplay.cfm&ContentID=13643.

34. Rob Bishop, U.S. Congressman, "House Republicans Launch New 10th Amendment Task Force," http://robbishop .house.gov/News/DocumentSingle.aspx?DocumentID =184458.

35. ALECWatch.org, "ALEC's Profits Before Patients Legislation," http://alecwatch.org/patientsbeforeprofits.html.

36. The Brennan Center for Voting Rights and Elections, "Voter ID Laws Passed Since 2011," accessed June 15, 2012.

37. Robert Costa, "It's Ed: Gillespie Named RSLC Chair," *National Review*, Jan. 25, 2010, http://www.nationalreview .com/corner/193613/its-ed-gillespie-named-rslc-chair/robert -costa.

38. Republican Governors Association, "About: Why the Comeback Begins Here," http://www.rga.org/homepage/about /why-the-comeback-begins-here/.

39. Caesar Rodney Institute, "Caesar Rodney Institute Launches Transparency Web Site," http://www.caesarrodney.org /index.cfm?ref=21200&ref2=9.

40. Kenneth P. Vogel, "For right, Wis. was years in making," Politico, Feb. 28, 2011, http://dyn.politico.com/printstory.cfm ?uuid=611D3199-9CEE-48D5-AA2F-E2B5C3DF28B3.

41. Bill Lueders, "How Trustworthy Is MacIver News Service?" The Daily Page, Oct. 28, 2010, http://www.thedaily page.com/isthmus/article.php?article=31025.

42. Andy Kroll, "Media Trackers, the Right's New Oppo-Research Attack Dog," *Mother Jones*, May 21, 2012.

43. Ibid.

ALSO AVAILABLE FROM
THE NEW PRESS

**The Betrayal of Work: How Low-Wage Jobs Fail
30 Million Americans**
Beth Shulman

The book *Newsweek*'s Anna Quindlen said "should be required reading
for every presidential candidate and member of Congress."

**The Color of Wealth: The Story Behind the U.S.
Racial Wealth Divide**
*Meizhu Lui, Bárbara Robles, Betsy Leondar-Wright, Rose Brewer, and
Rebecca Adamson*

An eye-opening field guide to the wealth gap.

**Economic Apartheid in America: A Primer on
Economic Inequality and Insecurity**
Chuck Collins and Felice Yeskel; foreword by Juliet Schor

Following the 2004 presidential election, a graphic portrait of the growing gap between the rich and everyone else in America.

Economics for the Rest of Us: Debunking the Science That Makes Life Dismal
Moshe Adler

The Independent Publisher Association's Gold Medal winner, a book that David Cay Johnston called "a brilliant eye-opener" because it turns the conventional wisdom about economics upside down.

Founding Myths: Stories That Hide Our Patriotic Past
Ray Raphael

The highly praised book in which cherished stories from American history are exposed as myths.

From Cairo to Wall Street: Voices from the Global Spring
Edited by Anya Schiffrin and Eamon Kircher-Allen

The book Bob Herbert praised as "the first essential text of a new and remarkably dynamic era of social activism that has already brought profound change to the world."

Fuel on the Fire: Oil and Politics in Occupied Iraq
Greg Muttitt

A groundbreaking investigation confirming what many have long felt: oil interests lay at the very heart of the Iraq War—a legacy that continues to haunt us.

Howard Zinn: A Life on the Left
Martin Duberman

From the award-winning historian and activist Martin Duberman, a sweeping political biography—the first—of Howard Zinn, "the people's historian" who himself made history, changing forever how we think about our past.

Kids for Cash: Two Judges, Thousands of Children, and a $2.8 Million Kickback Scheme
William Ecenbarger

From a Pulitzer Prize–winning *Philadelphia Inquirer* reporter, a gripping work of true crime about the Pennsylvania case in which judges in a rural county took cash payments for sending children to a privatized juvenile detention facility.

Labor Rising: The Past and Future of Working People in America
Edited by Daniel Katz and Richard A. Greenwald

A timely and urgent look at the twenty-first-century prospects of working people and the labor movement, from leading activists and historians.

Mismeasuring Our Lives: Why GDP Doesn't Add Up
Joseph E. Stiglitz, Amartya Sen, and Jean-Paul Fitoussi

A major, timely new report on why GDP is a deeply flawed indicator of economic performance and social progress—and how to develop better indicators of societal well-being—by renowned Nobel Prize–winning economists.

The Moral Underground: How Ordinary Americans Subvert an Unfair Economy
Lisa Dodson

The untold story of a silent movement for economic justice as featured on *Marketplace*, in the *Boston Globe*, and in the *American Prospect*.

Muckraking!: The Journalism That Changed America
Edited by Judith Serrin and William Serrin

More than one hundred classics of American investigative journalism, from Tom Paine to Bob Woodward.

"Multiplication Is for White People": Raising Expectations for Other People's Children
Lisa Delpit

From the MacArthur Award–winning education reformer and author of the bestselling *Other People's Children*, a long-awaited book on how to fix the persistent black/white achievement gap in America's public schools.

The New Jim Crow: Mass Incarceration in the Age of Colorblindness
Michelle Alexander

The "explosive debut" (*Kirkus*) from a rising legal star in America arguing that we have not ended racial caste in America—we have simply redesigned it.

Political Awakenings: Conversations with History
Harry Kreisler

Stories of insight and inspiration from twenty leaders and thinkers who have changed the world—including Howard Zinn, Amira Hass, and Ron Dellums.

Protest Nation: Words That Inspired a Century of American Radicalism
Edited by Timothy Patrick McCarthy and John McMillian

From Eugene Debs to Paul Robeson, Angela Davis, and Harvey Milk—a compendium of words that spurred American radical thought and action, from the early twentieth century to the present.

The Radical Reader: A Documentary History of the American Radical Tradition
Edited by Timothy Patrick McCarthy and John McMillian; foreword by Eric Foner

Key documents illustrate the richness of radicalism in American society.

So Rich, So Poor: Why It's So Hard to End Poverty in America
Peter Edelman

An uncompromising look at the increasing poverty in America today—especially among young people—by the man who famously resigned from the Clinton administration to protest the treatment of the nation's poor.

Who's Afraid of Frances Fox Piven?: The Essential Writings of the Professor Glenn Beck Loves to Hate
Frances Fox Piven

A primer on the ideas of the leading progressive thinker Glenn Beck considers one of the nine most dangerous people in the world.

CELEBRATING INDEPENDENT PUBLISHING

Thank you for reading this book published by The New Press. The New Press is a nonprofit, public interest publisher. New Press books and authors play a crucial role in sparking conversations about the key political and social issues of our day.

We hope you enjoyed this book and that you will stay in touch with the New Press. Here are a few ways to stay up to date with our books, events, and the issues we cover:

- Sign up at www.thenewpress.com/subscribe to receive updates on New Press authors and issues and to be notified about local events
- Like us on Facebook: www.facebook.com/newpress books
- Follow us on Twitter: www.twitter.com/thenewpress

Please consider buying New Press books for yourself; for friends and family; or to donate to schools, libraries, community centers, prison libraries, and other organizations involved with the issues our authors write about.

The New Press is a 501(c)(3) nonprofit organization. You can also support our work with a tax-deductible gift by visiting www.thenewpress.com/donate.